D0512740

Dynamics of Internatic

ASIA-PACIFIC BUSINESS CASES

Dynamics of International Business: Asia-Pacific Business Cases brings the challenges and complexities of the contemporary international business environment into the classroom. These authentic case studies, based on recent research and events, enable students to engage with the economic, social, political and intercultural factors that impact on international business. They also enable students to explore and understand how these factors are addressed in the real world.

Designed to facilitate a problem-based learning approach to the study of international business and management, the cases in this book:

- draw on a diverse range of businesses and industries – from seafood to video games to renewable energy
- illustrate fundamental themes and concerns within global business, including ethics, sustainability, emerging markets, and cultural and legal differences
- span many countries across the Asia-Pacific region, reflecting the growing importance of trade and business ties within this area
- include discussion questions that encourage students to apply international business theory and develop critical thinking skills in the context of realistic scenarios
- include references and suggestions for further reading.

Extra resources for instructors, including case synopses, learning objectives and guided answers to the discussion questions, are available at www.cambridge.edu.au/academic/internationalbusiness.

Prem Ramburuth is Professor of International Business and President of the Academic Board at the University of New South Wales, Australia.

Christina Stringer is Senior Lecturer in the Department of Management and International Business at the University of Auckland, New Zealand.

Manuel Serapio is Associate Professor of International Business at the University of Colorado Denver, United States.

Praise for *Dynamics of International Business*

'It is not often that a case collection provides the depth, scope and clarity that make it a useful companion for both teaching and research. This collection does just that, providing an interdisciplinary lens with which to observe, reflect on, and, most importantly, understand complex business problems, in particular in the Asia Pacific region.'

Oded Shenkar
Ford Motor Company Chair in Global Business Management Fisher College of Business,
The Ohio State University

'A case book we've been waiting for! Its objective is to encourage and enable faculty and teaching staff to infuse IB content into business courses at all levels. . . . It fills the gap of lacking case studies from outside the US or Europe. It's a must for any IB teacher who wants to gear-up his/her teaching towards the Century of the Asia Pacific.'

Klaus Macharzina
Emeritus Professor and AIB Fellow, Hohenheim University

'This is a very informative and well constructed collection of case studies . . . Particularly refreshing and insightful are unique conditions, whether institutional and regulatory or sociocultural and economic, facing multinationals or domestic firms competing in the region, making it a very useful book for instructors and students interested in business landscapes and strategies unfolding there.'

Yadong Luo,
Emery Findlay Distinguished Chair and Professor of International Business,
University of Miami

'Congratulations to PACIBER for its major accomplishment of this Case Book . . . This Case Book is further evidence of the role of PACIBER in advancing International Business Education in this region. With more than 20 cases from academics across the Asia-Pacific region, I believe this Case Book will provide valuable learning experiences for readers, both academics and practitioners.'

Emeritus Professor Khunying Suchada Kiranandana
Chairperson, Chulalongkorn University Council

'. . . a thoughtful and valuable collection of cases written by international business professionals who have vast experiences in countries across the Asia Pacific Region. Through these cases, highly relevant scenarios in the international business environment can be brought into an educational setting to engage participants on decidedly relevant Asia Pacific topics and issues.'

Dr. Stefanie Lenway
Eli and Edythe L. Broad Dean, Eli Broad College of Business, Michigan State University

'This is an excellent set of short cases useful in any business school class that prepares folks to understand, and work in, any of the dynamic and rapidly growing Asian economies.'

Raj Aggarwal
Sullivan Professor of International Business, University of Akron

'. . . an impressive collection of cases and teaching notes. The true extent of globalization in the world economy is not often well represented, but in this one volume, you will find true diversity in topic, country, and industry . . . With the diversity of cases, and the increased need for students to understand global economies, this collection is a great resource for faculty at institutions all around the world.'

Kenneth G. Brown
Professor, University of Iowa, USA

Dynamics of International Business

ASIA-PACIFIC BUSINESS CASES

Edited by

PREM RAMBURUTH, CHRISTINA STRINGER AND MANUEL SERAPIO

Cases from the Pacific Asian Consortium for International Business Education and Research (PACIBER)

CAMBRIDGE
UNIVERSITY PRESS

CAMBRIDGE UNIVERSITY PRESS
Cambridge, New York, Melbourne, Madrid, Cape Town,
Singapore, São Paulo, Delhi, Mexico City

Cambridge University Press
477 Williamstown Road, Port Melbourne, VIC 3207, Australia

Published in the United States of America by Cambridge University Press, New York

www.cambridge.org
Information on this title: www.cambridge.org/9781107675469

First published 2013

Cover design by Marianna Berek-Lewis
Typeset by Integra Software Services Pvt. Ltd
Printed in Singapore by C.O.S. Printers Pte Ltd

A catalogue record for this publication is available from the British Library

*A Cataloguing-in-Publication entry is available from the catalogue of the National Library
of Australia at* www.nla.gov.au

ISBN 978-1-107-67546-9 Paperback

Additional resources for this publication at www.cambridge.edu.au/academic/internationalbusiness

This book is dedicated to
Dr NH Paul Chung, Professor
Founder of the Pacific Asian Management Institute
His great vision inspired the creation of PACIBER.

Foreword

Globalisation of capital markets, developments in information technology and advances in communications and transportation are transforming business practices around the world. Successfully engaging in business in the international arena requires knowledge of the wide variety of cultures, national backgrounds, business practices and languages spoken throughout the area. Leading business schools in the Asia-Pacific region are becoming essential players in providing knowledge and skills for current and prospective business professionals.

The Pacific Asian Consortium for International Business Education and Research (PACIBER) was created in 1988 as a consortium of universities dedicated to establishing linkages to promote international business education, research and exchanges of information, faculty and students. PACIBER member schools benefit by increased access to and networking with the leading business schools in North America, Asia and Oceania. Collaborative activities between PACIBER member schools add value to member universities through a range of activities. These include joint research projects, recruitment and exchange of students, faculty exchange and networking, placement of students in member school programs, joint curriculum development, access to the latest developments in business education, increased research funding opportunities from private and government agencies, and invaluable networks with leading business schools.

With its secretariat at the crossroads of the Pacific, in the University of Hawai'i's Pacific Asian Management Institute, PACIBER strives to widen the scope of cooperation, facilitate communication and expand consciousness about the Asia-Pacific region among its members, and in the business community at large. PACIBER representatives gather every year in the location of a member school to receive updates on current international business issues, discuss curriculum development and present new initiatives for the consortium. Research panels and keynote speeches are also part of the program. These annual meetings of PACIBER provide a forum for the exchange of ideas, where members can network and learn from one another. Through faculty exchanges and other mutually beneficial alliances, member universities can raise the level of their business education programs to world-class standards.

This casebook is a product of the type of integrated research and curriculum development projects in which PACIBER members are engaged. The goal of the book is to help faculty – particularly those in the Asia-Pacific region – integrate current and relevant Asia-Pacific business content into their curriculum. It is also designed to increase active learning, as well as develop communication and cross-cultural skills in all business students – skills that are known to be extremely important to employers.

The book represents a collaborative effort by over 30 authors and editors from throughout the Asia-Pacific region. It would not have been possible without the contributions of cases by dozens of scholars. We acknowledge their diligent work in preparing and revising their cases and providing teaching materials to complement the cases.

The book benefited substantially from the capable management and commitment of our editorial trio, led by Professor Prem Ramburuth and her assistant, Irene Ellul, at the University of New South Wales, who organised and coordinated the process with the publishing company. Our other co-editors, Dr Christina Stringer of the University of Auckland and Dr Manuel Serapio of the University of Colorado Denver, each managed cases in their areas of expertise, and provided ongoing input on all aspects of the book. This team of three editors worked diligently over a two-year period to solicit cases, manage the review and revision process, and organise the content into a usable and user-friendly volume. The diversity, range and quality of the cases is testimony to their hard work and talent.

We also acknowledge the assistance of André Everett, Grant Kim, Rochelle Macarthur, Tamira Reed, Cindy Qin, Nisarg Desai and Nikki Serapio, and the tremendous support of David Jackson, the Commissioning Editor-Academic of Cambridge University Press.

We are pleased to present this volume at the celebration of PACIBER's 25th anniversary in 2013. We encourage scholars who are interested in our programs to consult our website at <http://www.paciber.org>.

Shirley J Daniel, Director
Pacific Asian Management Institute
Secretariat of PACIBER
Shidler College of Business
University of Hawai'i at Manoa
Honolulu, Hawai'i

Contents

Contributors

Eliseo A Aurellado is Professor and Chair of the Finance Cluster of Faculty at the Ateneo Graduate School of Business, Ateneo de Manila University, Makati City, the Philippines.

Sergio Biggemann is a Senior Lecturer in Marketing in the Business School at the University of Otago, New Zealand. He is also Associate Editor for International Business with the *Journal of Business Research*.

Amanda Budde-Sung is a Lecturer in International Business at the University of Sydney, Australia. She has twice been nominated for the Australia New Zealand Management Educator of the Year award.

Chintana Bunbongkarn is an Associate Professor and Senior Researcher at Unisearch, Chulalongkorn University, Bangkok, Thailand.

Dan V Caprar is a Lecturer in the Australian School of Business, University of New South Wales, Sydney, Australia. He also teaches at the Australian Graduate School of Management in Hong Kong.

Pachsiry Chompukum is an Associate Professor at Chulalongkorn Business School, Bangkok, Thailand.

Alejandro Cisneros works in the design and manufacturing of customised training equipment for industries and research institutions.

Graham Elkin is an Associate Professor in the Department of Management, University of Otago, Dunedin, New Zealand.

André M Everett is Professor of International Management at the University of Otago, Dunedin, New Zealand, and Adjunct Professor at Huazhong University of Science and Technology, Wuhan, China.

Maris Farquharson is Assistant Professor in Entrepreneurship and Innovation at Nottingham University Business School China, Ningbo, China.

Sascha Fuerst is an Associate Professor in the Department of International Business at the Universidad EAFIT in Medellin, Colombia.

Sally Anne Gaunt is a Lecturer in the undergraduate Cross-Cultural Management course in the Australian School of Business at the University of New South Wales, Sydney. She also runs a successful training company in Australia.

Gloria Lan Ge is a Senior Lecturer at Griffith University, Queensland, Australia, and Director of the Griffith Bachelor of Business in Hong Kong.

Evan Goodwin is an international business student in the Grant MacEwan University Business School, Edmonton, Alberta, Canada.

Raymund B Habaradas is Assistant Professor at the Management and Organization Department of De La Salle University, Manila, the Philippines.

Zhu Hang is Associate Professor of Entrepreneurship and Strategy at Sun Yat-sen Business School, Sun Yat-sen University, Guangzhou, China.

Kimberley Howard is a project manager and term faculty member in the Grant MacEwan University Business School, Edmonton, Alberta, Canada.

Shih-wei Hsu is Assistant Professor in Organizational Behaviour, Nottingham University Business School China, Ningbo, China.

Anders Örtenblad is Associate Professor in Organizational Behaviour and Director of Teaching Development at Nottingham University Business School China, Ningbo, China. He is also an Associate Editor of the *International Journal of Management Reviews*.

Cindy Qin teaches international business, strategic management and cross-cultural management at the University of San Francisco in the United States.

Prem Ramburuth is Professor in International Business in the Australian School of Business and President of the Academic Board at the University of New South Wales, Sydney, Australia.

Eugene Rees is a Senior Projects Analyst at the New Zealand Ministry for Primary Industries.

Cheryl Rivers is a Senior Lecturer in International Business at Victoria University of Wellington, New Zealand.

Adriana Roldán-Pérez is an Associate Professor and Academic Coordinator of the Asia Pacific Studies Centre at EAFIT University, Medellín, Colombia.

Peter K Ross is a Senior Lecturer at the Department of International Business and Asian Studies, Griffith University, Queensland, Australia.

Julie Rowney is Professor in Human Resources and Organizational Dynamics at the Haskayne School of Business, University of Calgary, Canada.

Diane Ruwhiu is a Lecturer in the Business School, Otago University, New Zealand.

Massoud Saghafi is Professor of Marketing at the San Diego State University, San Diego, California.

Asuncion Sebastian is a PhD candidate in Development Studies at De La Salle University, Manila, the Philippines.

Manuel G Serapio is Associate Professor of International Business and Entrepreneurship at the Business School, University of Colorado Denver, in the United States. He is also Faculty Director of the university's Institute for International Business and Center for International Business Education and Research.

Yan Shi is a Senior Lecturer at Fuzhou University, China.

Glenn Simmons is a PhD candidate in the Department of Management and International Business, University of Auckland, New Zealand.

Jessica Smart works in recruitment, and recently graduated from the University of Otago, Dunedin, New Zealand with a Master of Business.

Christina Stringer is a Senior Lecturer in the Department of Management and International Business, University of Auckland, New Zealand.

Henry T Tsuei is International Executive-in-Residence and Co-Chair of the Global Advisory Board at the Institute for International Business, University of Colorado Denver, United States.

Yue Wang is Associate Professor of International Business in the Department of Marketing and Management, Macquarie University, Sydney, Australia.

William X Wei is Chair, Asia Pacific Management Program, Institute of Asia Pacific Studies at Grant MacEwan University Business School, Edmonton, Alberta, Canada. He is Vice Chair of the Sino-Canada Asia Pacific Economic Research Institute, and a Senior Researcher with the Center for China and Globalization.

Chai Wenjing is a Senior Researcher in the 21st Century Media Group and reporter for the *21st Century Business Herald*.

Su Xing is Senior Editor of the *21st Century Business Review*.

Haina Zhang is a Lecturer in Management, Adam Smith Business School, University of Glasgow, Scotland.

Wu Ziwei is pursuing a Master of Science in International Branding Management at Euromed Management in Marseilles, France.

■ Preface

It is widely acknowledged that actively engaging students is vital to the learning process. Unfortunately, our education systems have all too often fostered one-way communication and information flows from teacher to student. As a result, it is sometimes difficult to get students to participate actively in class discussions, and this is probably more true in the Asia-Pacific region than in the United States and Europe. However, most of us are familiar with the Chinese proverb: 'Tell me and I'll forget; show me and I may remember; involve me and I'll understand.' This book is designed to help teachers of international business implement this sage advice in their classrooms through the use of cases.

While there are a number of experiential learning techniques that can be used in higher education, case-based teaching is one of the most efficient and flexible methods for actively involving and encouraging students to make the transition from classroom to practice. Cases provide an opportunity for students to apply technical knowledge and theories derived from lectures and textbooks to real-world situations. Effective integration of cases as part of a course can allow students to cultivate an array of skills that will be useful in their careers. Specifically, Edge and Coleman (1986) list nine action skills that are reinforced through the use of cases – skills that enable a person to:

1. think clearly in complex ambiguous situations
2. devise reasonable, consistent, creative action plans
3. apply quantitative tools
4. recognise the significance of information
5. determine vital missing information
6. communicate orally in groups
7. write clear, forceful, convincing reports
8. guide students' careers
9. apply personal values to organisational decisions.

The use of cases as part of course pedagogy is particularly useful in teaching international business, where global skills development is essential, exposure to cross-border understanding and cultural contexts is required, and 'primary experience' in global contexts on a large and frequent scale is not feasible (Ramburuth & Daniel 2011).

Unfortunately, teachers are often challenged when it comes to finding appropriate cases from affordable sources that address international topics and situations (Coulthard & Dooley 2010; Ramburuth & Welch 2005). In a study that examined syllabi for core strategy courses at 51 leading business schools, Ghemawat (2007) found that 33 per cent of courses he reviewed with colleagues did not have a single case study that took place outside the United States, and most did not teach global strategy concepts or tools. In addition, as the required business school curriculum content topics continue to increase, many faculty members find it difficult to squeeze more assignments and topics into an already extensive class syllabus. In many core courses, it is not feasible to devote a whole class period to a single case discussion.

However, a shorter case can be integrated more easily, and provide a valuable opportunity to engage students in the theories and topics they are already studying.

The goal of this casebook is to encourage and enable more faculty and teaching staff to infuse international business content and active learning into business courses at all levels. The book is designed specifically to provide up-to-date, realistic, concise and easy-to-integrate international business case situations from the Asia-Pacific region. Each case is designed to include a concise scenario and discussion questions. The questions provide options for stimulating discussion at undergraduate and graduate levels, are formulated for the involvement of individual and group work, and include extension questions aimed at facilitating advanced levels of learning.

Frequently, an obstacle to finding and integrating the 'right' case occurs when no teaching notes are available to help the instructor efficiently understand the case concepts, demonstrate how they might be integrated into a class or suggest potential answers to the questions. This casebook addresses these issues and provides insightful teaching notes and potential answers to the questions set, offers alternate questions to be tailored to class needs and suggests references for further reading. Instructors and students who are novices at using the case method of instruction will be able to experience a more lively and meaningful class discussion.

The cases included will provide a valuable complement to any course in which the instructor would like to include an international business component, particularly with an Asia-Pacific focus. Example courses and topics could include:

- Introduction to International Business
- Global Business Environments
- Business Strategy
- International Entrepreneurship
- Cross-cultural Management
- Organisation Design and Behaviour
- Globalisation and Society.

To facilitate the integration of cases into existing international business and management courses and topics, the cases are organised into four broad categories:

- Part I: The Environment of International Business, including issues relating to political, legal, economic, cultural, ethical and sustainable environments
- Part II: Strategy and Entrepreneurship, including issues relating to globalisation, entry modes, strategic alliances, leadership, innovation, and opportunities and risks in international business
- Part III: Managing People in International Business, including issues relating to international management, human resources, cross-cultural management, expatriation, and training and development for global contexts
- Part IV: Operating in International Markets, including issues relating to sourcing, global competition, market share, foreign direct investments, exports and imports, and other issues encountered in engaging in business in foreign environments.

The cases are 'real-life' examples written by academic and practitioners in international business. They aim to provide authentic learning experiences covering the many topics listed.

▪ References

Coulthard, M & Dooley, L 2010, *Cases in international business: strategies for internationalization*, Tilde University Press, Melbourne.

Edge, A G & Coleman, D R 1986, *The Guide to Case Analysis and Reporting*, 3rd edn, System Logistics, Honolulu.

Ghemawat, P 2007, 'The globalization of business education: through the lens of semi-globalization', *Journal of Management Development*, vol. 27, no. 4, pp. 391–414.

Ramburuth, P & Daniel, SJ 2011, 'Integrating experiential learning and cases in international business', *Journal of Teaching in International Business*, no. 22, pp. 38–50.

Ramburuth, P & Welch, C 2005, *Casebook in international business: Australian and Asia-Pacific perspectives*, Pearson Education, Sydney.

Part

The Environment of International Business

1

AWB and the Iraqi Oil-for-Food scandal: Just a cost of doing business?

Peter K Ross

In 2005, the Australian government initiated an inquiry into 'certain Australian companies in relation to the UN Oil-for-Food program', subsequently known as the Cole Inquiry. This inquiry investigated what was to become Australia's biggest international corruption scandal – the A$300 million paid in kickbacks to the Saddam Hussein-led Iraqi government by the Australian Wheat Board (AWB), an exporting monopoly (Holmes 2006). Even more damning was the fact that this money had been paid to the same dictatorial regime against which Australian soldiers had fought two wars. The seeds of this corruption went back to the introduction of a UN-administered Oil-for-Food Program (OFFP) that was negotiated with the Iraqi government following the First Gulf War.

■ First Gulf War 1990–91

In 1990, under a government led by Saddam Hussein, Iraq invaded Kuwait. Following an international outcry, a United Nations-endorsed, United States-led coalition force subsequently liberated Kuwait in 1991, in a military action named 'Operation Desert Storm'. The peace terms required Saddam Hussein to open up Iraq to UN weapons inspectors, including the inspections of sites suspected of being linked to the development of 'weapons of mass destruction' (WMDs) (UN Security Council Resolution 687) (Fisher 2004, p. 462). The responsibility for finding weapons, including WMDs, was given to the UN Monitoring, Verification, and Inspection Commission (UNMOVIC) and the International Atomic Energy Agency (IAEA).

UNMOVIC and IAEA inspectors had some success in finding and disposing of weapons. This included the destruction of '38,500 munitions, 480,000 litres of chemical agents, and 1.8 million litres of precursor chemicals' (Squassoni 2003, p. 4). But Iraqi officials became increasingly obstructive over time. This included delaying tactics and blocking access to 'sensitive sites'. Inspectors also complained that interview rooms frequently were bugged by the Iraqi government. Some observers therefore suggested that 'Iraqi compliance was superficial and oriented to facilitating the process of inspections, rather than on providing cooperation in substantive matters' (Squassoni 2003, p. ii). By 1998, the Iraqi government had become emboldened by increasing disunity amongst UN Security Council members and evicted all UNMOVIC personnel from the country. Following pressure from the United States and the United Nations, UNMOVIC personnel eventually were allowed back into Iraq in 2002, but there had now been a four-year period with effectively no UN inspections of Iraqi sites.

The period following the First Gulf War was, therefore, typified by a high degree of distrust amongst the parties. Further, many coalition force country governments – particularly the United States – believed that Iraq had not fully complied with UN Security Council Resolution 687, which required it to provide *unrestricted* access to its weapons facilities.

■ The UN Oil-for-Food Program and sanctions

Following the invasion of Kuwait in 1990, the UN Security Council voted for economic sanctions against Iraq (Harris 2007). These sanctions effectively prohibited UN member states from trading with Iraq, and included an embargo on the purchase of Iraqi oil – the country's predominant export revenue source. The UN Security Council hoped that the sanctions might apply sufficient economic and political pressure on the Iraqi government to persuade it to withdraw its forces from Kuwait. However, sanctions have often proven to be ineffective in changing regime behaviour – US trade sanctions against Cuba, Iran and Burma, for example, have failed to change the nature of the targeted regimes (Griswold & Lukas 1999). In this instance, the UN sanctions failed to induce Saddam Hussein to withdraw his forces from Iraq, resulting in the First Gulf War. Following the war, the UN Security Council renewed and maintained the sanctions because of the Iraqi government's apparent failure to fully comply with UN Resolution 687. Much of the pressure to maintain this approach came from the US government.

A problem with implementing wide-ranging sanctions is that they are, by their nature, a blunt economic instrument. While sanctions aim to change a regime's behaviour, the elite within the targeted countries often find ways to get around the sanctions and/or simply skim off a bigger percentage of a shrinking economy. Saddam Hussein, for example, continued to build new palaces and his family maintained a life of relative opulence throughout the sanctions period. Further, 'the regime remained as brutal and uncompromising in its treatment of political opponents as it was prior to sanctions' (Boone, Gazdar & Hussain 1997, p. 3).

Saddam Hussein was also prepared to use the economic plight of ordinary Iraqi people to pressure the United Nations to lift its sanctions, and overseas reporters who visited the country routinely were taken on state-organised tours of hospitals and other impoverished institutions. While much of this was a cynical ploy on the part of the Iraqi regime to pressure the United Nations into changing its stance, the fact remained that ordinary Iraqi people continued to suffer. Boone, Gazdar and Hussain (1997, p. iii) advise that real earnings for Iraqis:

> fell by around 90 per cent in the first year of the sanctions, and then fell by around 40 per cent more between 1991 and 1996 ... observations on the type of survival strategies that Iraqis are resorting to confirm this impression that in many ways Iraq is now very much like some of the poorest countries in the world, whereas before the sanctions it could be placed on par with the upper Middle Income countries.

Clearly, the sanctions had created an ethical and political dilemma for UN Security Council members, not to mention a public relations nightmare. In 1995, the *New York Times* published an article entitled 'Iraq Sanctions Kill Children' (Crossette 1995). Observers also suggested that the ongoing situation had led to 'sanctions fatigue' among UN Security Council members (Squassoni 2003).

▨ The Oil-for-Food Program

A UN strategy to help address this problem was the creation of the OFFP, whereby limited amounts of Iraqi oil could be exported for defined essential goods such as foodstuffs and medicines. The United Nations passed an initial resolution to initiate such a program as early as 1992, but the Iraqi government rejected the initial UN terms and a negotiated agreement was not finalised until late 1996 (Harris 2007). In finalising this agreement, the United Nations made a significant concession by agreeing that the Iraqi government, *not* the United Nations, would make the final decision on who could buy its oil and which firms could supply the humanitarian goods (Holmes 2006). This allowed Saddam Hussein to exert a far greater influence over the OFFP process than the United Nations had intended initially, further increasing the potential for corruption of the program. In line with this agreement, the Iraqi government refused to approve any OFFP purchase of wheat from US farmers because of the US government's continued support for the sanctions (Mayman 2003). Given that the United States is a major wheat exporter, the Iraqi government's stance gave other competitor wheat-exporting nations, such as Australia, a major advantage in terms of securing wheat sales to Iraq.

The OFFP agreement stipulated that all monies received under the program were to be paid into a UN escrow account, which in turn would monitor the receipt and disbursement of all the funds. Between December 1996 and 2003, Iraqi oil worth US\$64 billion was sold under the auspices of the OFFP, with US\$34 billion spent on humanitarian goods and US\$18 billion spent on reparations. (Volcker, Goldstone & Pieth 2005a; Harris 2007).

In 2003, continuing tensions between the United States and Iraq boiled over into the Second Gulf War. Debate over the causes and responsibility for this war are wide-ranging and beyond the scope of this case study, but in 2003 the United States led an invasion force dubbed the 'Coalition of the Willing' into Iraq – Australia was a member of this coalition invasion force. Disagreements among UN Security Council members meant that, in contrast to the First Gulf War, this coalition force was not backed by the UN Security Council.

Rumours concerning the corruption of the OFFP had been circulating for some years, but it was not until the defeat of Saddam Hussein's forces in this Second Gulf War that significant amounts of evidence supporting these rumours emerged from Iraqi government files and archives. Following the discovery of this evidence, the then UN Secretary General, Kofi Annan, initiated an inquiry into the administration and workings of the OFFP, chaired by Paul Volcker. The Volcker Inquiry discovered that, while the OFFP had improved the lives of ordinary Iraqis, the process had also systemically been corrupted. *Time Magazine* put this more bluntly, calling the OFFP a 'massive scam' (Sullivan 2005, p. 112). The inquiry estimated that more than 2200 foreign firms had paid bribes and/or kickbacks to the Iraqi government (Harris 2007), with an estimated value of at least US\$1.8 billion. The inquiry also found that the Iraqi government had been able to smuggle a further US\$11 billion worth of oil out of the country, again in direct contravention of UN sanctions. Of all the firms linked to illicit kickbacks and the OFFP, the company that was found to have paid the highest amount in corrupt payments to the Iraqi government was the Australian firm AWB. The Volcker inquiry estimated that, between 1999 and 2003, the AWB paid US$221 million in illicit payments – approximately A$300 million at the then exchange rate – which totalled an incredible 14 per cent of all the illicit funds paid to Saddam Hussein's regime under the OFFP (Harris 2007).

AWB

AWB's origins were in the government-owned Australian Wheat Board before it was privatised in 1999. Importantly, AWB was the beneficiary of the Australian government's 'single-desk' policy, which gave AWB the power to veto any other firm's application for a licence to export wheat from Australia (Aulich & Botterill 2007). This gave AWB a virtual monopoly on all wheat exports from the country. The logic behind the single-desk policy was to improve AWB's bargaining power. Australia is one of the world's biggest wheat exporters, and selling all its wheat exports through one source gave AWB – and, by extension, Australian wheat farmers – more power to negotiate deals in a competitive global market. The single-desk policy had broad general support from Australian wheat farmers and the National Party, a rural based political party that was a junior member of the ruling conservative Liberal/National Coalition that governed Australia from 1996 to 2007.

AWB gained a reputation for aggressively courting markets, which was in part related to the power it gained from its monopoly status. Aulich and Botterill (2007) further advise that, following privatisation, government regulatory oversight of AWB's export activities was relatively weak. Australia had sold wheat to Iraq for more than 50 years, and Iraq had developed into one of AWB's biggest export markets. Australian hard wheat was well suited to making Iraqi bread, while Iraq itself did not have the arable land available to grow its own requirements (Holmes 2006). The AWB therefore actively tendered for wheat sales to Iraq under the OFFP. Further, as outlined above, under the OFFP terms agreed upon by the United Nations in 1996, the Iraqi government was able to prohibit wheat imports from the United States, thereby eliminating a major trade competitor. In 2002, the year before the OFFP finished, Australia exported A$800 million worth of wheat to Iraq and by 2005 the Iraqi wheat market represented around 10 per cent of AWB's entire wheat exports for that year (Tucker 2006). Clearly, Iraq had developed into a lucrative market.

Kickbacks: Wheat exports to Iraq

AWB's success in Iraq had raised suspicions. Canadian wheat farming representatives, for instance, had complained to UN personnel about rumours of kickbacks being paid by the Australian firm to the Iraqi government (Volcker, Goldstone & Pieth 2005b). However, the United Nations did not initiate any large-scale investigation. Australia has solid democratic and transparent institutions, and is generally perceived as having relatively low levels of corruption (see Transparency International 2010). The idea that a large, long-established, former Australian government-owned firm could be engaging in such high-level illicit activity appears to have been anathema to UN officials at the time (Holmes 2006).

Nevertheless, the kickbacks being paid by AWB to the Iraqi government began in 1999. During this year, two AWB representatives visited Iraq and were told that they would need to pay a US$12 per ton 'trucking fee' on all wheat sold to Iraq (Cole 2006a, p. xiv). The Iraqi officials explained that this money was required to transport the grain from the port to the various inland regions of Iraq where it was required. The trucking fee would be added to the overall price that the Iraqi government was paying for the wheat, so AWB would not lose any money from the deal. This meant that AWB would receive an extra US$12 per ton for its wheat, but this extra US$12 would then be paid back to a transport firm nominated by the Iraqi government. Given that the US$12 per ton was well above actual transport costs, this was in effect a kickback to the Iraqi government. Although this payment, in US dollars to an Iraqi-nominated company, was in direct contravention of UN sanctions, AWB simply inserted a clause in its contract advising that: 'Discharge costs will be maximum of US$12 . . . And shall be paid by sellers to nominated maritime agents in Iraq.' (Holmes 2006) In July 1999, AWB submitted the contract to the Australian Department of Foreign Affairs and Trade (DFAT) for its scrutiny, and DFAT then forwarded the contract on to the United Nations for its approval (Holmes 2006). In the event, neither DFAT nor the United Nations appears to have uncovered or queried this clause.

Because UN sanctions did not allow AWB to pay the 'trucking fee' directly into any Iraqi financial institution, the Iraqi government asked AWB to pay the money to a Jordanian transport company, 'Alia Transportation'. During the Cole Inquiry, it emerged that this firm was 49 per cent owned by the Iraqi Ministry of Transport, and the monies for the 'trucking fees' that it received were later transferred to the Iraqi government (Holmes 2006). Between 1999 and 2003, the AWB entered into 26 contracts under the OFFP, but 'neither the fact nor the amount of the payments for the trucking fee made to Alia was shown on the face of any of the 26 contracts' (Cole 2006b, p. 9). During this period, the 'trucking fees' also increased from US$12 to more than US$50 per ton (Holmes 2006).

The Cole Inquiry

Following public pressure, in 2005 the Australian government initiated an inquiry into the activities of Australian firms in relation to the OFFP. The subsequent 'Inquiry into certain Australian companies in relation to the UN Oil-for-Food Program' (Cole 2006a, p. iii), focused on the activities of AWB and was presided over by Commissioner Terence Cole. The Cole Inquiry called many witnesses, including senior AWB management, and its published findings suggested that AWB knew that its payments of trucking fees to Alia contravened UN rules (Cole 2006a, 2006b). Its report further claimed that AWB management had engaged in a pattern of deliberate obfuscation in order to hide the true nature of the trucking fee payments from UN officials (Cole 2006a, 2006b). In 2006, the now public nature of AWB's activities with the previous Iraqi regime caused the new Iraqi government to ban all imports of Australian wheat, subject to the outcome of the Cole inquiry investigation (Tucker 2006). In his summing up of events, Commissioner Cole was scathing about AWB's behaviour:

> The consequences of AWB's actions have been immense. AWB has lost its reputation. The Federal Court has found that a 'transaction was deliberately and dishonestly structured by the AWB so as to misrepresent the true nature and purpose of the trucking fees and to work a trickery on the United Nations'. Shareholders have lost half the value of their investment. Trade with Iraq worth more than A$500 million per annum has been forfeited. Many senior executives have resigned, their positions being untenable. Some entities will not deal with the company. Some wheat holders do so unwillingly but are, at present, compelled by law to do so. AWB is threatened by lawsuits both in Australia and overseas. There are potential further restrictions on AWB's trade overseas. And AWB has cast a shadow over Australia's reputation in international trade. (Cole 2006, p. xi)

Commissioner Cole also recommended that criminal charges be made against 11 former AWB executives (Minder 2006). The inquiry also led to the resignation of AWB's CEO, Andrew Lindberg (Moldofsky 2006).

AWB could have approached the Cole inquiry quite differently. In 2005, it hired the services of an American-based crisis-management consultancy expert, Dr Peter Sandman, to give advice on the Iraqi wheat kickbacks crisis. Dr Sandman advised AWB that it would be in its best interests to admit that it had been paying bribes to the Iraqi regime and publicly 'over apologise' for its actions (McManus 2006, p. 7). In fact, he advised AWB to overstate its responsibility and set out how it was addressing the issue. But senior AWB management chose to ignore this advice, instead opting to 'tough it out'. In hindsight, it is impossible to say with certainty whether the Sandman strategy would have led to a better outcome for the firm. But the approach taken by AWB management appeared to accentuate, rather than minimise, the negative publicity associated with the scandal.

The Cole Inquiry was significant in another way: the then Prime Minister of Australia, John Howard, and two senior ministers – the Minister for Foreign Affairs, Alexander Downer, and the Minister for Trade, Mark Vaile – were called to give evidence. All claimed to have had no prior knowledge of AWB's illicit activities. While some diplomatic cables alluding to rumours of AWB's activities were found, none of these could be linked directly to the ministers concerned – the Minister for Foreign Affairs, for example, claimed not to have seen them (Holmes 2006; Silkstone 2006). Nevertheless, Australia traditionally has operated under the Westminster system, whereby government ministers are supposed to take ultimate responsibility for the actions of their departments. In this regard, AWB's transactions with the UN-administered OFFP were supposedly scrutinised by DFAT. Yet, following the release of the full evidence surrounding AWB's illicit activities, neither of the above two ministers resigned, despite the fact that A$300 million was paid in kickbacks to the

Iraqi government while they were the responsible ministers. Further, these two ministers had been part of the 2003 Cabinet, the executive arm of government, which agreed to commit Australian troops to the Second Gulf War.

The Cole inquiry did find that growing rumours and evidence about AWB's activities in Iraq had induced DFAT to make some internal inquiries into the matter prior to the Cole Inquiry (Silkstone 2006). But reports suggest that simple reassurances from AWB senior management were enough to satisfy DFAT officials that no wrongdoing had occurred (Holmes 2006; Silkstone 2006). Bartos suggests that this follows a pattern whereby 'there was a tacit understanding permeating the policy-making levels of government that AWB was a reliable, trustworthy partner to government, one not to be subjected to scrutiny' (2007, p. 1). Bartos further likens this to the BBC series *Yes, Prime Minister*, which invokes the 'Decent Chap Rule' – that is, 'decent chaps don't check up on decent chaps to see if they're behaving decently!' (2007, p. 6).

■ Aftermath

As outlined above, the negative publicity surrounding AWB's activities led to Iraq placing a ban on Australian wheat imports in 2006. Following extensive Australian government lobbying, the Iraq government subsequently agreed to receive limited imports of Australian wheat, provided they were not supplied by AWB (Pash 2006). The findings of the Cole Inquiry led the Australian government to then suspend AWB's veto power over Australian wheat exports and the government subsequently approved export applications from alternative firms; the veto power was transferred to the Federal Minister for Agriculture, Fisheries and Forestry (Minder 2006). After a long and detailed review of the industry, a new body – Wheat Exports Australia (WEA) – was created in 2008 to review and accredit applications from firms wishing to engage in the bulk export of Australian wheat (Aulich & Botterill 2007; Wheat Exports Australia 2009). AWB had lost its bulk wheat export monopoly.

Australia is a signatory to the UN Convention Against Corruption (2005) (Bartos 2007), and the Australian government agreed to follow up on the Cole inquiry's recommendations to tighten up laws to better address the contravention of UN sanctions by Australian firms (Australian Government 2007). The government further set up a task force to investigate possible criminal charges against AWB managers, and in 2007 the Australian corporate regulator, the Australian Securities and Investments Commission (ASIC), instituted civil proceedings against six former AWB executives, with possible criminal charges to follow (ASIC 2007; Fry 2007). After a long and involved examination of the evidence, the criminal investigation into AWB was dropped in 2010, but ASIC resumed its civil case against the former AWB executives in what had become a long and protracted legal battle (ABC 2010).

In 2010, AWB agreed to pay out A$39.5 million to settle a class action from AWB shareholders, who had sued the firm for losses incurred because of the Iraqi wheat scandal – including a sharp fall in the share price. The original action was for A$100 million (Sexton 2010; Smith 2010). AWB also remains 'one of more than 90 companies involved in a civil case being brought by the Iraqi government' (Smith 2010, p. 16). A depressed AWB share price and associated financial problems, in part brought about by the fallout from the Iraqi kickbacks scandal, persuaded AWB shareholders to accept a takeover bid from the Canadian firm Agrium in late 2010 (Urban 2010). The former Australian government-owned entity was now owned by an overseas-based multinational corporation.

The OFFP scandal also embarrassed and arguably reduced the credibility of the United Nations. The sheer size of the corruption unearthed by the Volcker Inquiry, and the apparent ease by which it was manipulated by Saddam Hussein's regime, seriously questioned the United Nations' governance processes and its ability to effectively administer such programs. While the AWB was the biggest offender, the Volcker inquiry found evidence that firms from around the world had provided kickbacks to the Iraqi government.

Some would say that AWB's activities in Iraq were simply a cost of doing business in the region. But interestingly, a former chairman of the AWB in the 1980s and 1990s, Clinton Condon, disputed the idea that bribery is just a part of doing business in the Middle East. He advised:

> In the Middle East, of all the time when I was chairman for nine years, I was never, ever asked to pay kickbacks or bribes to anyone. In Iraq they were the same. No one ever asked me or put any pressure on in the slightest way for any sort of kickbacks. (Holmes 2006, p. 2)

The case therefore highlights the fact that firms – and, by extension, management and employees – have choices, and that short-term gains may not always accord with the best long-term interests of a firm.

■ Discussion questions

1.1 Do you think AWB's conduct was wrong, or is engaging in bribery and corruption 'just a cost of doing business' in countries such as Iraq under the Saddam Hussein regime?

1.2 A check on Transparency International's list of business perceptions of corruption across countries (http://www.transparency.org/policy_research/surveys_indices/cpi/2010/results) suggests that Australian institutions and businesses are generally not considered to be corrupt. What do you think went wrong in this case?

1.3 In your opinion, which of the following organisations/people were responsible for AWB's behaviour? Give reasons for your answer.
   a. Saddam Hussein and his Iraqi government
   b. AWB management
   c. the United Nations
   d. the Australian government
   e. other organisation(s)/people

1.4   How would the following ethical perspectives/frameworks view AWB's behaviour?
    a. utilitarian approach
    b. deontological approach
    c. rights and justice approach
    d. light of day approach

5.   Do you think the crisis-management strategy advocated by Sandman would have been a better strategy for AWB to implement? Why or why not?

■ References

Aulich, C & Botterill, L 2007, *A very peculiar privatisation: the end of the statutory Australian Wheat Board*, Proceedings of the Australasian Political Studies Association Conference, Melbourne.

Australian Broadcasting Corporation (ABC) 2010, 'ASIC seeks to resume civil cases against AWB execs', ABC Rural, 30 June 2010, viewed 20 December 2012, <http://www.abc.net.au/rural/news/content/201006/s2941210.htm>.

Australian Government 2007, *Australian government response to the Report of the Inquiry into Certain Australian Companies in Relation to the UN Oil-for-Food Programme*, Attorney-General's Department, Canberra.

Australian Securities and Investments Commission (ASIC) 2007, 'ASIC launches civil penalty action against former officers of AWB', 19 December 2007, viewed 20 December 2012, <http://www.asic.gov.au/asic/asic.nsf/byheadline/07-332+ASIC+launches+civil+penalty+action+against+former+officers+of+AWB?openDocument>.

Bartos, S 2007, *Policy Implications of the AWB scandal*, paper presented to the Public Policy Network conference, Adelaide, February.

Boone, P, Gazdar, H & Hussain, A 1997 *Sanctions against Iraq: costs of failure, a report prepared for the Center for Economic and Social Rights on the Impact of United Nations-Imposed Economic Sanctions on the Economic Well-Being of the Civilian Population of Iraq*, United Nations, New York, November.

Cole, T 2006a, *Report of the Inquiry into Certain Australian Companies in Relation to the UN Oil-for-Food Programme. Volume 1: summary, Recommendations and Background*, Commonwealth of Australia, Canberra.

——2006b, *Report of the Inquiry into Certain Australian Companies in Relation to the UN Oil-for-Food Programme. Volume 4: finding*, Commonwealth of Australia, Canberra.

Crossette, B 1995, 'Iraq sanctions kill children', *New York Times*, 1 December, viewed 20 December 2012, <http://www.nytimes.com/1995/12/01/world/iraq-sanctions-kill-children-un-reports.html>.

Fisher, WB 2004, 'Iraq', in L Dean (ed.), *The Middle East and North Africa*, 50th edn, Europa, London, pp. 443–522.

Fry, E 2007, 'Six AWB executives face Iraq charges', *Financial Times*, 20 December, p. 16.

Griswold, DT & Lukas, A 1999, *Trade sanction – Cato Handbook for Congress: policy recommendations for the 106th Congress*, Cato Institute, Washington, DC, pp 555–63.

Harris, H 2007, 'Through public inquiry: Oil-for-Food, the Volcker and Cole Inquiries, and Australia's wheat exports to Iraq', *Business and Society Review*, vol. 112, no. 2, pp. 215–26.

Holmes, J 2006, 'Cash crop (Parts 1 and 2)', *Four Corners*, ABC TV, 10 April (Part 1), 17 April (Part 2), viewed 20 January 2013, <http://abc.net.au/4corners/content/2006/20060417_awb/video.htm>.

Mayman, J 2003, 'War over wheat: Australian farmers fret that the US farm lobby may invade their lucrative market in Iraq', *Far Eastern Economic Review*, vol. 166, no. 17, p. 41.

McManus, G 2006, 'AWB ruled out coming clean', *Courier-Mail*, 25 March, p. 7.

Minder, R 2006, 'Canberra grants permits to grain exporters', *Financial Times*, 23 December, p. 6.

Moldofsky, L 2006, 'Head of AWB resigns in Iraq kickbacks scandal', *Financial Times*, 10 February, p. 8.

Pash, R. 2006, 'Iraq to buy $134m of wheat', *The Age*, 30 March, viewed 22 January 2013, <http://www.theage.com.au/news/national/iraq-to-buy-134m-of-wheat/2006/03/29/1143441216087.html>.

Sexton, E 2010, 'Why did AWB shareholders settle for so little?', *The Age*, 20 February, viewed 22 January 2013, <http://www.theage.com.au/business/why-did-awb-shareholders-settle-for-so-little-20100219-olx0.html>.

Silkstone, D 2006, 'Downer, Vaile to go before Cole Inquiry', *The Age*, 8 April, viewed 22 January 2013, <http://www.theage.com.au/news/national/downer-vaile-to-go-before-cole-inquiry/2006/04/07/1143916721670.html?page=2>.

Smith, P 2010, 'Australian wheat exporter settles over Iraq kickbacks', *Financial Times*, 16 February, p. 16.

Squassoni, SA 2003, *Iraq: UN inspections for Weapons of Mass Destruction*, CRS Report for Congress, Congressional Research Service/Library of Congress, Washington, DC.

Sullivan, A 2005, 'The year we questioned authority', *Time Magazine*, vol. 166, no. 26, 26 December, p. 112.

Transparency International 2010, 'Corruption Perception Index: 2010', Transparency International, viewed 21 January 2010, <http://www.transparency.org/policy_research/surveys_indices/cpi/2010/results>.

Tucker, S 2006, 'Canberra fury as Iraq suspends wheat deal', *Financial Times*, 14 February, p. 9.

Urban, R 2010, 'Investors approve Agrium's bid for AWB', *The Australian*, 17 November, viewed 20 January 2013, <http://www.theaustralian.com.au/business/investors-approve-agriums-bid-for-awb/story-e6frg8zx-1225954630044>.

Volcker, PA, Goldstone, RJ & Pieth, M 2005a, *Independent Inquiry Committee into the United Nations Oil-for-Food Program: the management of the United Nations Oil-for-Food Program. Volume I – the report of the committee*, United Nations, New York.

—— 2005b, *Independent Inquiry Committee into the United Nations Oil-for-Food Program: the management of the United Nations Oil-for-Food Program. Volume III – report of the investigation*, United Nations, New York.

Wheat Exports Australia (WEA) 2009, 'About us', Wheat Exports Australia, 24 June, viewed 20 January 2013, <http://www.wea.gov.au/AboutUs/default.htm>.

2

Walking the blurry line in China: Negotiating deals and staying out of jail

Cheryl Rivers

On Sunday, 5 July 2009, four Rio Tinto (Rio) staff who were engaged in selling and supplying iron ore to Chinese steel mills were arrested in Shanghai. The event made headline news in Australia, where Rio's iron ore operations are head-quartered, and across the globe. In November 2010, an eminent American expert on Chinese law noted that putting a rival in prison is an increasingly common tactic in business negotiations (*Sydney Morning Herald* 2009). Was the arrest and subsequent imprisonment of the four Rio staff a negotiation tactic by the Chinese because of the importance of the iron ore to the Chinese economy? Or did the four men who were found guilty of violating Chinese law knowingly cross the line from making *guanxi* (which means connections or relationships) payments to paying bribes? What lessons can foreign companies operating in China learn from the Rio Tinto case?

The four men described in this case are now in jail in China. They are Stern Hu, who was Rio's manager in Shanghai and is Chinese-born with Australian citizenship, as well as Wang Yong, Liu Caikui and Ge Minqiang, all Chinese citizens.

■ Why were they jailed? Rumours and speculation

Initially, the four men were held without charge, and access was denied to Australian consular officials. The lack of access by both Australian officials and by Rio Tinto meant that until charges were laid on 12 August 2009, the rumour mill worked overtime. The men's arrests were labelled a spy scandal.

There were suggestions that the arrest of the four men was 'payback' for Rio Tinto Board's decision, on 5 June 2009, to scrap a strategic partnership with Chinalco (the Aluminium Corporation of China). Rio had been in discussions with Chinalco for months over a deal that would have seen Chinalco buy a stake in Rio's iron ore, copper and aluminium assets. Newspaper articles suggested that Rio's decision had caused a loss of face to the Chinese. China's official news agency, Xinhua, said: 'Rio Tinto is like a dishonourable woman: once she loved the money in Chinalco's pocket but she actually did not love the man himself. Now she is breaking faith and kicking down the ladder.' (Garnaut 2009a)

Their arrest was also linked to Chinese government anger about an Australian Government Defence Department White Paper that highlighted concerns about Chinese military power. However, as more information emerged, it seemed that the arrests were about the Chinese improving their negotiation position and a battle between the Chinese government and smaller steel companies (McDonald 2009). To understand this suggestion, it is necessary to have an appreciation of both how iron ore negotiations occur, and the role and importance of the negotiations between Rio Tinto and the Chinese Iron and Steel Association (CISA).

▥ Chinese demand for iron ore

China is the world's largest producer of iron ore as well as leading the world in steel, ahead of Brazil, which produced 380 megatonnes and Australia, which produced 370 megatonnes (Allen 2010). However, these numbers need to be adjusted because Chinese ore is of a much lower grade than Brazilian and Australian ore. Adjusted for equivalence, China produces about 400 million tonnes equivalent. Chinese production is made up by over 5000 iron ore mines in China and many of them are small and some are illegal. China does not produce enough iron ore to meet the demands of its own steel mills, so it relies on importing iron ore from Brazil and Australia.

▥ The iron ore benchmark pricing system

When the Rio staff were arrested, iron ore was sold under contract into the Chinese market (and other markets) using a 40-year-old *annual* benchmark system, and involved three major mining companies – Rio Tinto (an Australian company), BHP Billiton (an Australian-based company) and Vale (a Brazilian company). Under this pricing system, the first price agreed upon between one of the three dominant iron ore mining companies and one of their major customers in any market set the 'benchmark' that was followed by all the sellers (the iron ore producers) and all the customers (the steel mills) in that market for the next 12 months. Two former negotiators of iron ore contracts for the Australian producers describe these negotiations as 'six-months-of-mating-dance-meets-Fight-Club' (Dines & Kirchlechner 2010, p. 8). They say that those who have experience of the format 'cannot think of any process better designed to introduce tensions and discord into relationships between sellers and buyers' (2010, p. 8).

A benchmark price was set in each of the main iron ore markets in Asia: Japan, Taiwan, Korea and China. It is important to understand that the significance of agreeing to this first price (the benchmark) was that it set the price for an entire year. Thus Rio Tinto and CISA were not negotiating the price for a one-off shipment of iron ore, but rather the price that would be paid for a 12-month period. The benchmark system accounts for about 70 per cent of iron ore sales.

Steel mills can also buy iron ore on the spot market, where the price is based on supply – the iron ore that is available in the ports or on nearby ships – and demand – the number of steel mills that want to buy ore on a particular day. The spot price fluctuates widely, and in China had been the cause of considerable unhappiness. In late 2008, the spot price had nudged a 40 per cent premium over the benchmark price and Rio had diverted iron ore from its contracted sales into the spot market so it could make more money. Although Rio had, according to Stern Hu, 'acted in accordance with the letter of the contract, but not the spirit' (Garnaut 2009c, p. 1), many of the Chinese steel mills were displeased.

The 2009 benchmark price set in Japan

By 1 June 2009 (a month before the arrests), Rio had announced that it had agreed prices for its iron ore contracts with South Korean steelmaker POSCO and Taiwanese steelmakers CSC and Dragon on the same terms that it had agreed with Nippon Steel, its main Japanese customer. These terms were a 33 per cent price drop on the 2008 benchmark. This was the first time in six years that iron prices had fallen (recall that June 2009 was just eight months after the Global Financial Crisis had hit).

The Chinese position

A 33 per cent price cut was offered to the Chinese, but CISA would not accept it. Instead, the Chinese negotiators requested a 45 per cent drop on the 2008 benchmark. This demand created a tense atmosphere. Comments that appeared in the press prior to the arrests give a sense of how the Chinese viewed the situation.

Shan Shanghua, the head of CISA, denied reports that had appeared on the Steel Business Briefing website (http://www.steelbb.com), stating that his association might reverse its decision to reject the 33 per cent price cut for iron ore agreed between Rio Tinto and Nippon Steel: 'We absolutely will not accept a 33 per cent price cut.' (Garnaut 2009a, p. 1) He had publicly stated his goal to the Chinese press: 'the price of iron should be reduced by more than 40% and return to 2007 levels' (McDonald 2009, p. 11). He also said that Chinese steelmakers in CISA had no right to negotiate iron ore prices individually with overseas miners, and that any separate agreements reached with miners would be invalid (Garnaut 2009a).

The dual goals of CISA

It is this second comment that provides an insight into the objectives of CISA in the 2009 negotiations. CISA was new to the negotiations with Rio, as the Chinese government had decided to replace the negotiating team from the state-owned and second largest steel enterprise in the world, Baosteel, which had been in charge of negotiations for years. Baosteel had lost political support after it agreed to a 79 per cent price rise in 2008, which led to increased costs of Chinese steel production (Garnaut 2009c).

Recall that Shan Shanghua had said Chinese steelmakers had no right to negotiate iron ore prices individually with overseas miners (Garnaut 2009a). They were concerned because China has a two-tiered system for purchasing iron ore. The big steel mills can access the negotiations with iron ore producers and secure long-term fixed-price contracts, while the smaller and medium-sized steel mills are obliged to buy iron ore on the spot market – which is much more volatile. The system allows the large mills to buy more iron ore than they need on fixed-price contracts and then sell the ore that they do not need on to the smaller mills (Baroboza 2009d). According to Xu Zhongbo, an industry expert, 'there are 112 enterprises that are qualified importers.

But China has thousands of small mills, all of them waiting to get iron ore. So that gives big steelmakers a great chance to arbitrage.' (Baroboza 2009c, p. A8) The state-owned mills benefited from on-selling benchmark-priced iron ore – often at very large mark-ups – and the profits from these sales flowed through to the state mills, their executives and their middlemen friends (Garnaut 2010b).

When the small mills in China had complained about the two-tier pricing system, the Chinese government had responded by regulating against speculation by the larger mills. However, 'regulators rarely enforce rules' (Baroboza 2009d). In 2007 and 2008, there was surging demand for iron and commensurately high prices on the spot market. The incentive was in place for the smaller mills to bribe the larger mills and purchase the ore through them. A general manager of a trading company observed that 'the government had been trying to stop small steel producers from importing ore or buying it on the black market … the program had not been successful' (Baroboza 2009c, p. A8).

During the trial of the Rio negotiators, it became apparent that some Chinese steel mills had procured iron ore directly from Rio in approaches that did not involve the state-controlled state system. If these companies bought and sold iron ore directly from Rio, it would reduce the bargaining power of the benchmarking process, as well as take away some (illegal) earnings from the state-owned mills. Following the arrests of the Rio Tinto negotiators, an online newsletter, the *Economic Observer*, quoted a Baosteel source as saying that the 'Rio Tinto affair is really a struggle between the market power of China's steel companies and the political power of China's govern-ment planners' (McDonald 2009).

■ The different perspectives of the two sides

It is interesting to note that the CISA negotiators had been criticised publicly in China, even prior to the arrests. A newspaper report cited steel academic Xu Zhongbo as appraising CISA's head, Shan Shanghau, as having 'good experience for planning economies but not for international co-operation and business'. He appraised Deputy President Luo Bingsheng as being similarly incompetent, noting that: 'If someone has a higher position than him, then he will always follow that position. And he can change that position very quickly.' (Garnaut 2009c, p. 1).

On one side of the negotiations were the Chinese team members, who were political appointees and relatively inexperienced in negotiations with commercial counterparts like the Rio Tinto team. If they were to keep their bosses in government happy, they needed to keep the benchmark system in place, ensure that the smaller mills bought iron ore through the state-controlled system, and seek to achieve CISA chief Shan Shanghua's publicly stated goal that 'the price of iron should be reduced by more than 40% and return to 2007 levels' (McDonald 2009).

On the Rio Tinto side of the negotiations, there were negotiators who were tough and talented enough to have achieved a 79 per cent price rise the previous year. They also had an excellent understanding of the Chinese steel market. In October of 2008, Rio Tinto had commissioned a Chinese consultancy company, CBI, to collect data about iron ore production in China. According to press reports, Rio Tinto had sent a survey team across China to find out about what was going on, and get a reliable sample of how much iron ore China's 5000 mines were producing (Freed & Garnaut 2009). They used this information to calculate how much of China's local production would be shut down at different prices – Rio estimated which mines would close when the price of iron ore dropped to certain levels. Rio Tinto had released an earlier version of this financial model in May 2007, and it had been 'adjusted and re-labelled by investment bank analysts to become the industry standard' (Garnaut 2009b, p. 6). Rio used the monthly steel production figures published by the Chinese government to make an estimate of future steel production and gain a sense of the demand side of the Chinese steel production equation.

The Rio team relied on its analysis of the Chinese iron ore production and steel demand to hold firm on its negotiating position and resist the cut of more than 33 per cent of the 2008 benchmark. Rio kept arguing to the CISA team that demand for imported iron ore in China was strong. When Rio referred to facts and figures in the underlying data about profits and production in the Chinese steel and iron-ore mining industries, CISA's negotiators would reply with 'political diatribes' (Garnaut 2009c, p. 1). CISA's 'conclusions about the market were driven by politics and wishful thinking' (Freed & Garnaut 2009). Garnaut (2009b, p. 6) notes:

> Rio's vast negotiating advantage over its Chinese customers, was, and continues to be, that it collates information systematically and analyses it rigorously. Rio is dealing with a steel association that acts as if it has no idea how far its industry has moved beyond its powers of command.

The different perspectives and impact are also highlighted by Freed and Garnaut (2009, p. 11) in their observation that 'Rio would say the market is strong and CISA would deny this; Rio turns out to be right and for CISA it was beyond humiliating'.

Paying bribes and stealing state secrets

A stalemate was reached in the negotiations between CISA and Rio Tinto in early July. On 5 July, four members of the negotiating team were arrested. It was widely speculated that the men were being held for two crimes: paying bribes and obtaining Chinese state secrets. The Chinese and Australian press were using terms like 'espionage' and 'spying'. By 15 July, the China Daily newspaper was publishing allegations that the Rio Tinto staff had paid bribes to all 16 of China's major steel mills to gain access to industry data. China Daily was quoting an unnamed senior manager at a large steel company, who said that if the companies did not accept the bribes then Rio would have cut supplies. The allegations were that the Rio staff had accessed confidential government documents that showed production and inventory levels at state-owned mills (Baroboza 2009c).

Legal experts on Chinese law confirm that the country's state secrets laws are vague and could be applied to commercial secrets of state-owned companies (Baroboza 2009c). The state secret laws are vague enough to be used to punish political opponents or those who pose a threat to national interests. Legal scholars note that the Chinese government was considering revising the laws to bolster its credibility. A Chinese law specialist, Jerome Cohen of New York University, is quoted as saying 'the reason it is up for revision is there is widespread dissatisfaction with it. It lends itself to arbitrary treatment. Police can take advantage of stretching the law.' (Baroboza 2009a, p. 10)

In early July, the Australian Foreign Affairs Minister, Stephen Smith, voiced what many foreign business people were thinking: 'Frankly, it's difficult for a nation like Australia to see a relationship between espionage or national security and what appear to be suggestions about commercial or economic negotiations.' (Baroboza, 2009b, p. A4) An Australian academic who studies Chinese law, Peter Yuan Cai (2009), explained that the state secrecy laws covered all matters concerning national security and interests and section 4 of Article 8 classifies secret matters relating to economic and social developments as state secrets. Accordingly:

> it is highly probable that matters relating to iron ore negotiations, such as figures for current iron ore stockpiles at state-owned mills, procurement plans, and net profits made by steel mills can all be regarded as state secrets. Importantly, Article 11 of the State secrecy law empowers state entities that produce these secrets to classify them accordingly. (Cai 2009, p. 1)

This means that CISA could classify its information as a state secret.

In a media release dated 17 July, Rio's Head of Iron Ore, Sam Walsh, said that his employees had acted with integrity at all times and in accordance with Rio Tinto's strict and publicly stated code of ethical behaviour (Rio Tinto 2009a). The Rio Tinto code of ethics prohibits bribery and facilitation payments, as well as gifts and entertainment that could be intended or interpreted as a reward or encouragement for a favour or preferential treatment (Rio Tinto 2009b). The company's detailed 'business integrity guidance' mentions that accepting 'bribes or backhander payments relating to the award of supply or other contracts' is unacceptable (Rio Tinto 2003, p. 11). Rio also actively monitors operations by requiring managers to complete an annual survey on how well they are fulfilling their ethical obligations (PriceWaterhouseCoopers 2008) and trains its staff about business integrity – including anti-bribery and anti-corruption training (Rio Tinto 2010).

In early August, new allegations were published on an official website, administered by the Secrets Office of China's Central Committee. These suggested that Rio Tinto was involved in a six-year clandestine operation against China's steel mills. Specifically, it said Rio had been involved in 'winning over, buying off, prying out, routing one by one, and gaining things by deceit' (Garnaut & Murphy 2009a, p. 1). The site said that 'Rio's activities led China to pay A$123 billion (700 billion yuan, about US$102 billion) more for iron ore than they otherwise would have' (2009a, p. 1), even though the money was more than Rio's total iron ore sales to China during that period (2009a).

Charges: taking bribes and stealing commercial secrets

Five weeks after being arrested, the Rio executives were charged on 12 August, 2009. The Australian Department of Foreign Affairs said the men were suspected of using improper means to obtain commercial secrets about China's steel enterprises under Article 219 of Chinese criminal law, and of commercial bribery – which involves the offence of taking bribes from individuals not employed by state organisations – under Article 163 of the Chinese criminal law (O'Mally 2009). Commercial or trade secrets are defined as 'technical information and business information which is non-public, can bring economic benefits to the party that has rights therein and is practical, and for which the party that has rights therein has adopted measures to maintain its confidentiality' (Downing 2006, p. 7). The Chinese Criminal Code provides criminal sanctions for any serious trade secret offence that causes material losses to the owner of the trade secret (Zhou 2006). The charges were different from those originally mooted in the Chinese press: the men were charged with taking bribes, not paying them, and with obtaining commercial secrets, not state secrets.

The blurry line

When the Rio employees were first arrested, the Chinese government was quick to point to the obligation of foreign companies to obey China's laws. In mid-July, Qin Gang, a representative of the Chinese Foreign Affairs Ministry, said: 'There is an old Chinese saying: A man of noble character acquires his wealth by honourable means. What does honourable mean? First the law. We request foreign enterprises in China to abide by the laws and regulations of China.' (Sainsbury 2009) However, it is often easier to stay on the correct side of Chinese laws in theory than it is in practice, because they are ambiguous (as is the case with the trade secrets law) and/or are arbitrarily applied. Personal relationships are important in the way the law is applied in China. Although the Chinese government has undertaken a huge number of reforms (and continues to do so), it has failed to create a stable legal structure, and enforcement continues to be subject to personal accommodation such as intervention by local or regional government officials (Zhou & Poppo 2010).

Although the bribery law is fairly straightforward, the application of it is lackadaisical. On 19 May 2010 (a month and a half after the four Rio staff were sentenced), the Supreme People's Procuratorate of China and the Ministry of Public Security issued a joint document confirming that enterprises that offered bribes of more than 200 000 yuan (US$29 412) to non-governmental personnel in enterprises and other work units would face prosecution (Bin 2010). The amount of money that changed hands in the case of the Rio staff violated this figure. Yet only one of the 20 steel companies that had offered bribes to the Rio Tinto staff had been prosecuted when this case was written (in late 2010).

Another challenge for foreign companies is juggling their obligation to conform to the bribery and corruption laws while still participating in the gift-giving rituals around *guanxi* (Millington, Eberhardt & Wilkinson 2005). One way for Western companies to get around these challenges is to recruit local staff who have the necessary cultural understanding. Indeed, we could infer that part of Rio Tinto's motivation in recruiting Stern Hu and the other Chinese staff was to help bridge the cultural differences, or potential cultural misunderstandings, that might arise between the Australian and Western staff and the company's Chinese customers.

With regard to the trade secrets law, what a foreign enterprise can and cannot do is still ambiguous. It is also somewhat ironic that, although the Rio Tinto staff were charged and found guilty of stealing trade secrets, Rio Tinto was aware that its computing system was attacked by hackers in China around the time of the negotiations (ABC 2010), and that CISA was obtaining 'real-time updates about its negotiation position from whoever was listening to its phones and watching its email traffic' (Freed & Garnaut 2009, p. 1).

From August 2009 until March 2010, speculation about the four Rio employees continued in Chinese and international newspapers. After they were charged, they were allowed visits from their lawyers, and Stern Hu received visits from Australian consular staff. The Chinese prosecutors continued to collect information and interviewed numerous Chinese steel mill employees. The spot price for iron ore in China continued to rise. By August 2009, the spot price for iron ore had increased to US$110 per tonne (Garnaut & Murphy 2009b) – a considerable premium on the price offered to the Chinese by Rio Tinto. Rio Tinto continued to support its employees, and stated that it was not aware of any wrong-doing by them. In December 2009, Rio announced that it was restructuring its iron ore business in Asia. A new chief negotiator, Danny Goeman, was appointed to take responsibility for the negotiations in his role as Rio Tinto's Iron Ore Asia's general manager of marketing (Murphy 2009). On the Chinese side, it was announced that Baosteel would resume its role as head of the negotiations – although there was never a public statement about why this decision was made.

On 29 March 2010, the four men were tried and found guilty of the following accusations, as published in the *Wall Street Journal* (Areddy & Lin 2010):

- Stern Hu was accused of taking 6.4624 million yuan (US$950 000), including a 1 million yuan (US$146 000) bribe from Hebei Jainye Company and US$748,600 from Tanshang Steel. With regard to the obtaining commercial secrets, Stern Hu had met with Tan Yixin of Shougang Steel group on 8 June 2009 to get information about CISA's next price in the negotiations.
- Wang Yong, who was a sales director of a subsidiary of Rio Tinto, took bribes worth 75.1443 million yuan (US$11 million) including a US$9 million bribe from Du Shanghau of Rizhao Steel and a 1 million yuan (US$146 000) bribe from him to buy a house in Shanghai. On 17 June 2009, Wang Yong met Tan Yixin and obtained information about how Chinese companies were negotiating with Brazilian iron ore producer Vale.

- Ge Minqiang, a sales manager at the Shanghai representative office of Rio Tinto Singapore Co., was accused of taking 6.9453 million yuan (US$1 million), of which he kept 2.474 million yuan (US$362 000). In January 2008, Ge Minquiang obtained information about the content of a CISA meeting in Nanning, China from Handan Steel.
- Liu Caikui, also a sales director at the Shanghai representative office of Rio Tinto Singapore Co., took bribes totalling 3.7862 million yuan (US$554 000). He also obtained information about a CISA document concerning steel company bids on iron ore prices, and in October 2008 obtained information about steel output cuts that had been discussed in a CISA meeting.
- The information obtained was reported and emailed to the headquarters of Rio Tinto.

In conclusion, the judge said that the men had used illegal means to obtain commercial secrets that put the Chinese steel industry in a powerless position, and he added that their action had a direct cause-and-effect relationship on the industry's weakened position in negotiating iron ore prices.

Stern Hu was imprisoned for 10 years, Wang Yong was sentenced to 14 years' imprisonment, Lui Caikui was sentenced to seven years in prison and Ge Minqiang was sentenced to eight years in prison. Rio Tinto terminated their employment.

Discussion questions

2.1 What is the relationship between business ethics and the law? Should multinational companies take different approaches to their business activities in different countries/regions due to differences in the laws and/or cultural practices, or should they operate according to the same ethical standards globally?

2.2 Rio Tinto had a stringent code of ethics in place and audited conformance to its code. What could Rio have done differently in the circumstances?

2.3 Before charges were laid, the Chinese press published some information that was designed to shame Rio – recall that Xinhua was quoted as saying that Rio Tinto was like a dishonourable woman and an official Chinese government website alleged that Rio Tinto had been involved in clandestine affairs with Chinese steel mills that caused China to pay $123 million more for iron ore than it otherwise would have. Shaming tactics are common in China because the Chinese care about 'face' (*mianzi*). How did 'face' influence the actions of the different players in this case? How can foreign companies balance the desire to 'get the best deal' with preserving the 'face' of their Chinese counterparts?

2.4 Rio Tinto adopted a predominantly polycentric staffing policy for its Shanghai office, with its recruitment of local staff and appointment of Stern Hu (a Chinese-born Australian citizen) as manager. Identify some advantages and disadvantages of a polycentric approach for a multinational corporation that has to sell its products into China. In your answer, discuss the ability of staff to build relationships (*guanxi*) with customers and the need for a multinational company to ensure conformance with its codes of ethics. Based on your analysis of the pros and cons of a polycentric staffing policy, what sort of policy do you recommend Rio Tinto adopt going forward: ethnocentric, polycentric or geocentric? Explain your recommendation in light of Rio's experiences.

References

ABC 2010, 'Rio hacked at time of Hu arrest', *ABC News*, viewed 20 December 2013, <http://www.abc.net.au/news/strories/2010/14/19/2877042.htm>.

Allen, T 2010, 'Iron ore company review: exploration, development & production, March quarter 2010', viewed 20 February 2013, <http://www.rcresearch.com.au>.

Areddy, JT & Lin, B 2010, 'Court stenographer at Rio Tinto verdict', *China Real Time Report*, 29 March.

Baroboza, D 2009a, 'China says Australian is detained in spy case', *New York Times*, 10 July, p. A10.

—— 2009b, 'Espionage charges in China may be linked to negotiations over iron ore prices', *New York Times*, 11 July, p. A4.

—— 2009c, 'Mining company inquiry puts focus on a black market in China's steel industry', *New York Times*, 15 July, p. A8.

—— 2009d, 'Rio Tinto gave bribes to many, China says', *New York Times*, 16 July, p. A4.

Bin, X 2010, Anti-bribery laws extended to private sector', 20 May, viewed 15 January 2013, <http://China.org.cn>.

Cai, Y 2009, 'The long arm of the Chinese state secrecy law', paper presented to East Asia Forum, Australian National University, Canberra.

Dines, C & Kirchlechner, P 2010, 'Let the annual ironmen tussle begin', *The Age*, 20 January, p. 8.

Downing, KJ, 2006, 'Trade secret law and protecting your client's process', ABA Section of Litigation, viewed 20 December 2012, <http://www.foley.com>.

Freed, J & Garnaut, J 2009, 'Exit the dragon', *Sydney Morning Herald*, 6 June, p. 1.

Garnaut, J 2009a, 'China ire over Rio's Chinalco "dishonour"', *The Age*, 9 June, p. 1.

—— 2009b, 'Rio's market intelligence gives it iron edge over China', *The Age*, 17 August, p. 6.

—— 2009c, 'Trade secrets: the iron ore wars', *The Age*, 22 August, p. 1.

—— 2010a, 'Pluck up corporate courage in China', *Sydney Morning Herald*, 30 November, p. 6.

—— 2010b, 'A year on, secrets, lies and corruption remain at the heart of the Rio Tinto case', *Sydney Morning Herald*, 6 July, p. 6.

Garnaut, J & Murphy, M 2009a, 'China's $120bn Rio spy claim', *The Age*, 10 August, p. 1.

—— 2009b, 'Rio spied for six years: China', *Sydney Morning Herald*, 9 June, p. 1.

McDonald, H 2009, 'China thought we wouldn't care for Hu', *Sydney Morning Herald*, 25 July, p. 11.

Millington, A, Eberhardt, M & Wilkinson, B 2005, 'Gift giving, *guanxi* and illicit payments in buyer–supplier relations in China: analysing the experience of UK companies', *Journal of Business Ethics*, no. 57, pp. 255–68.

Murphy, M 2009, 'Rio marketing boss takes over ore price talks', *Sydney Morning Herald*, 12 December, p. 3.

O'Mally, S 2009, 'Stern Hu faces "lesser charges" in China, *The Age*, 12 August.

PriceWaterhouseCoopers 2008, *Confronting corruption: the business case for an effective anti-corruption programme*, PriceWaterhouseCoopers, Sydney.

Rio Tinto 2003, *Business Integrity Guidance*, Rio Tinto, London.

—— 2009a, *Shanghai employees – Update 1*, viewed 12 December 2012, <http://www.riotinto.com/media/18345_media_releases_18235.asp>.

—— 2009b, *The way we work: our Global Code of Business Conduct*, Rio Tinto, London.

—— 2010, *2009 annual report*, Rio Tinto, London.

Sainsbury, M 2009, 'Beijing warns Australia against "noisy" interference in Stern Hu case', *The Australian*, 17 July.

Sydney Morning Herald 2009, 'China: get rich, go to jail', *Sydney Morning Herald*, 29 November, p. 16.

Zhou, KZ & Poppo, L 2010, 'Exchange hazards, relational reliability, and contracts in China: the contingent role of legal enforceability', *Journal of International Business Studies*, no. 41, pp. 861–81.

Zhou, LW 2006, *Criminal sanctions for trade secret offences: China law and practice*, Euromoney Institutional Investor (Jersey) Ltd, Hong Kong.

3

The feasibility of solar energy in el Junco

Julie Rowney and Alejandro Cisneros

Access to energy is critical to ensuring development in the world's poorest countries; however, an estimated 1.5 billion people in developing countries have no such access. This problem is most severe in remote areas, where the majority of the population live without electricity. In such instances, access to even a small amount of electricity could lead to life-saving improvements in agricultural productivity, health, education, communications and access to clean water (Grimshaw & Lewis 2010). Almost all developing countries, including Latin America, have enormous solar power potential (WHO, UN Development Program 2009). What is unfortunate is that the countries that receive solar energy support are often also those least able to benefit from the development, due to a lack of knowledge and capacity to take advantage of the solar power and facilitate conversion to electricity (Grimshaw & Lewis 2010).

Renewable energy: Latin America and the Caribbean

In 2007, in Latin American and Caribbean countries, installed capacity for power generation grew at a yearly rate of 3.51 per cent – 0.29 per cent higher than the previous 10 years (OLADE 2007). Most of the region's power was generated by hydroelectric plants (56.7 per cent) followed by thermoelectric (39.7 per cent). The countries with electricity coverage rates of over 96 per cent and are Chile, Costa Rica, Barbados, Uruguay, Brazil, Suriname and Venezuela, while those with the lowest coverage levels are Honduras (67 per cent) and Haiti (34 per cent) (OLADE 2007). Energy demand in the region has increased by an average of 35 per cent over the last decade and, despite the global recession, it is currently experiencing a positive flow of funding from investors.

There are some projects in renewable energy development in Latin American countries. For instance, Argentina is building its first solar energy park in the north-western province of San Juan. This park is meant to be the most powerful solar energy park in Latin America (Valente 2010). It has the support of Brazilian, German and Spanish companies, which together with the provincial government will provide an estimated US$120 million dollars. Likewise, Brazil is developing solar, wind and tidal energy projects throughout the country (2010). In the southern region of the continent, Chile is focusing on the huge solar capacity of the Atacama Desert with the Atacama Solar Platform Project, which has the potential to become the world's largest power-generation plant (Origlia 2009). Berliant (2010) believes Latin America is ready for solar and other forms of renewable power. Experts say that Latin America is being electrified, with US$100 billion in power generation projects underway. They see nuclear and renewable energy as being a major part of the energy mix (Berliant 2010).

Ecuador and renewable energy

Ecuador is located in western South America, bordering the Pacific Ocean to the west, between Colombia and Peru. Thus Ecuador is located in the middle of the world, so its solar potential is enormous. Because of its geographical location, the climate in Ecuador varies from region to region, from tropical along the coast and the Amazonian jungle, cooler at higher elevations and temperate in cities located in the Andes corridor. Due in part to the wide variety of conditions, it is obvious that Ecuador has a huge amount of natural resources to be exploited for sustainable energy development.

Ecuador produces mainly oil and some natural gas; crude oil is used in domestic refineries and for export. Residential energy consists mainly of electricity, traditional biomass and petroleum products. Ecuador has a net electricity surplus, but it often faces supply shortages during the October–March dry season, when hydroelectricity output declines. To make up for these shortfalls, Ecuador must import electricity from Colombia (Developing Renewables 2006). Even though a large percentage of electricity production comes from hydro, the energy production is dominated by the use of hydrocarbons, especially oil. New renewable technologies (wind, solar, geothermal) are not represented in the total energy supply (Developing Renewables 2006).

The Ecuadorian Constitution (2008) states that the government will promote the use of new technologies that are environmentally friendly and that utilise renewable sources of energy to reduce environmental impact and the country's dependency on energy generated from fossil fuels (Asamblea Nacional Constituyente 2008). Moreover, the Constitution states that the government will encourage the use and development of non-conventional electric resources with the aid of public organisations, financial institutions, universities and private institutions. According to CONELEC (2008), the state energy entity, a total of 49.66 per cent of Ecuadorian energy is produced by hydraulic power (see Figure 3.1). However, Ecuador is not self-sufficient, and there is a lack of equal access to energy among its inhabitants, especially in the rural areas (Ministerio de Electricidad y Energía Renovable 2010). At the end of 2009 and the start of 2010, Ecuador experienced its latest energy

Figure 3.1: Electric energy generation in 2007 (%) *Data Source:* CONELEC (2008). Figure is authors' elaboration.

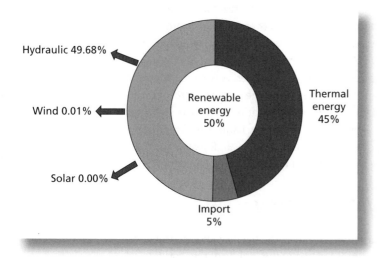

shortages due to a lack of rain, which caused a lowering in the flow of rivers that feed the hydroelectric plants. Having this kind of problem in a country that has abundant natural resources is unacceptable, and as a result there are emerging ideas and concrete projects for diversifying the sources of energy and generating energy from photovoltaic cells and wind turbines (Ministerio de Electricidad y Energía Renovable 2010). According to the new Hydroelectric Matrix provided by the Ministerio de Electricidad y Energía Renovable (MEER) (2010), Ecuador is planning to increase the percentage of hydroelectric energy from 42 per cent up to 86 per cent by 2020 and to reduce thermal energy from 34 per cent to 3 per cent (Tech4CDM 2008).

The El Dorado Company and the El Junco Project

The community of El Junco, located in the central part of the province of Manabí, has daily energy shortages which are limiting its development. The province of Manabí is located along the central part of the Pacific coast between the provinces of Esmeraldas, Santa Elena and Guayas, while the west side of the province faces the Pacific Ocean (Impulsar Beta 2012). Manabí does not have many elevations, with its highest point just 500 metres above sea level. Manabí is known for its vast cultural and ancestry heritage. It was the home of early cultures, and its legacy can still be found in local activities and traditions (Manabi Gobierno Provincial 2012). The province has a 350-kilometre coastline and also encompasses many fluvial systems coming from the Andes; these give Manabí an average temperature of 25°C during the months of June through December; however, the climate might change abruptly due to the effect of El Niño. Manabí is also known for its beaches, fishing villages, commercial centres such as Manta – one of the major ports in Ecuador – and Machalilla National Park, which has rich vegetation and variety of species of fauna as unique as the Galapagos Islands (Manabi Gobierno Provincial 2012).

El Dorado Road Construction (ERC), an Ecuadorian company, established its operations base camp in El Junco. Its core business is road construction consultancy. Until now ERC has produced energy through diesel generators, which barely meet the company's energy needs in terms of either quality or quantity. Moreover, diesel generators produce nitrogen oxide (NOx) emissions; NOx is considered to be responsible for the formation of ground-level ozone, or smog. It also contributes to acid rain and adversely affects the human respiratory system.

As part of the firm's expansion plan, ERC is assessing the feasibility of implementing a renewable source of energy and developing a strategy for implementation. Because El Junco is located in the coastal region of Ecuador, it has the privilege of continuous access to resources such as wind, sun and water, which seems promising for the enterprise's interest in producing and supplying its own energy. According to the Ministerio de Electricidad y Energía Renovable (MEER) (2010), the country's potential for producing renewable energy has been poorly exploited. ERC wants to be the pioneer in this area. Implementation of the project will not only benefit ERC, but also the community, and government support would be an added advantage. After an in-depth analysis, ERC's board of directors decided to study the possibility of implementing a photovoltaic system so ERC could supply its own energy and eliminate the use of diesel. Designing policies, strategies and measurements to increase the usage of renewable sources of energy will benefit and prompt development in rural areas, where the quantity, availability and distribution of a renewable resource is present (Corporacion para la Investigacion Energetica 2008). This goal has the support of local authorities such as the Consejo Nacional de Electricidad (CONELEC), Corporación de Investigación Energética (CIE) and MEER (2008).

In order to convert energy from the sun, it is necessary to have a solar cell that turns sunlight directly into electricity without fuel, moving parts or waste products. All of the current sources of energy produce undesirable by-products, such as spent fuel and wasted heat; in the case of fossil fuels, carbon dioxide is produced and released into the atmosphere. The same effect can be seen in small-scale electricity production using diesel generators (Lynn 2010). Solar cells work silently and effortlessly, which makes them a model of operational simplicity; however, the technology's efficiency is not yet well developed (Lynn 2010). Demand for solar power is rising as individuals and societies express increasing concern about the environment.

ERC also planned to create a Technology Transfer Centre. Engineers would be trained and thus improve their skills; this would translate into 'know–how' for ERC and would give the company a competitive advantage. In addition, ERC is considering a Strengths, Weaknesses, Opportunities and Threats (SWOT) analysis. Hence, a decision to implement a photovoltaic system could fit the image ERC wants to acquire: as a company that performs environmentally friendly activities within a socially responsible framework (ERC 2010).

◼ Designing the photovoltaic system

The proposed photovoltaic system will be incorporated into ERC's base camp, which consists of a four-storey building. The ground floor is the workshop and parking space, and the first floor houses the reception area, the general manager's office and five spaces for employees. The second floor provides housing for the field engineers and workers. It consists of seven rooms, which can accommodate up to 14 workers. The third floor, under construction, will be the general manager's office. Importantly, the property is large enough to hold a significant number of photovoltaic panels. Additionally, the façade of the building can do the same task, as well as improving the aesthetics of the building.

The size of the system will depend on the amount of loads – the amount of volts needing to be supplied. Depending on the size, the costs will vary. In order to provide different options to the company in terms of energy requirements, the total loads have been divided into four categories:
1. *Basic:* refers to the lighting system including all light bulbs together with rooms' loads (TV sets, radios, cable decoder, etc.).

2. *Office:* includes all the office appliances that need to be used during working hours.
3. *Workshop:* refers to the electric tools used for maintenance of equipment and tools that are being used in the construction of the building, such as welders.
4. *Overall:* the final category will be the total loads, which will include all the three categories.

In order to properly determine the financial viability of the proposed project, the following financial indicators have been used: net present value (NPV), the internal rate of return (IRR) and the payback period. If the NPV is bigger than zero, then the project is feasible and will produce income for ERC. The IRR is the percentage profitability of the project, considering each year's cash flow; this rate is to be compared with the cost of capital – if the IRR is bigger than the cost of capital, then it is worthwhile to invest in the project. Finally, the payback period will show the period of time required for a return on an investment to repay the sum of the initial investment (*New York Times* 2010).

For each of the four categories, the source of financing is 50 per cent shareholder financing and 50 per cent bank loan – a 15-year term loan at an interest rate of 9.78 per cent (PICAVAL 2010) . The initial investment for all of the categories will depend on the quantity of batteries, PV cells, controllers and inverters needed to operate the system (see Table 3.1).

Importantly, ERC will save money by not buying energy from the government, thus increasing its cashflow. Currently, ERC provides its own energy through the diesel generator only when there are blackouts at the base camp. ERC's income is generated by two main activities: learning income, since the company will develop a Technology Transfer Center (ERC 2010); and the consultancy services that have been the company's core business (ERC 2010) (see Table 3.2).

In order to analyse the feasibility of the project, it is necessary to obtain the NPV. All the future cash flows were brought back to the present with a discount rate of 9.78 per cent. If the NPV is greater than zero, the investment will add value to ERC, making the project feasible. Moreover, if the present value is equal to zero, the project is still feasible because ERC will neither gain nor lose value but in turn there will be other

Table 3.1: Initial investment				
	Basic	Office	Workshop	Overall
Solar Panel Exmork Wp/24V DC	$769 440.00	$ 3 600.00	$161 280.00	$ 964 320.00
Charge Controller Morningstar Tristar 45	$13 080.48	$ 571.20	$2 741.76	$ 16 393.44
Inverter 192 VDC 10.000VA 11VAC	$ 53 860.80	$ 2 352.00	$11 289.60	$ 67 502.40
Millenium Batteries	$195 840.00	$ 8 640.00	$40 320.00	$ 244 800.00
Total initial investment	$ 1 032 221.28	$ 45 163.20	$ 215 631.36	$ 1 293 015.84

Source: Authors' elaboration.

Table 3.2: Monthly savings and income				
	Basic	Office	Workshop	Overall
Monthly savings	$ 100.38	$ 4.24	$ 20.86	$ 125.48
Learning	$ 2 000.00	$ 2 000.00	$ 2 000.00	$ 6 000.00
Consultancy services	$ 20 000.00	$ 20 000.00	$ 20 000.00	$ 60 000.00
Total inflows	$ 22 100.38	$ 22 004.24	$ 22 020.86	$ 66 125.48

Source: Authors' elaboration.

gains, such as the company's image. The payback period is better when the investment is recovered faster and the IRR will be considered better when it is greater than the opportunity cost. In this case, the opportunity cost will be the rate at which the loan is obtained (9.78 per cent). The results are presented in Table 3.3.

Table 3.3: Principal economic indicators				
	Basic	Office	Workshop	Overall
Net present value	$ 806 246.05	$ 179 829.04	$ 9 530.83	$ 1 066 783.93
Payback time (years)	4.54	0.22	1.54	5.27
Internal rate of return (IRR)	2.13%	48.72%	10.21%	1.68%

Source: Authors' elaboration.

As shown in Table 3.3, the largest NPV, the lowest payback time (2.5 months) and the biggest IRR are in the office category.

▦ Environmental footprint analysis

All electricity generation produces CO_2 and other greenhouse gases. In order to be able to compare the impacts of these emissions, the total CO_2 amounts emitted throughout the system's lifetime have to be calculated (Parliamentary Office of Science and Technology 2006). For this purpose, emissions can be divided into two groups: direct emissions, which arise during the operation of the system; and indirect emissions, which arise during other non-operational phases of the life-cycle. Among the energy production technologies, coal, oil and gas have the largest carbon footprints, because these fuels burn during operation. Non-fossil fuel technologies such as wind, photovoltaic, hydro, biomass, wave/tidal and nuclear are known as 'low carbon' or 'carbon neutral' because they do not emit CO_2 during their operation. However, they are not 'carbon free', since CO_2 emissions appear during other phases of their life-cycle (2006).

The total amount of CO_2 and other greenhouse gasses emitted during the full lifetime of a process or product is known as the carbon footprint (Parliamentary Office of Science and Technology 2006). It is expressed in grams of CO_2 equivalent per kilowatt hour of generation ($grCO_2Eq/kWh$). A carbon footprint can be calculated using the Life Cycle Assessment (LCA) methodology. This analyses the commutative environmental impacts of a process or product through all the stages of its life; this methodology is also called the 'cradle-to-grave' approach. It takes into account the energy input and emission output in the production process, during operation and while decommissioning (Parliamentary Office of Science and Technology 2006).

In order to perform the LCA, it is necessary to know the process by which the solar panels are produced. Panels are mainly produced in North America and, given the energy share described by the US Department of Energy (2010), the power that built the panels potentially comes from a mixture of energy generation: coal, oil, natural gas, nuclear, hydro and/or wind. Those energies produce emissions while being generated, and need to be considered as part of the carbon footprint of the photovoltaic system.

The office category represents the lowest investment to ERC. Table 3.4 provides the information required by this category. The data have been obtained from the potential PV panels that ERC will use if the project is implemented.

Table 3.4: 'Office' PV system characteristics	
Amount of PV Panels, units	80
Amount of PV Panels, m^2	8870
System lifetime, years	30
Days in a year	360
System output, kWp	12

Source: Authors' elaboration.

Using the above data, it is possible to calculate the total amount of electricity consumed in the production process of the system, which is approximately 2410 MWh. To provide a better understanding of the energy used by the PV panels' manufacturing and the energy created by them, the energy payback time (EPBT) needs to be calculated (Blakers & Weber 2000). EPBT is the time the energy production of the PV system will take to match the energy consumed by it, after which the system can be considered carbon neutral. For the system that ERC would utilise, the estimated EPBT is 3.72 years. In approximately four years, the system will produce the amount of energy used to build it, after which it can be considered carbon neutral (Paul Scherrer Institute 2009).

The emissions from the PV system during its manufacturing process have been calculated, and the figure is 1.71E6 kgCO$_2$E. It is important to mention that the PV system has a lifetime of 30 years, which needs to be taken into consideration. In order to compare the emissions that are going to be avoided, it is necessary to calculate the amount of emission incurred by the diesel generator during its 24-year lifetime. This is the amount of time that the system will be fully functional and actually decreasing CO$_2$ emissions after the payback period. Assuming that the generator is going to be used 24 hours a day for 360 days a year, the total emissions of the generator are 3.62E6 kgCO$_2$. To take into consideration the decommissioning emissions, using the mentioned rule of thumb leaves a value of 48,203.59 kWh, which translates into an energy requirement of $3.41E4 \, kgCO_2E$. In order to explain how these comparisons work, as explained above, the LCA consists of three main areas: manufacturing, operation and decommissioning. Table 3.5 provides a summary of the LCA results for ERC.

Table 3.5: LCA for ERC	
Life-cycle analysis for ERC	
Manufacturing	$1.71E6 \, KgCO_2E$
Emissions savings	$(3.62E6 \, KgCO2)$
Decommissioning	$3.41E4 \, KgCO2E$
Total	$1.88E6 \, KgCO2$

Community involvement and relations

Energy significantly influences life. It is influential in practically all aspects of human welfare, including access to water, productivity, health care, education, job creation, climate change and environmental sustainability (WHO, UN Development Programme 2009). This argument is no different from the reality that ERC is facing in operating in a rural area of Ecuador. Electricity is neither reliable nor available consistently. For ERC, this creates many disadvantages in terms of performance of the company's daily activities; however, this issue has partly been solved by using a diesel generator. The surrounding area of ERC has a small village, comprising 20–30 families, which has been affected by the company's operations (ERC 2010). When there was no company, people were dedicated to subsistence agricultural activity, which was difficult as the soil was too arid and the amount of rain insignificant (ERC 2010). But when ERC settled in el Junco, it created small economies.

Community involvement has played a major role during ERC's activities in el Junco, and if the Board of Directors decides to implement the project, more people will be employed for each of the new activities (ERC 2010). The company's management is committed to training local people to operate the system, and it knows all the details involved in photovoltaic power generation (ERC 2010). The scope of this project does not involve a phase during which the community can directly benefit from the generation produced from the photovoltaic system; however, the indirect effect is a cleaner environment (ERC 2010) and employment opportunities. In addition, ERC and members of the community will gain knowledge about mounting and operating the system.

Discussion questions

3.1 Evaluate this project in terms of qualitative and quantitative benefits for ERC, for the community and for the government.

3.2 What are the strengths, weaknesses, opportunities and threats (SWOT) relating to this project?

3.3 Which are the factors to be improved in order to decrease costs for ERC?

3.4 Briefly discuss the strategy presented by the company. What changes could you suggest that will enable this strategy to increase the benefits of the project?

3.5 Should the company implement the PV system? Why or why not?

References

Asamblea Nacional Constituyente 2008, *Constitución del Ecuador*, Government of Ecuador, Quito.

Berliant, L 2010, 'Energy Boom', viewed 1 June 2010, <http://www.energyboom.com/solar/latin-american-solar-takes>.

Blakers, A & Weber, K 2000, *The energy intensity of photovoltaic systems*, Australian National University, Canberra.

CONELEC 2008, 'Atlas Solar del Ecuador', viewed 1 June 2010, <http://www.conelec.gov.ec/downloads/Atlas.pdf>.

Corporacion para la Investigacion Energetica 2008, *Atlas Solar del Ecuador con fines de generacion electrica*, CONELEC, Quito.

Developing Renewables 2006, *Renewable energy in emerging and developing countries: current situation, market potential and recommendations for a win–win–win for EU industry, the environment and local socio-economic development*, Developing Renewables, Quito.

ERC 2010, Interview with A Cisneros.

Grimshaw, D & Lewis, S 2010, *Solar power for the poor: facts and figures*, Science and Development Network, viewed 20 February 2013, <http://www.scidev.net/en/features/solar-power-for-the-poor-facts-and-figures-1.html>.

Impulsar Beta 2012, *Impulsar Beta*, viewed 20 November 2012, <http://www.impulsar.org>.

Lynn, P 2010, *Electricity from sunlight: an introduction to photovoltaic*, Wiley, London.

Manabi Gobierno Provincial 2012, 'Manabi Gobierno Provincial', viewed 20 November 2013, <http://www.manabi.gob.ec>.

Ministerio de Electricidad y Energía Renovable 2010, *Ministerio de Electricidad y Energía Renovable*, viewed 1 June 2010, <http://www.meer.gov.ec/Meer/portal_meer/internaView.htm?code=1160&template=meer.internas>.

New York Times 2010, New York Times *glossary of financial terms*, New York Times Publishing, New York.

OLADE 2007, *Energy statistics report*, OLADE, Quito.

Origlia, G 2009, 'Atacama Desert could become the largest power', *GreenMomentum*, 4 March.

Parliamentary Office of Science and Technology 2006, *Carbon footprint of electricity generation*, Postnote, London.

Paul Scherrer Institute (PSI) 2009, *Life cycle analysis of photovoltaic energy systems*, PSI, Villigen, Switzerland.

PICAVAL 2010. *Reporte de Mercado*. Quito: PICAVAL.

Tech4CDM 2008, 'Proyecto Tech4CDM', viewed 1 June 2010, <http://www.tech4cdm.com/uploads/documentos/documentos_La_Electrificacion_Rural_en_Ecuador_d6701fbe.pdf>.

US Department of Energy 2010, 'Energy sources: US Department of Energy', viewed 30 June 2010, <http://www.energy.gov/energysources/index.htm>.

Valente, M 2010, 'Energy – Latin America: moving towards renewables, viewed 230 June 2010, <http://globalgeopolitics.net/wordpress/2010/03/17/energy-latin-america-moving-towards-renewables>.

World Health Organization (WHO), United Nations (UN) Development Programme 2009, *The energy access situation in developing countries*, WHO, New York.

4

Colombian coffee: Issues of sustainability?

Christina Stringer and Adriana Roldán-Pérez

Colombia is renowned internationally for growing high quality Colombia mild Arabica coffee beans, characterised by a rich flavour and aroma. (Colombia mild Arabica coffee is an official type of coffee designated by the International Coffee Organisation.) Principally grown for the export market, Colombian coffee commands a premium price internationally, and is widely sought after by buyers. In 2007, the European Union granted a 'Protected Designation of Origin' order for Colombian coffee.

In recent years, Colombia's ranking in production terms has dropped from second to fourth place, with the country losing ranking first to Vietnam in 1999 and more recently to Indonesia in 2009. The drop in ranking is largely a result of changing climatic conditions. Coffee exports from Colombia declined for a second consecutive year, from 12.5 million bags in 2007 to 7.8 million bags in 2011 (ICO 2013). The 2009 production level was the industry's lowest since 1976 (USDA 2010), and much lower than initial forecasts of 11 million bags for 2010. Between 2005 and 2008, production levels averaged 11.71 million bags, guaranteeing surety of supply for international buyers. The decrease of three million bags of coffee represented a substantial loss of income not only for the local industry, but also for international traders and buyers – many of whom were unable to deliver the coffee for which they had entered into a forward purchase agreement and that they had on-sold due to the special characteristics of Colombian coffee. On the quality dimension, however, at the same time as production has been decreasing, quality has been increasing, due to the industry's focus on improving quality.

▦ The global coffee industry

There are two principal commercial coffee varieties: Arabica and Robusta. Coffee grown in different geographical locations has distinctive characteristics in terms of flavour and aroma. Arabica coffee beans, which are grown at altitudes above 1000 metres, are known for having a richer flavour and aroma, so Arabica coffee is able to command a higher market price. Robusta beans are grown at lower altitudes and in higher temperature climatic zones. While Robusta beans demonstrate a greater resistance to disease, the bean is considered to have a woody and bitter taste in comparison to Arabica beans, and hence is classified as an inferior bean.

Arabica beans, comprising 60 per cent of world production, are predominately grown in Brazil and Colombia. The International Coffee Organisation has divided world coffee production into four groups, based on the types of coffee grown in particular countries: Colombian mild Arabicas; other mild Arabicas; Brazilian; and other natural Arabicas Robustas (Roldán-Pérez et al. 2009). Brazil, Indonesia and Vietnam are the leading producers of Robusta beans. Together, these four countries controlled 60.5 per cent of total world production in 2011 (see Table 4.1).

Table 4.1: Total production of selected exporting countries (000 bags)							
	Type	Crop year	2007	2008	2009	2010	2011
Brazil	(A/R)	Apr-Mar	36 070	45 992	39 470	48 095	43 484
Colombia	(A)	Oct-Sep	12 515	8 664	8 098	8 523	7 800
Ethiopia	(A)	Oct-Sep	5 967	4 949	6 931	7 500	6 500
Guatemala	(A/R)	Oct-Sep	4 100	3 785	3 835	3 950	3 750
Honduras	(A)	Oct-Sep	3 842	3 450	3 575	4 326	4 500
India	(A/R)	Oct-Sep	4 319	4 062	4 827	5 033	5 333
Indonesia	(R/A)	Apr-Mar	4 474	9 612	11 380	9 129	8 250
Mexico	(A)	Oct-Sep	4 150	4 651	4 200	4 850	4 300
Peru	(A)	Apr-Mar	3 063	3 872	3 286	4 069	5 443
Uganda	(R/A)	Oct-Sep	3 250	3 197	2 797	3 290	3 212
Vietnam	(R)	Oct-Sep	16 405	18 438	17 825	19 467	20 000
Total world production			116 635	128 263	122 658	134 498	13 1253

Source: Table generated from data obtained from the International Coffee Organisation (2013).

There are a number of differences between the coffee industry in each of these four countries. For example, Brazil is a low-cost producer of coffee. Growers have achieved economies of scale through large-scale plantations methods that require intensive fertiliser application and utilise mechanised harvesting. In contrast, due to high levels of humidity in Colombia, coffee beans are hand-picked and washed; the care taken with the beans not only ensures a quality bean but gives Colombia a competitive advantage. The 1990s saw a significant period of growth for the Vietnamese coffee industry. Aided by government subsidies, the industry expanded production by planting over one million acres to emerge as a significant exporter. This resulted in Vietnam flooding the market with cheap Robusta beans. Indonesia is divided into more than 17 000 islands and the quality of coffee grown can vary greatly, depending on the region in which it is grown. The focus of this case study is the Colombian coffee industry.

Colombian coffee industry

In Colombia, coffee is grown by 566 000 growers in over 500 municipalities located in 18 different provinces (FNC 2010). Coffee exports represent around 5 per cent of Colombia's exports. The coffee industry in Colombia is a 'critical motor of social development' (Roldán-Pérez et al. 2009, p. 53); it is an economically sensitive industry that makes a significant contribution to social welfare. Over 94 per cent of coffee is grown on farms of less than 5 hectares, with 60.59 per cent grown on less than 1 hectare (FNC 2010). The prevalence of small holdings means that most coffee growers operate at a subsistence level. Furthermore, coffee may not necessarily be the only crop grown on the land. Growers have the option of selling to domestic cooperatives, MNCs and domestic exporting firms. Colombia exports over 90 per cent of its production with the United States as its principal export market, followed by Japan and Germany.

The decline in production that began in 2008 has been attributed to a number of factors. One such factor is the El Niño climate phenomenon, which resulted in a water deficit and sharp increases in the prices of fertilisers and chemicals on the international market. Another factor has been an increase in the strength of the peso against the American dollar. Declining production, coupled with less income due to unfavourable exchange rates, resulted in growers not having the necessary income to buy sufficient fertiliser and chemicals to take care of their plantations. In turn, this resulted in a number of trees becoming affected by increased infestation levels of rust disease, which destroys coffee trees. The industry has also been affected by coffee berry borer disease, which has the potential to wipe out whole harvests in affected areas. Both the coffee borer and rust have a greater impact at lower altitudes, and in Colombia coffee is grown at altitudes of up to 2500 metres. Yet another factor impacting the decline in production was the onset of La Niña in 2010, resulting in increased rainfall.

In addition to climatic conditions and price volatility, production has been negatively impacted by the age of the trees. On average, coffee trees produce less yield after nine years, and it is estimated that Colombia has 330 000 hectares of low-yielding trees. Under a government-subsidised program, the Federación Nacional de Cafeteros de Colombia (FNC) implemented a coffee renovation program to replant in the vicinity of 330 000 hectares of trees (USDA 2009). Between 2007 and 2009, 212 000 hectares of old and low-yielding trees were taken out of production in order to plant new trees. It takes between three and four years for coffee to reach its harvesting point, with mature trees yielding coffee beans for between two and three months of the year. The coffee renovation program has been hindered by small-scale, subsistence-level growers resisting the replacing of older trees because of an immediate loss in income. While there is concern about the short-term benefit, it is the long-term sustainable production level that is of greater concern.

Federación Nacional de Cafeteros de Colombia (FNC)

> The work of the Federation revolves around the coffee growers and their families ensuring Colombian coffee is grown in a sustainable manner, strengthening common interests within coffee-growing communities while positioning Colombian coffee as the best coffee in the world. (FNC 2011a)

As a key player in the industry, the FNC seeks to ensure growers receive a fair price for their coffee. While the FNC is a private capital firm with public objectives, it has a special agreement with the Colombian government by which the FNC manages resources from the National Coffee Fund. The FNC collects and manages taxes obtained from coffee exports. It represents over 500 000 coffee-growing families (Roldán-Pérez et al. 2009).

The FNC was established by Colombian growers in 1927, as they were concerned about foreign companies purchasing coffee beans from Colombian growers at prices below market value (Bentley & Baker 2000; Rettberg 2010). Growers sought not only to gain greater market access and a fair price for coffee beans, but also to provide economic and social benefits to the growers. The establishment of the FNC was seen as 'an ambitious project: in the beginning, the Federation had no shipping, banking or storage facilities and no scientific assistance' (Bentley & Baker 2000, p. 3). Today, the FNC – governed by the growers – is a significant player in the industry. Growers elect their representatives at the local, provincial and national levels; thus the FNC is a legitimate representative of coffee growers. Growers have the choice of selling to the FNC, MNCs or other domestic companies. The FNC functions as a buyer, processor and exporter of coffee, as well as undertaking quality-management programs, and involving itself in marketing and advertising. Buying around 30 per cent of Colombian coffee, the FNC operates 512 purchasing sites around Colombia as well as controlling a number of value-adding nodes along the value chain through investment in vertically related industries. A key function of the FNC is the enforcing of quality standards, the undertaking of research and development, and the provision of technical assistance to growers. Strategically, when world market prices are low, the FNC has the ability to store greater quantities of coffee beans in its warehouses to sell when the market price increases. It has invested significant resources in building up the market reputation of Colombian coffee: 'Since the 1920s, the FNC has built up markets based on its reputation for quality – Colombian coffee enjoys a premium of about 20 per cent.' (Bentley & Baker 2000, p. 5)

The FNC offers a guaranteed minimum purchase price to growers. The Coffee Policy Agreement (2008–11) provides $1.4 trillion Colombia pesos ($US737 billion) in economic aid to the coffee industry (Roldán-Pérez et al. 2009). Included in the agreement is a 'Price Protection Contract', wherein growers are guaranteed 474 000 Colombian pesos (approximately $US250) per 125 kilogram bag (Roldán-Pérez et al. 2009). The scheme administered by the FNC offers both price protection and a fixed income, which is essential for an industry characterised by subsistence-level growers. The guaranteed purchase price helps ensure quality standards as well as surety for the growers. Colombia is the only coffee-growing country 'that pays a subsidy when international prices are low and provides social services and infrastructure improvements in coffee-growing regions' (Global Exchange n.d.). The purchase price, based on the world price for coffee and the exchange rate, is communicated daily and ensures transparency within the industry:

> In this way the FNC accomplishes its aim of ensuring that all Colombian coffee growers receive the best possible price and minimizes the possibility that intermediaries and speculators take a portion of the price paid by international markets. (FNC 2011b)

Specialty coffee

The FNC produces and markets a range of specialty coffees, including indigenous, organic and environmentally responsible coffee, fair trade coffee and regional coffees with unique attributes. Specialty coffees, produced from green beans which are of exemplary or superior quality, or are produced under particular circumstances, are priced higher than regular coffee products. In 2009, specialty coffee comprised approximately 27 per cent of coffee exports, of which the FNC had a 43 per cent share. Specialty coffee can earn growers up to 200 per cent more than regular coffee (Zaino 2010).

The coffee industry is governed by a variety of international certification schemes, which fall under three main pillars: (1) economic; (2) environmental; and (3) social. In the economic pillar, UTZ CERTIFIED verifies that the coffee product has been produced in a socially and environmentally responsible manner. UTZ CERTIFIED 'helps coffee growers to be more professional and competitive in production and selling' (UTZ CERTIFIED 2011). In contrast, the environmental certification process is based upon sustainable agricultural practices. The Rainforest Alliance focuses on the conservation of biodiversity and protection of the environment and workers, whereas organic certification guarantees that 95 per cent of coffee beans have been grown organically. The social pillar encompasses fair trade, which is based on fairer trading practices for disadvantaged small-scale coffee producers. Under the fair trade scheme, producer groups are paid a social premium. Fair trade also incorporates environmental practices. The recent increase in Colombian coffee prices as a result of decreased production has meant that there is less incentive for customers to purchase Colombian fair trade coffee because of the differential in price (FNC 2010). Customers are less willing to pay a higher price for fair trade coffee from Colombia and are buying their fair trade coffee from other markets. In contrast, organic coffee has less effect on differential prices, so exports of organic coffee from Colombia remain stable.

When a grower considers becoming certified, the FNC often recommends that the grower starts with the 4C Association because it is simpler to implement. The 4C Association has developed a Common Code of the Coffee Industry (4C), with the goal of eliminating the worst practices in the coffee industry. Once growers have achieved 4C, they can then choose to move up to fair trade and Rainforest Alliance certification schemes (Interview FNC 2010). Some of the benefits of certification schemes for growers include market access and higher returns. However, there can be substantial costs associated with certification, which is a significant barrier to entry for many growers. Furthermore, the FNC itself cannot certify all the crops because they don't have the resources (FNC 2010).

Initiatives of the Federación Nacional de Cafeteros de Colombia

In 1940, as a result of lobbying by the FNC, the Colombian government established the National Coffee Fund (NCF) to undertake social, environmental and technological initiatives and sustainability. The NCF was commissioned with the purpose of purchasing of the majority of the domestic crop in order to ensure price stability for growers in Colombia. The FNC manages the NCF, which is funded from contributions by growers, coffee sales and Juan Valdez® royalties. The fund has financed 'a substantial number of social, infrastructure, environmental, diversification, agricultural counseling projects that rival the achievements of any NGO in the world' (Colombian Coffee Federation 2002). Some of the initiatives undertaken by the FNC include the following.

■ *Juan Valdez®*

In 1960, the Juan Valdez icon was launched to help market Colombian coffee:

> Juan Valdez, the friendly small-scale coffee grower, was rightly chosen by the Federation to epitomize and market internationally the image of widespread welfare, opportunity and wholesomeness associated with the Colombian coffee economy. (Rettberg 2010, p. 115)

Juan Valdez has achieved remarkable marketing success, particularly in the United States – the main export market for the FNC. In 1981, the Juan Valdez® brand was created to further promote Colombian coffee internationally. The success of Juan Valdez® was such that in 1985 it was voted 'America's Favourite Advertising Icon'. In 2002, Juan Valdez® Cafés were opened in domestic and international markets to continue to promote Colombian coffee and achieve greater returns for growers, as well as to compete more directly with companies such as Starbucks.

The cafés are owned and operated by Procafecol, a subsidiary of the FNC. Growers were given the opportunity to purchase shares in Juan Valdez Cafés. The cafés were opened in key locations in the United States, including Times Square in New York and Seattle, Starbucks' home city. Juan Valdez Cafés also expanded into Spain, Ecuador and Chile. Unfortunately, as a result of the economic crisis and resultant declining coffee consumption habits, Juan Valdez Café stores in the United States and Spain were closed. The FNC closed its flagship store in New York in 2010, the same year that they announced a worldwide expansion through a franchising scheme promoting upscale specialty coffee.

■ *Regional Coffee Guarantee Fund*

Through the Coffee Fund Guarantee program, the FNC underwrites loans from private banks to coffee growers. Small-scale coffee growers have limited access to collateral, and thus the program removes a major obstacle, giving growers the opportunity to improve production. Through the program, growers have access to lower interest rates, formal identification and bank accounts. There are some regions where ownership of land is not clear, and the identification guarantees growers' rights.

■ *Manuel Mejía Foundation*

In 1960, the FNC established the Manuel Mejía Foundation, a non-profit organisation established to improve the well-being of people in coffee-growing regions through formal and informal education. The Foundation enters into partnerships with corporations in order to contribute to improving the quality of education in Colombia. Partnerships have been established with Occidental Petroleum Corporation and the Genesis Foundation. Recent projects implemented by the Foundation include educating young people in social and vocational competencies, and teaching information and communication technology to coffee growers. In 2006, the FNC and the Manuel Mejía Foundation introduced the Virtual Classroom for Coffee Growers program, which trains coffee growers in information and communication technologies (ICT). Approximately 4500 growers have participated in the program, with a focus on improving the levels of coffee production as well as improving the quality of life for the growers and their families (FNC 2011c).

■ *Social and environmental initiatives*

The FNC is committed to social and environmental initiatives in order to strengthen the social fabric within coffee-producing regions. Bentley and Baker (2000, p. 6) state that 'nearly all the public works in the Central Coffee Belt are funded by the Federation [schools, roads, electricity] ... therefore, the Federation operates as a kind of competent, alternative government in the Colombian Coffee Belt'. The FNC receives a tax on coffee exports, to be spent on public goods (infrastructure, water systems, health clinics, schools), as well as receiving funds from non-profit organisations and companies for investment purposes. Key partners and donors include Nestlé, Sara Lee and USAID. The FNC takes on the role of the welfare state through the provision of social programs, including health care, education and food aid. (See http://www.federaciondecafeteros.org/particulares/en/sostenibilidad_en_accion/nuestra_trayectoria for details of social initiatives undertaken by the FNC between 1965 and 2007.)

■ Issues of sustainability

In 2009, the FNC estimated production to be 11 million bags of coffee, but in fact production was 8.09 million bags. Despite production increasing to 8.5 million bags in 2010, it was still short of the 10 million bags forecasted and the ideal 11 million to 12 million bags needed under normal conditions in order to ensure the sustainability of the industry (Stillman 2011). Furthermore, in 2011 production decreased further to just 7.8 million bags.

Coffee remains a vital commodity for Colombia, and the loss in production has had both enormous economic and social consequences. If production does not exceed 11 million bags, then there are likely to be serious implications for the growers – in particular, subsistence-level growers. Not only does the shortfall in production mean a significant loss of income for growers – some of whom are switching to planting other crops – but it also has an effect on the export markets, with buyers switching to purchasing coffee from other countries. Indeed, recent reports have questioned the future of the FNC due to the coffee crisis and the organisation's inability to more accurately predict production (Gomez Carmona, Guevara Gil & Velez 2010).

Discussion questions

4.1   Is there a new model that the FNC should be pursuing in order to respond to and meet international demand? How can Colombia reposition itself in the international coffee market?

4.2   What are the key differences between the work the FNC undertakes in areas of social development and the benefits obtainable through fair trade?

4.3   What might the different certification schemes mean for the promotion of Colombian coffee? Are the certification schemes competing? Discuss.

4.4   What can the FNC do to stimulate demand in the internal market?

References

Bentley, JW & Baker, PS. 2000, *The Colombian Coffee Growers' Federation: organised, successful smallholder farmers for 70 years*, Agricultural Research and Extension Network Paper No. 100, Overseas Development Institute, London.

Colombian Coffee Federation 2002, 'National Federation of Coffee Growers of Colombia (FNC)', paper presented to Global Grassroots Entrepreneur Trading Network Workshop, The World Bank, Washington DC, viewed 23 June 2010, <http://siteresources.worldbank.org/INTPOVERTY/Resources/335642-1124115102975/1555199-1124741378410/fnccs.pdf>.

Federation of National Coffee Growers (FNC) 2010, Interview.

—— 2011a, 'About us', viewed 11 January 2011, <http://www.federaciondecafeteros.org/particulares/en/quienes_somos>.

—— 2011b, 'FNC information', viewed 11 January 2011, <http://www.federaciondecafeteros.org/particulares/en/quienes_somos/fnc_en_cifras>.

—— 2011c, 'Extension services', viewed 31 January 2011, <http://www.federaciondecafeteros.org/caficultores/en/servicios_de_extension>.

Global Exchange n.d., 'Fair trade farmers in Colombia', viewed 15 December 2010, <http://www.globalexchange.org/campaigns/fairtrade/coffee/ColombiaFlyer.pdf>.

Gomez Carmona, S, Guevara Gil, J & Velez, ME 2010, 'The coffee decline' (translated from Spanish), *Poder 360°*, viewed 27 May 2010, <http://www.poder360.com>.

International Coffee Organisation (ICO) 2013, 'Total production of exporting countries', viewed 5 January 2013, <http://www.ico.org/prices/po_files/sheet001.htm>.

Rettberg, A 2010, 'Global markets, local conflict: violence in the Colombian coffee region after the breakdown of the International Coffee Agreement', *Latin American Perspectives*, no. 37, pp. 111–32.

Roldán-Pérez, A, Gonzalez-Perez, MA, Huong, PH & Tien, DN 2009, 'Coffee cooperation and competition: a comparative study between Colombia and Vietnam', report presented to the Virtual Institute of the United Nations Conference on Trade and Development (UNCTAD), viewed 10 October 2010, <http://vi.unctad.org/component/frontpage/?start=125>.

Stillman, A 2011, 'Colombian coffee growers face tough year', *BBC News Latin America and Caribbean*, viewed 25 January 2011, <http://www.bbc.co.uk/news/world-latin-america-12216419>.

USDA 2010, 'Colombia coffee annual: increased production and exports in prospect', *GAIN Report*, viewed 12 December 2010, <http://gain.fas.usda.gov/Recent%20GAIN%20Publications/Coffee%20Annual_Bogota_Colombia_6-10-2010.pdf>.

UTZ CERTIFIED 2011, 'FAQ', viewed 1 February 2011, <http://www.utzcertified.org/index.php?pageID=110>.

Zaino, J 2010, 'Special cup of Joe', *RFID Journal*, May/June, pp. 16–18.

5

Preserving paradise: Shell's sustainable development programs in the Philippines

Raymund B Habaradas

A global company like Shell faces multiple challenges whenever it operates in a developing country such as the Philippines, which still struggles with poverty and related problems like hunger, joblessness and disease. When dealing with local communities, Shell takes the stance of a good neighbour, continuously finding ways to contribute to the general well-being of the communities within which it operates. Its involvement in the anti-malaria program of Palawan, as illustrated in this case study, is evidence of how Shell has remained true to its commitment to sustainable development and stakeholder engagement.

■ Palawan, Philippines

The setting of this case study is a tropical paradise called Palawan, a narrow archipelago of 1700 islands on the western border of the Philippines. Stretching from Mindoro in the north-east to Borneo in the south-west, it lies between the South China Sea and the Sulu Sea. With a land area of more than 1.7 million hectares, Palawan is the country's largest province, and is composed of the long and narrow Palawan Island plus a number of other smaller islands that surround the main island. The Calamianes Group of Islands, to the north-west, consists of Busuanga Island, Culion Island and Coron Island. Durangan Island almost touches the western-most part of Palawan Island, while Balabac Island is located off the southern tip, separated from Borneo by the Balabac Strait. Palawan also includes the Cuyo Islands in the Sulu Sea. The disputed Spratly Islands, located a few hundred kilometres to the west, are considered part of Palawan by the Philippines, and are locally known as the Kalayaan Group of Islands (Palawan 2012).

Palawan's irregular coastline stretches for almost 2000 kilometres and is indented by numerous coves and bays that feature spectacular rock formations and pristine beaches. The terrain is a mix of coastal plains, craggy foothills, valley deltas and 'a vast stretch of virgin forests that carpet its chain of mountain ranges' (Palawan 2012). Palawan is home to two UNESCO World Heritage sites: the Puerto Princesa Subterranean River National Park and the Tubbataha Reef Marine Park. Also referred to as the country's last frontier, it is witness to the quest of a global company – Shell – to simultaneously achieve business, social and environmental goals through two major undertakings: (a) the Malampaya Deep Water Gas to Power Project; and (b) the Movement Against Malaria.

■ Shell in the Philippines

Shell has had a rich history of doing business in the Philippines ever since its kerosene products reached the country in 1897. Since then, the company has continually expanded its operations and has widened the range of its products and services for the Philippines market. These products, important to the progress and development of the country, include fuels – for example, Shell V-Power, Shell V-Power Diesel, Shell Diesel, Shell Super Unleaded E10; oils and lubricants – such as Shell Helix engine oils and Shell Advance motorcycle oils; others, like Shellane LPG and kerosene. Shell also provides card services to enhance its customers' experience with Shell's products. The company has card services that fit different needs, from fleet owners who are in search of better and more efficient ways to track fuel and oil expenses to private motorists who want to benefit from their loyalty in choosing Shell fuels to power their vehicles. The impact of Shell's presence in the Philippines is evident in the fact that, today, Shell has almost a thousand service outlets nationwide.

Table 5.1: Shell Philippines' historical milestones	
Year	**Milestone**
1897	Shell's kerosene products reached the Philippines for the first time.
1914	Shell established a corporate presence in the country. Through its trading centre, it imported kerosene and sold it to households in Manila and adjacent areas.
1940s	Encouraged by the growing economy, Shell offered more products and established numerous installations and depots throughout the country.
1960s	Shell built its first crude refinery in Tabangao, Batangas. Taking advantage of the rapidly growing agricultural sector, Shell engaged in the marketing and sales of chemicals and crop protection.
1970s	Shell began its oil and gas exploration efforts. These were meant to lessen the country's dependency on imported oil and gas products.
1980s	Shell started to supply LPG products to the Philippines and its neighbours in Asia when its refrigerated LPG terminal became operational in 1983.
1982	The Pilipinas Shell Foundation, Inc. (PSFI) was established and became active in providing livelihood and entrepreneurship training, and in undertaking other community-development endeavours.
1986	Shell bought majority ownership of Philippine Petroleum Corporation, then the country's only lube refinery.
1990s	Shell Philippines Exploration B.V. (SPEX) signed a service contract with Occidental Philippines, Inc. in 1990, paving the way for investments in oil and gas exploration in north-western Palawan.
1993	A bigger and more advanced refinery was built near Shell's existing facility in Tabangao. This new refinery, which increased Shell's production capacity, also produced unleaded gasoline and low-sulphur diesel fuel.
1998	Shell started developing and constructing the Malampaya field, which led to the production of natural gas in the country by the early part of the next decade.

Source: Compiled from Shell Philippines (2012).

The growth of Shell in the Philippines and the highlights of its corporate existence in the country are shown in Table 5.1.

Today, the Shell companies in the Philippines (SciP) include various companies engaged in oil and gas exploration, production, oil refining, distribution, sales and customer service (see Appendix). SciP has grown to be one of the Philippines' largest investors, directly employing over 4000 people throughout the archipelago.

▣ Vision, mission and core values

Like good corporate citizens, the Shell companies in the Philippines (SciP) seek to adhere to the vision-mission and values of the Shell Group. These values-driven statements guide Shell and all of its affiliates around the world in conducting business and providing the company's products with efficiency, profitability and responsibility in meeting the growing energy needs of the world (Shell 2010). Shell Group's vision-mission statement demonstrates its commitment to combining profitability with responsible and sustainable practice, evident in the description below:

> We believe that oil and gas will be integral to the global energy needs for economic development for many decades to come. Our role is to ensure that we extract and deliver them profitably and in environmentally and socially responsible ways.
>
> We seek a high standard of performance, maintaining a strong long-term and growing position in the competitive environments in which we choose to operate.
>
> We aim to work closely with our customers, our partners and policymakers to advance more efficient and sustainable use of energy and natural resources.

Shell employees are required to uphold the organisation's core values, which include honesty, integrity and respect for people, and to adhere to the fundamental practices of trust, openness, teamwork, professionalism and pride in what they do.

Shell's guiding principles

Shell companies in the Philippines take the organisation's guiding principles in relation to the areas of economic development, competition, business integrity, political activities, health, safety, security and the environment, local communities, communication and engagement, and compliance very seriously (Shell Philippines 2012). For example, when dealing with local communities, Shell companies strive to be good neighbours by helping members of the community (e.g. out-of-school youth) achieve their social and economic goals. Aside from providing jobs, Shell companies also implement a comprehensive set of programs (e.g. skills development, livelihood and enterprise development, health programs and other basic social services) that contribute to the general well-being of the communities within which they operate. They also work with other groups 'to enhance the benefits to local communities, and to mitigate any negative impacts' from their activities (Shell Philippines 2012).

Commitment to sustainable development and stakeholder engagement

Of particular interest to the communities in the Philippines (and to this case study) are the Shell companies' commitment to sustainable development, expressed in terms of generating robust profitability, delivering value to customers, protecting the environment, managing resources, respecting and safeguarding people, benefiting communities and working with stakeholders. Taken together, 'they help find a balance between Shell's long- and short-term goals' (Shell Philippines 2012).

Shell also recognises five areas of particular responsibility: to its shareholders, customers, employees, business partners and society. As stated in Shell's General Business Principles, it commits 'to conduct business as responsible corporate members of society, to comply with applicable laws and regulations, to support fundamental human rights in line with the legitimate role of business, and to give proper regard to health, safety, security and the environment' (Shell Philippines 2012). Recognising the varied circumstances within which its companies operate, and the potential for both opportunities and challenges, Shell encourages its corporate managers to continuously 'assess the priorities and discharge these inseparable responsibilities on the basis of that assessment' (Shell Philippines 2012).

Shell's commitment to sustainable development was clearly influenced by the intense international criticism of its environmental and human rights record in the Delta region of Nigeria and its controversial decision to dispose of the Brent Spar oil terminal in the North Sea. Organised campaigns against Shell, including consumer boycotts, cost the company millions of dollars in revenue and severely affected its reputation (Herz, La Vina & Sohn 2007). Because of the public backlash, Shell formalised its sustainable development policies and re-examined its approach to stakeholder engagement, which now actively sought the approval of the local community in addition to the official consent of authorities (Solleza & Barns 2003). In the Philippines, Shell authorities clearly had the lessons of the recent past in mind when they invested in the Malampaya Project.

■ The Malampaya Deep Water Gas-to-Power Project

Because the Philippines historically has relied on imported fuel for most of its industrial power requirements, the Malampaya Deep Water Gas-to-Power Project was a significant undertaking because it signalled the birth of the natural gas industry in the country (Pilipinas Shell Foundation 2002). It is probably the largest industrial investment in the Philippines to date. A joint undertaking of the national government and the private sector, the project is spearheaded by the Department of Energy, and is developed and operated by Shell Philippines Exploration B.V. (SPEX) on behalf of joint-venture partners Chevron Malampaya LLC and the PNOC Exploration Corporation (Malampaya 2009).

In 1989, a small gas reservoir called Camago was discovered in the area of Service Contract 38 (SC38). In 1990, upon acquisition of a 50 per cent participating interest in SC38, SPEX joined the search for natural gas reserves. Two years later, the Malampaya gas field was discovered, and it was later found to be connected to the Camago structure. After drilling five wells to determine the amount of gas available in Malampaya, SPEX confirmed the presence of 'a formidable power source' 80 kilometres northwest of Palawan island – about 2.7 trillion cubic feet of natural gas reserves and 85 million barrels of condensate, located some 3000 metres below sea level. After comprehensive studies were undertaken, it was concluded that 'Malampaya presented an extraordinary opportunity for commercial gas development in the Philippines' (Malampaya 2009).

Three years after the former President of the Philippines, Fidel V Ramos, signed the declaration of commerciality of the venture, and after overcoming 'myriad ... daunting logistical, social, environmental, and financial challenges', the Malampaya Deep Water Gas-to-Power Project was inaugurated in a special ceremony at the onshore gas plant in Batangas in 2001 (Malampaya 2009). Production of natural gas to fuel three gas-fired power stations with a combined capacity of 2700 megawatts has met as much as 50 per cent of Luzon's power-generation requirements, reduced oil imports, provided a stable supply of energy, contributed billions of pesos in revenues for government, and offered a cleaner source of power (Malampaya 2011).

The Malampaya Project is just one of the several initiatives of Shell in support of the energy-reform agenda of the Philippine government, which seeks to address the concerns of energy security, energy diversity, energy efficiency and carbon dioxide (CO_2) management. Shell also increased the number of its retail stations selling 10 per cent ethanol-blended gasoline, or E10, and increasing the coco methyl ether (CME) component in Shell Diesoline from 1 to 2 per cent. Both these moves highlight Shell's immediate compliance with the *Biofuels Act* of 2006, which mandates that by 2011 all gasoline fuel products distributed and sold by oil companies should have at least 10 per cent bioethanol, and that all ethanol to be blended with gasoline should be locally sourced (Villasanta 2010). By meeting its legal obligations and being a good corporate citizen, Shell demonstrated its long-term commitment as a major investor in the country.

On 9 August 2011, President Benigno S Aquino III launched the next-phase development of the Malampaya Deepwater Gas-to-Power project with a visit to its Onshore Gas processing Plant in Batangas. Malampaya's next-phase development aims to maintain the level of production of, and maximise the recovery of, indigenous natural gas from the Malampaya and Camago reservoirs. Malampaya Phase 2 will entail drilling and development of two additional wells by 2014, while Malampaya Phase 3 will involve the installation of a new platform where additional equipment and facilities will be housed by 2015. These new investments, according to SPEX Communications, 'are seen to further benefit the Philippines in energy self-sufficiency and government revenues, and will continue to be a major source of power for Luzon's energy requirements in the years to come' (Malampaya 2011). For the people of the region, this means greater employment opportunities and increased economic activity brought about by such large-scale investments.

▪ Going beyond business: Shell's sustainable development programs

The Malampaya Project provided Shell with an opportunity to demonstrate a more enlightened approach to doing business – one that considered the economic, social and environmental bottom lines. Even before the project gained steam and reaped commercial benefits, SPEX consciously integrated the value of sustainable development in its operations. SPEX did this in partnership with the Pilipinas Shell Foundation, Inc. (PSFI), an independent non-profit organisation that also serves as the social development arm of the Shell companies in the Philippines. Established in

1982, PSFI has a solid track record of implementing social investment projects designed to help disadvantaged people to become more productive and responsible members of society (Shell 2010). By collaborating closely with PSFI, SPEX was able to actively engage the communities that hosted the sites where the Malampaya project's installations operated. The goal was for the host communities to enjoy long-term benefits far beyond the life of the project.

The partnership between SPEX and PSFI gave birth to sustainable development programs in several sites, including programs in Palawan, the main site and source of deep water gas, in Tabangao, Batangas, where the on-shore gas plant is located, in Subic, where the Concrete Gravity Structure or the base platform was built, and in Oriental Mindoro, where the gas pipelines traverse from Palawan to Batangas (Pilipinas Shell Foundation 2002). Keeping in mind the framework of sustainable development, which considers the needs of the present generation without compromising the ability of future generations to meet their own needs, Shell – through PSFI – introduced a comprehensive – though varied – set of interventions meant to enhance the quality of life of the residents of the above-mentioned host communities. The programs were introduced only after PSFI consulted community members and stakeholders to determine their specific needs. In Oriental Mindoro, for example, farmers and fishermen were trained and organised into a cooperative, and fishing communities by the coast were taught coastal resource management. PSFI also trained the Mindoro residents – especially the women and youth of Calapan City (the provincial capital) – to become entrepreneurs (e.g. training in activities such as hog raising, dressmaking) so that they could generate alternative sources of income.

In Subic, PSFI focused on the needs of Sitio Agusuhin, whose residents previously depended largely on fishing for their income. Opportunities for other sources of income were introduced when Sitio Agusuhin was chosen as the site for the Concrete Gravity Structure, a fundamental aspect of the Malampaya Deep Water Gas-to-Power Project. The Sitio Agusuhin Development Program had several components. The Livelihood and Enterprise Development component involved micro-lending activities, a Consumer Cooperative Store, a community-based forest management project and an aqua-culture development project. The Organisation Development and Capability Building component resulted in the establishment of several community associations and a cooperative. Moreover, the rehabilitation of the elementary teachers' quarters, playground, community centre, chapel and high school building widened the community's access to basic services and education. Through the Education and Human Resource Development component, several hundred individuals were sent to high school, while others were given scholarships that allowed them to enrol in technical/vocational courses. Finally, through the Environmental Protection and Stewardship component, a 20-hectare area of land planted with more than 20 000 fruit-bearing trees now serves as a feeding area for endangered bats, through the Bat Habitat Restoration Project (Pilipinas Shell Foundation 2002).

In Batangas, PSFI implemented a sustainable development program geared towards helping the communities surrounding the Shell Tabangao Refinery and the Malampaya

On-Shore Gas Plant (MOGP). These communities are collectively known as TALIM (Tabangao, Ambulong, Libjo, San Isidro and Malitam). Among the programs PSFI implemented in TALIM is Job Link, which was a response to expectations that job vacancies created by industrial projects be filled in by residents of the communities hosting the business. When Shell embarked on the construction of the MOGP in Tabangao, thousands of workers were required to build the plant. Since the locals initially did not possess the skills required by the contractors, Shell considered bringing in workers from elsewhere. To address local demands for employment, however, PSFI convened a Job Link committee that included contractors, project managers and community representatives. This led to the hiring of deserving local workers and the provision of skills-upgrading courses to selected beneficiaries.

PSFI also introduced local capability-building programs, which developed the leadership potentials of TALIM youth, strengthened the Barangay Development Councils and trained women for community service. Using a participatory planning approach to harness the communities' potentials, PSFI supported the local organisations in the community by providing them with various capability-building workshops, such as vision-mission-goal exercises and community action-planning workshops.

Shell combats malaria in Palawan

Beyond creating employment and educational opportunities, Shell also introduced a comprehensive set of other programs. In Palawan, it established technical/vocational training programs for the local youth, an agricultural skills training program designed to improve farm productivity and management, and an integrated farming bio-systems training program for farmers. Shell also introduced projects such as the rehabilitation of the Palawan Adventist Hospital, rural electrification using Solar Home Systems and a mud crab livelihood project in partnership with the Centre for Renewable Resources and Energy Efficiency (CREE). Such activities served to upgrade the quality of life of the members of the community.

But there major challenges with which to contend. What Palawan badly needed was a solution to a problem that had plagued it for decades: malaria. Controlling the disease has been difficult, especially in remote areas where access to basic health care services and facilities is limited. Prevention and cure are further hampered by issues such as widespread misconceptions about the disease, the dwindling number of health service providers, the increasing resilience to treatments, limited resources to effectively control the disease and competing priorities with other leading illnesses in the country. According to the Department of Health, malaria remains endemic in 65 of the country's 79 provinces, and those most at risk are Filipinos who belong to indigenous communities (Rebueno-Trudeau & Diaz 2006).

While PSFI had initial doubts about its capability to address health concerns, not having the medical expertise, it proceeded to implement a community-based malaria control project known as Kilusan Ligtas Malaria (KLM). PSFI's apprehensions quickly vanished because KLM generated enthusiastic support from practitioners, who had the technical and medical expertise needed to address Palawan's health problems. PSFI realised that its ability to mobilise resources and organise community leaders, local organisations and private entities to work together towards a common goal – a skill it has honed over more than two decades of social development work – was the key to KLM's initial success. Because of the collaborative approach adopted by PSFI and the particular strengths of KLM, the number of malaria cases in Palawan decreased from 42 394 in 2000 to only 8071 in 2009. Over the same period, deaths due to malaria also dropped dramatically by 91 per cent. For unknown reasons, the number of cases rose to 10 375 in 2010, but dropped to an all-time low of 5623 in 2011 (see Table 5.2).

Table 5.2: Malaria morbidity and mortality in Palawan, 1998–2011

	1998	1999	2000	2001	2002	2003	2004
Confirmed through microscopy	1 046	1 310	7 633	7 917	10 557	19 872	22 425
Diagnosed through signs and symptoms only	77 189	52 141	34 761	31 673	17 994	9 000	5 925
Total cases	78 235	53 451	42 394	39 590	28 551	28 872	28 350
Deaths	99	85	67	74	77	76	31
	2005	2006	2007	2008	2009	2010	2011
Confirmed through microscopy	16 339	13 084	17 088	10 799	8 071	10 375	5 623
Diagnosed through signs and symptoms only	148	–	–	–	–	–	–
Total cases	16 487	13 084	17 088	10 799	8 071	10 375	5 623
Deaths	20	26	11	9	6	6	3

Source: Pilipinas Shell Foundation 2002 (c/o Marvi Trudeau).

KLM's Program Manager, Aileen Balderian, attributed Palawan's success in bringing down malaria-related mortality and morbidity to enhanced early-case detection and treatment, very high mosquito net coverage, and intensive indoor residual spraying (IRS). She said Malaria Awareness Day celebrations, media engagement, multimedia campaigns and continuous advocacy also provided wider opportunities to educate communities on malaria (Dela Cruz 2010).

Media involvement was especially helpful in raising people's awareness of malaria. Radio plugs informing people about free nets and their uses, and reminders to hang their nets at dusk, are aired in all radio stations in the province at least six times a day. In addition, information on free diagnosis and treatment, and other malaria-related information, is aired three to five times daily (Dela Cruz 2010). These combined strategies and the support provided by SPEX and PSFI not only raised the awareness of people, but also showed how critical their participation can be in eradicating this disease.

How it all started

The success of the malaria-reduction campaign was not easy. It took a group of determined individuals to overcome the roadblocks that stood in the way. Marvi

Rebueno-Trudeau, who had served as PSFI's Program Manager for Palawan, recounted the beginnings of the anti-malaria campaign in the province (Diaz 2006). In 1999, when she was still working with the Provincial Government of Palawan as the Governor's adviser on economic development, she conceptualised a project that aimed to bring public services closer to the people through a mobile government that went around the islands and the most remote communities of Palawan. This project was aptly named Lakbay Bayanihan (LAKBAYAN) sa Palawan. One of the proposed activities was blood smearing to trace the incidence of malaria. Trudeau mobilised the Provincial Health Office, the Department of Health – Malaria Control Service, ALAYKA ng Palawan and the AGAPE Rural Health Program to get the program going. 'But the original proposal to smear 100 per cent of Palaweños had to be adjusted because we had limited resources,' she said.

When David Greer, then managing director of Shell Philippines Exploration B.V. (SPEX) visited Palawan to attend to business matters, Marvi approached him after his meeting at the provincial hospital and asked for five minutes to speak to him about malaria control. He said: 'Your five minutes start now.' She began presenting her ideas for the anti-malaria program while her staff scrambled to set up the screen and the projector in the hospital lobby. 'I knew I got his interest when David Greer and his team sat down and listened to the whole presentation,' she said. David invited Marvi to present a proposal before the SPEX Sustainable Development Council in Manila, which eventually agreed to fund the implementation of the anti-malaria program.

Marvi had originally planned to seek financial assistance from the Asian Development Bank (ADB), but saw Shell's planned investment in Palawan as an opportunity to generate some support from the private sector. She asked SPEX for P10 million (approximately US$250 000), hoping to use this as leverage to get additional support from ADB and other bilateral agencies to raise the proposed budget of P36 million (approximately US$900 000). However, the SPEX SD Council, decided to give the full amount on two conditions: that the provincial government would agree to contribute P5 million (approximately US$125 000) per year for 20 years to ensure that the project was sustainable after the SPEX grant had been exhausted, and that Marvi ran the program herself.

Both the governor and the vice-governor of Palawan received the news favourably, and agreed that Marvi should head the project. Marvi thus became the first project director of KLM, which was placed under the auspices of the provincial government. Together with two other individuals, Clyde Café and Yoyon Rebueno, she started to advocate the program to the local government units (LGUs), particularly the mayors. Municipal Technical Working Groups were organised during the first few months of the project. However, the project was stalled by politics, which dragged KLM into a series of congressional hearings. 'I decided to quit,' Marvi said.

Fortunately, Shell decided that the project was worth reviving. 'When David Greer and I met again in Palawan, he asked me to join Shell and to continue implementing KLM. We rehired the community organisers we had already trained and carried on with the program,' Marvi recalled.

When Marvi was with PSFI, KLM retained an office under the provincial government. She worked closely with Ray Angluben, who initially served as deputy director, and eventually became project director. Prior to his appointment, he worked on policies and legislation matters for the National Institute of Health. A major milestone that Marvi and Ray accomplished as partners was the completion of microscopy training in 344 barangays of Palawan. They did this while trying to rebuild the credibility of KLM after politics had earlier stalled its implementation for several months.

Learning from her experience, Marvi tried her best to shield KLM from politics – particularly from politicians with ulterior motives. 'As we were imposing a no-politics rule, it became difficult at first to get local support because the network we were using to implement KLM were political structures,' she admitted, 'but once community best practices started emerging, the others began to participate.' The local government officials realised the program's genuine desire to help people, and saw how the communities readily embraced KLM and took an active role in achieving its goals.

Marvi credits KLM's successful implementation to the dedication of the field staff and to the volunteers' commitment to help. 'The KLM staff are out in the field for as long as three months, non-stop. Sometimes, they hardly see their families,' she said. Others return from the field for a one-week assessment every quarter, then immediately go back to the field: 'What keeps this program alive are the people and their commitment to the cause of the program, which I want to call "missionary complex". Nobody embodies that complex more than Palaweños,' says Marvi, who is herself a Palawan migrant. Carefully selecting KLM has apparently paid off. 'When we engaged them,' Marvi said, 'the foremost consideration was to get people with the passion to be of service to other people, not exactly the ones with the right skills, because skills can be learned. That heart, which cannot be bought nor acquired, is the life of KLM.'

▨ Movement against malaria

KLM has since evolved into a strong public–private partnership among PSFI, the Malampaya Joint Venture Partners (SPEX, Chevron Malampaya LLC and the Philippine National Oil Company – Exploration Corporation), the Provincial Government of Palawan, the Department of Health, the Centre for Health Development of Region IV and the municipal LGUs.

Because of KLM's huge success, PSFI was able to secure a five-year grant from the Global Fund to Fight AIDS, Tuberculosis and Malaria (GFATM). Renamed Movement Against Malaria (MAM), the PSFI's anti-malaria program expanded its coverage to include four more provinces: Apayao, Quirino, Sulu and Tawi-Tawi. By 2009, malaria cases in all five provinces had dropped by 88 per cent over a six-year period. The number of deaths decreased from 150 in 2003 to only 17 in 2009.

In 2010, PSFI received an additional US$31.4 million from GFATM, which allowed it to expand MAM's coverage to 40 provinces with an estimated at-risk population of 16 million. And, as in the initial four provinces, malaria morbidity and mortality rates throughout the country have since declined substantially (see Table 5.3).

Table 5.3: Malaria morbidity and mortality in the Philippines, 2005–11

	2005	2006	2007	2008	2009	2010	2011
Population (000)	85 472	87 237	89 050	90 917	92 225	94 106	95 546
Cases	46 342	35 405	36 235	23 655	19 955	17 137	9 412
Morbidity rate	54.22	40.58	40.69	26.02	21.64	18.21	9.85
Deaths	150	122	73	56	24	22	6
Mortality rate	0.175	0.140	0.082	0.062	0.026	0.023	0.006

Source: Pilipinas Shell Foundation, Inc. (c/o Marvi Trudeau).

MAM has since been recognised as the UN Millennium Development Goal Warrior for Goal Number Six for its significant contributions in addressing the scourge of malaria. It was also conferred an Excellence Award in the Concern for Health category of the 9th Asian Corporate Social Responsibility (CSR) Awards, Asia's premier CSR awards program.

Appendix: Shell companies in the Philippines

Subsidiaries/affiliates	Description
Pilipinas Shell Petroleum Corporation (PSPC)	PSPC refines, blends, transports and sells a wide range of high quality fuels, lubricants, bitumen and other specialty oil-based products. It operates a 100-thousand barrels-per-day refinery, 22 oil distribution terminals/depots across the country and close to 1000 retail stations nationwide.
Shell Gas (LPG) Philippines, Inc. (SGLPI)	A fully owned subsidiary of PSPC, SGLPI provides cost-efficient, reliable and safe LPG energy solutions, tailored to customers' needs. Liquefied Petroleum Gas (LPG) is a clean-burning fuel with high combustion efficiency, and its portable and flexible use encourages a wide range of applications, including space and water-heating solutions, cooking and air-conditioning applications, industrial or agricultural processes, and powering vehicles and fleets.
Shell Philippines Exploration, B.V. (SPEX)	SPEX is at the forefront of the country's oil and gas exploration activities, operating the Malampaya Deepwater Gas-to-Power Project on behalf of the Department of Energy and its partners (Chevron Malampaya LLC and the Philippine National Oil Company – Exploration Corporation).
Shell Gas Eastern, Inc. (SGEI)	SGEI operates the only refrigerated propane and butane terminal in the Philippines, supplying local and regional customers.
Shell Shared Service Centre (SSSC) – Manila, B.V.	SSSC-Manila provides processing services related to finance, human resources, procurement, customer service and other business needs to Shell companies around the world. SSSC-Manila has grown from fewer than 50 staff in 2004 to over 2700 employees in 2010. It moved to a new building, Solaris One, in 2009, and has expanded its scope of work to accommodate additional migrated services. Its sustained growth is testimony to the Filipino professionals' world-class calibre and is a significant contribution to the Shell Group's operational excellence.
Pilipinas Shell Foundation, Inc. (PSFI)	Established in 1982, PSFI is an independent non-profit organisation that implements social investment projects in the country, which are designed to help disadvantaged people become more productive and responsible members of society. PSFI has benefited more than 2.5 million people all over the country through its community-development and health-care programs.

Source: Shell (2010).

Discussion questions

5.1 How does Shell seek to fulfil its corporate social responsibility in the Philippines?

5.2 Why do companies like Shell implement social development programs in the local communities where they operate?

5.3 How would you assess Shell's performance as a company, using the sustainable development framework?

5.4 Are there areas of sustainable development that Shell can further contribute to or that the Philippines can seek to address with support and assistance?

References

Dela Cruz, D 2010, 'Movement against malaria: project implementation review', *Milestones*, January, p. 25.

Diaz, M 2006, 'Infecting Palawan bottom-up', *Milestones*, August, pp. 8–10.

Herz, S, La Vina, A & Sohn, J 2007, *Development without conflict: the business case for community consent*, World Resources Institute, Washington DC, viewed 22 August 2012, <http://pdf.wri.org/development_without_conflict_fpic.pdf>.

Malampaya 2009, 'Power from the deep: overview of Malampaya', viewed 20 February 2013, <http://malampaya.com/?page_id=2>.

—— 2011, 'President Aquino kicks-off Malampaya's next-phase development', viewed 20 February 2013, <http://malampaya.com/?p=224>.

Palawan 2012, Wikipedia, viewed 20 February 2013, <http://en.wikipedia.org/wiki/Palawan>.

Pilipinas Shell Foundation 2002, psfi@twenty 2002, viewed 20 February 2013, <http://www.accessmylibrary.com/coms2/summary_0286-26800220_ITM>.

Rebueno-Trudeau, M & Diaz, M 2006, 'Movement against malaria: one scourge, one fight, one movement', *Milestones*, August, p. 25.

Shell 2010, *Sustainable Development in Action 2010: The Shell Companies in the Philippines*, viewed 20 February 2013, <http://issuu.com/sdinaction/docs/shellsdinaction2010>.

Shell Philippines 2012, Website, viewed 20 December 2012, <http://www.shell.com.ph>.

Solleza, C & Barns, J 2003, *Case Study on Shell Malampaya*,: Asian Institute of Management and Synergos Institute, Manila.

Villasanta, A 2010, 'No free ride to that low-carbon future', *Shell World Philippines*, no. 4, pp. 25 and 27.

Part II

Strategy and Entrepreneurship in International Business

Dewak: The positioning and growth of a born global software firm from a developing country

Sascha Fuerst

> We are not so interested in our home market [Colombia] because it is not very attractive related to profit and experience. Being in international markets provides us with more experience – experience regarding competitiveness. Our international market experience makes us look more attractive, more competitive. It is very different to do business with foreigners than with nationals. For instance, you have to deal with another language [English] and then there is the importance of punctuality. Here they are more relaxed concerning deadlines. The culture is very different. The learning we experience internationally definitely makes us more competitive.
>
> – Carlos Orozco, General Manager of Dewak, 2010

▦ Introduction

In February 2008, following the insolvency of their former employer (a small software company), Andres, Carlos, Daniel, Diego and Nicolas suddenly found themselves unemployed. They met for coffee in one of Medellín's shopping malls to discuss their future careers. Considering their educational and professional backgrounds in systems engineering and informatics, they decided to focus on a software business.

Andres, Carlos, Daniel, Diego and Nicolas started to work as a team of freelancers for Kayako customisation services. While working for their former employer, they had gained exposure to the open-source customer-support solutions of Kayako. Nevertheless, the business opportunity of customisation services for Kayako solutions was never exploited, due to the insolvency of their former firm.

Kayako's software solutions (Kayako 2012a) were introduced into the market in 2001, and by 2012 more than 30 000 customer organisations of all sizes and industries were making use of them (Kayako 2012a). Kayako is a self-funded, privately owned company run by 61 employees, with offices in the United States, the United Kingdom and India. The firm provides web-based customer-support solutions that allow companies to centrally manage their entire customer support channels through email, web, telephone or live chat. Kayako's customers can decide whether they would like to host the product on their own web server or make use of Kayako's on-demand service. Because the core web software code is open-source, firms are able to extend their help desk and build on top of Kayako's framework according to their own requirements.

The open-source nature of Kayako provided an interesting business opportunity because Kayako (the firm) was not interested in customisation services for its core product. As Carlos commented:

> They [Kayako] sell the software out of the box but are not interested in its customisation. They basically opened that market [customisation of Kayako]; it's totally open. NTT Communications [one of the largest telecommunications companies in the world, headquartered in Hong Kong], for instance, contacted Kayako to implement a modification of its software for NTT but Kayako wasn't interested and passed this opportunity on to us. (Orozco 2010)

The customisation of Kayako's software solutions seemed to provide an interesting business opportunity with global potential and reach. So how could this international business opportunity be exploited, and what were the advantages and disadvantages of working with Kayako? These were issues upon which Andres, Carlos, Daniel, Diego and Nicolas pondered.

■ The creation of Dewak

With the aim of establishing a company based on their professional experience and personal interests, the five entrepreneurs decided to distribute the roles within the team in the following manner. Carlos was assigned the role of the chief executive officer in charge of general management. Andres, as chief marketing officer, took care of business development and marketing. Nicolas performed the task of project manager and, together with Diego, worked on software development. Diego was also assigned the role of IT manager to oversee the deployment of technology. Daniel took over as web developer and designer. The company name was identified by introducing the letters 'D' and 'K' into a random word generator, and the most appealing name from the list – 'Dewak' – became the firm's name.

In order to start their business, men required laptop computers, internet access and work space in Carlos's house. A web page was created within two weeks, and the services announced on Kayako Internet forums among the Kayako community. Creating early expectations among their future customers seemed to be the perfect choice – the 'Our Team' page on Dewak's website proved to be the most visited section as visitors tried to identify the people behind the firm. Many visitors recognised the team from previous dealings with their former employer. These connections were truly beneficial for attracting potential customers. By the end of May 2008, the business had generated sufficient income for the five entrepreneurs to rent their own office space so they could move out of their colleague's house.

Their educational and professional backgrounds in systems engineering and informatics provided them with the knowledge and skills to perform the different programming tasks (see Appendix). Their professional experience, however, was limited to a few years because all of them had only recently completed their undergraduate studies before starting the business. Their English communication skills further helped them build and attend to a global customer base.

Dewak eventually became a born global firm (Gabrielsson et al. 2008) that internationalised less than two years after its foundation, with clients on five continents in 31 countries. In order to position the company in the global market of software customisation, Dewak needed to create and implement a strategy to overcome its liabilities of newness and foreignness.

NTT Communications in Hong Kong (NTT 2012), the international and long-distance service arm of NTT, one of the largest telecommunications companies in the world (ranked 31st in the Global Fortune 500 list of 2011 – see NTT 2012), was interested in including Dewak in its list of providers. The registration process required a business bank account, which Dewak obviously did not have as the company was not yet officially registered. So far, payment had been made exclusively via Pay Pal into one of the founders' personal bank accounts. Nevertheless, business was initiated with NTT Communications with a promise to provide the required information as soon as possible.

While the legal documents for the formation of Dewak were being drafted, Carlos's father recommended that the firm register itself in the nearby free trade zone to take advantage of fiscal benefits such as a lower income tax for goods and services produced within the zone and sold exclusively to customers abroad. This seemed to be an advantageous option, as Dewak intended to target customers abroad and not within Colombia.

Dewak was ultimately incorporated on 10 June 2008. The firm received certification as a member of the free trade zone a month later, on 28 August 2008. Subsequently, business bank accounts were opened in Colombia and the United States to facilitate receipt of payments from clients. Since then, Dewak has consisted of just the original five employees (the founders) and three administrative support staff (who handle accounting and legal issues).

Dewak's service portfolio and relationship with Kayako

Andres, Carlos, Daniel, Diego and Nicolas initially decided to concentrate on Kayako implementation, customisation, support and consultancy services. As of June 2010, customisation of Kayako applications generated 80 per cent of Dewak's income. Due to the successful completion of Kayako-related customisation projects, Kayako (the firm) invited Dewak to participate in the development of parts of its core product. Furthermore, Kayako featured Dewak on its website regarding customisation services. Dewak was also granted the status of 'authorised partner', which facilitated new client acquisition. After initial success with Kayako-related projects, Dewak began to diversify its product portfolio, offering website development and customised applications based on Joomla! and LAMP.[1]

A global customer base

Dewak's clients are primarily located in the United States (50 per cent), United Kingdom (20 per cent) and Australia (20 per cent), with the rest of the world accounting for the other 10 per cent (Figure 6.1). Although there are clients in Latin America and the Caribbean, they are few.

In the beginning, Dewak had a frequently changing customer base seeking assistance with small projects, but over time and with enhanced reputation, the firm began to implement larger projects with multinational clients. For instance, Dewak customised the Kayako-based help desk application of NTT Communications. Due to the positive results achieved through this project, NTT Communications then offered Dewak a support service agreement to support and sustain the previously customised help desk application. The agreement generates monthly payments and is renegotiated annually.

Asia and Oceania	North America	Latin America and the Caribbean	Europe	Africa
Australia	Canada	Chile	Cyprus	South Africa
Hong Kong	*United States*	Ecuador	Czech Republic	
India		Jamaica	Denmark	
Israel		Mexico	France	
New Zealand		Panama	Germany	
Philippines		Trinidad and Tobago	Italy	
Singapore		Uruguay	Lithuania	
Thailand			Moldova	
			Norway	
			Spain	
			Sweden	
			The Netherlands	
			United Kingdom	

Source: Dewak (2010).

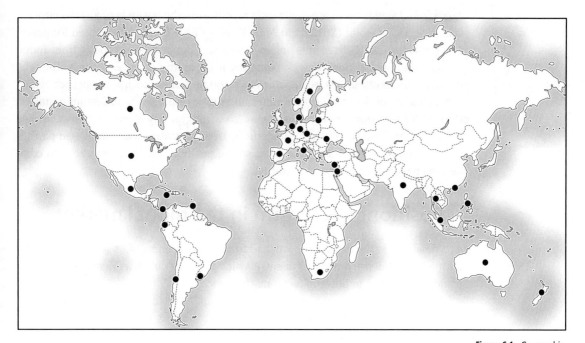

Figure 6.1: Geographic location of Dewak's clients

This provided Dewak with a fixed income superior to the sporadic payments of the previous ad hoc projects. Further, there are no restrictions placed on Dewak regarding the know-how, techniques, methods and skills acquired by providing these services. Any knowledge gained can be used in other client projects as well.

Cooperating with larger international firms provided an excellent opportunity for learning, as Carlos commented (Orozco 2010):

> It has many advantages. First, economically, they pay you monthly, and second, the learning experience has been very rich because we developed many different projects with them. New technologies are introduced, new standards that you have to learn. So we have to train ourselves in those standards, which provides an excellent learning experience, and that knowledge enters our firm as new know-how. Working with larger firms definitely provides many, many advantages.

Likewise, Dewak implemented and customised the help desk solution for Acer Australia's notebook business (ACER 2012). Working with renowned clients such as NTT Communications and Acer Australia added to Dewak's reputation and facilitated future client acquisition. Despite the importance of having larger international firms among its portfolio of clients, Dewak does not depend on them financially – those firms only contribute approximately 10 per cent of Dewak's annual income, and represent approximately 5 per cent of the customer base.

Competition

Apart from Dewak, there are only few competitors in the business of Kayako customisation services: Holbi (2012) and Aqua Develop (2012) from the United Kingdom, Modern-Help (2012) from the United States and SupportSkins (2012) from India. Despite the competition, Dewak perceives itself as the strongest firm within the market. This position has been achieved through a client-focused approach which considers fast project turnaround times and quick responses to follow-up inquiries. Due to this superior service, clients are also willing to pay more for Dewak service requests than for those of their competitors. Dewak's status as an authorised partner of Kayako also contributed to Dewak's strong position within the market (no competitors have been granted such status).

Positioning the firm in the global market

As a new firm in the market, Dewak had to create awareness of its services and build trust and confidence among its clients. Which particular internet marketing strategy could be deployed in order to facilitate this process?

The first approach was to announce Dewak's services within the forums on Kayako's website and the numerous freelance forums or directories related to Kayako. Paid advertising through Google AdWords provided additional leads to Dewak's website. One powerful strategy involved the development of free tools for Kayako, which created a lot of interest in Dewak. Therefore, Dewak opened a new thread within the Kayako forum called 'Review of Dewak', where users were asked to provide feedback about Dewak's free tools (Kayako 2012b). These reviews created more awareness of and confidence in Kayako among potential clients, and made Dewak appear more experienced.

Another strategy to create awareness, trust and confidence among potential clients involved obtaining Kayako's support as a referral partner and a listing in the third-party directory on Kayako's website. With an increasing customer base, Dewak also asked current clients to put the Dewak logo on their website to generate additional leads to Dewak's web page.

To overcome perceptions of Dewak as a small firm, operating virtually and solely from Colombia, Dewak decided to register both a phone number and PO Box address in the United States and the United Kingdom. As Carlos commented (Orozco 2010):

> Such a move was certainly beneficial because clients perceived us as a more international, larger, and experienced firm. Although we are always honest in this respect, and if someone asks, we tell them that our office is based in Colombia only.

There has been no need to provide Dewak's website in a language other than English, as most of the firm's clients are located in English-speaking countries. Even where English is not the native language of its clients, its use has proved sufficient. There is no version offered in Spanish, despite the company being located in Colombia, a Spanish-speaking country.

■ Adapting marketing activities to the growth of the firm

The growth of the firm and the diversification into new businesses (i.e. customisation is based on Joomla! and LAMP) caused Dewak to rethink their approach toward branding. Dewak's team had the idea to create a more 'serious', 'professional-looking' image of the firm, which basically involved a change of colours and typography (see Figure 6.2).

A larger, more diversified client base has also produced new opportunities by generating positive customer reviews on Dewak's website. The reviews create additional awareness and confidence among potential clients. Paid advertising on Google AdWords did not produce the expected effect. As an alternative, Dewak is experimenting with search engine optimisation and is exploring social networking tools such as Facebook and Twitter.

Multiple channels of communication with clients and potential customers are also becoming more important. The live-chat function on Dewak's website and the registered phone numbers in the United States and United Kingdom provide an important competitive edge for Dewak which, in contrast to many competitors and freelancers, demonstrates permanent visibility despite it being an internet-based firm. 'You can always "see" us, we are always visible and present if a client needs us,' Carlos affirmed (Orozco 2010). Such permanent availability has its limits, however, as Dewak's staff are not available 24 hours a day. Time differences between Colombia and clients from the Asia-Pacific region and Europe also constrain communication and response times, but so far any delays have been met with understanding by clients.

Despite the fact that Dewak's business operates through the World Wide Web and builds on the internet, Dewak appreciates the need to establish closer

relationships with clients through personal contact. On one occasion, Andres travelled to the United States to implement a project on site. If the same project had been implemented remotely from Colombia, it would have taken a month instead of two weeks. On-site support has also been contemplated within the service support agreement of NTT Communications, but has not yet been requested. Dewak perceives the implementation of projects on site as an important factor for future business. It intends to include this additional service in the product portfolio under the title 'Dewak Trip'.

■ How should Dewak develop from here?

Within just two years of its founding, Dewak experienced rapid growth – with clients in 31 countries – while maintaining its small size, which classifies it as a micro-firm (fewer than 10 employees) under Colombian law.

Increasing the expansion and diversification of Dewak remains a top firm priority. Carlos asked himself how this future expansion and diversification should take shape, considering how the firm had evolved so far.

The following factors have been taken into account by Carolos in his decision-making. Kayako customisation represents 80 per cent of Dewak's annual income. What if Kayako decides to restrict access to its source code or enters the business of customisation itself? Should Dewak make use of its position in the market and develop proprietary software product in order to reduce dependence on others? All Dewak's current clients are located outside the firm's home market, Colombia, and most of them outside Latin America. Should Dewak consider exploring more business opportunities within Colombia or the region?

Daily operations often make it difficult to think about and implement strategy. 'As we are all engineers, we are not sufficiently familiar with issues related to business strategy,' Carlos observed (Orozco 2010).

Appendix: A personal profile of the five entrepreneurs

Carlos (born 1982), Chief Executive Officer

Systems engineer, high level of English, two years of work experience in systems engineering within Colombia prior to foundation of Dewak.

....

Andres (born 1982), Chief Marketing Officer

Systems engineer, fully bilingual (Spanish, English), five years of work experience in systems engineering prior to foundation of Dewak, including 18 months in Florida (United States).

....

Nicolas (born 1983), Project Manager and Software Developer

Informatics engineer, high level of English, two and a half years of work experience in informatics within Colombia prior to foundation of Dewak.

....

Diego (born 1983), IT Manager and Software Developer

Informatics engineer, intermediate level of English, two and a half years of work experience in informatics within Colombia prior to foundation of Dewak.

....

Daniel (born 1986), Web Developer and Designer

Graphic designer, intermediate level of English, four years of work experience in web design and programming prior to foundation of Dewak.

Source: Dewak (2010).

Discussion questions

6.1   Describe the process of business idea development and firm creation in relation to Dewak. What critical events can you identify, and how did they shape the development of the firm?

6.2   Critically examine Dewak's Kayako customisation services. What are the advantages and disadvantages of that particular business in relation to Dewak's growth?

6.3   Evaluate Dewak's approach to positioning itself in a global market despite its small size. How have the various elements of Dewak's internet marketing strategy contributed to its positioning?

6.4   Based on Dewak's strengths and weaknesses, what recommendations would you make concerning the company's future expansion and diversification?

▤ Note

1   Joomla! is an open-source content management system platform for publishing content on the internet and intranet. LAMP is the acronym for a bundle of open source software solutions, originally coined from the first letters of Linux (operating system), Apache HTTP Server, MySQL (database software) and PHP (scripting language to produce dynamic web pages).

▤ References and further reading

ACER 2012, Website, viewed 20 February 2013, <http://www.acer.com.au>.

Aqua Develop 2012, Website, viewed 20 February 2013, <http://www.aquadevelop.com>.

Arenius, P, Sasi, V & Gabrielsson, M 2005, 'Rapid internationalisation enabled by the internet: the case of a knowledge-intensive company', *Journal of International Entrepreneurship*, vol. 3, no. 4, pp. 279–90.

Dewak 2010, Website, viewed 20 February 2013, <http://www.dewak.com/clients>.

Gabrielsson, M, Kirpalani, VHM, Dimitratos, P, Solberg, CA & Zucchella, A 2008, 'Born globals: propositions to help advance theory', *International Business Review*, vol. 17, no. 4, pp. 385–401.

Holbi 2012, Website, viewed 20 February 2013, <http://www.holbi.co.uk>.

Kayako 2012a, 'About-Kayako', viewed 21 April 2012, <http://www.kayako.com/company>.

—— 2012b, 'Review of Dewak S.A.', viewed 21 April 2012, <http://forums.kayako.com/threads/review-of-dewak-s-a.15460>.

Modern-Help 2012, Website, viewed 20 February 2013, <http://www.modern-help.com>.

Moen, O, Endresen, I & Gavlen, M 2003, 'Executive insights: use of the internet in international marketing: a case study of small computer software firms', *Journal of International Marketing*, vol. 11, no. 4, pp. 129–49.

NTT 2012, 'About Us', viewed 21 April 2012, <http://www.ntt.com/aboutus_e>.

Orozco, C 2010, Personal communication, June.

Sarasvathy, SD 2001, 'Causation and effectuation: toward a theoretical shift from economic inevitability to entrepreneurial contingency', *Academy of Management Review*, vol. 26, no. 2, pp. 243–63.

—— 2004, 'Making it happen: beyond theories of the firm to theories of firm design', *Entrepreneurship Theory and Practice*, vol. 28, no. 6, pp 519–31.

SupportSkins 2012, Website, viewed 20 February 2013, <http://www.supportskins.com>.

Qingdao Applied Chemistry Company (Kingking): Pivoting into a new global strategy

Henry T Tsuei and Manuel G Serapio

August 2010 marked an important milestone for Qingdao Applied Chemistry Company (Kingking). In this month, the company opened its flagship store in Beijing's fashionable Wang-fu-jing district. The store opening signalled an important shift in the company's strategy. Until recently, Kingking had positioned itself primarily as a world-class manufacturer-supplier of wax (candle) products and relied heavily on exporting to major retailers in the United States and Europe. However, in recent years the company has focused on the expansion of its business in China, while maintaining its global footprint as a supplier to the world's largest retailers and customers in more than 50 countries. The key elements of the company's new strategy are to: (1) establish Kingking as a prominent global brand, both in local and international markets; (2) grow significantly in the Chinese market; and (3) sharpen the company's manufacturing advantages in order to increase its share of the export market. The challenge for Kingking's top management was to determine how to best coordinate and implement this new strategy.

■ The Kingking story

Kingking was established in 1993 by Chen Suo-Bin, a native of Qingdao in China's north-east Shandong province. Chen grew up in Shandong during the tail end of China's Cultural Revolution. Like most young people of his generation, after completing his formal education he was assigned to work for a government-owned business – a State Owned Enterprise (SOE) in Beijing. His assignment was to be the assistant to the company's chairman and president. While this post would have been a dream job for many, Chen sensed little room for advancement and growth. Not willing to take the traditional seniority-based career path, he became restless and resigned from the company after two years. Chen's timing was auspicious, as China was in the midst of its economic reform in the early 1990s, providing aspiring entrepreneurs like Chen with unprecedented opportunities.

While China's economic reform began more than 30 years ago, the pace accelerated in earnest during the late 1990s. Changes that included the introduction of legislation to protect personal property and the formation of capital markets that provided funding for private sector businesses generated a flurry of entrepreneurial activities.

Returning to his home province of Shandong, and borrowing US$2500 from family and friends, Chen bought into a recycling business to begin the pursuit of his entrepreneurial dream. Using profits from his modest recycling operation, Chen started making glass holders for candles and eventually settled on candle manufacturing as his main focus. He landed contracts with major US and European retailers, and his business was soon deriving 90 per cent of its revenue from exports. As mentioned above, the company sells its products in more than 50 countries, with the lion's share of its sales going to the world's largest global retailers: Walmart (USA), IKEA (Sweden), Carrefour (France) and Metro (Germany). In 2006, Kingking became a publicly listed company on China's Shenzhen Stock Exchange. The company's market capitalisation grew from US$147 million in 2007 to more than US$400 million in

2012. Based on its 2012 filing, Kingking had revenues of $66 million and net profits of $4 million.

The global candle industry

The global yearly sales value of candles and wax products exceeded US$10 billion in 2012. The European and US markets accounted for more than 50 per cent and 30 per cent of the global candle market respectively, and market consumption levels have remained steady in recent years.

Yankee Candle Company and Blyth are two of the world's largest candle companies. Established in 1969 and headquartered in Massachusetts, Yankee Candle Company had sales of US$785 million, net income of US$33 million and total assets of US$1.2 billion in 2011. The company has more than 500 retail outlets selling candles, home fragrance and decorative items, and car and room sprays. Blyth was established in 1976 and is headquartered in Connecticut. Its 2011 revenues were US$900 million, with net income of US$25 million and total assets of US$500 million. Blyth has three subsidiaries: Candle Corporation of America, Party Lite and Midwest Company. In addition to selling candles, the company sells home decorative and fragrance items, photograph albums, and gourmet coffee and tea. As far as the US candle market is concerned, more than 400 candle manufacturers supply 90 per cent of the market; the balance is made up of products imported from abroad. It is likely that this figure will change as more Chinese candle companies target the United States as an export market.

Kinking is small in comparison to both Blyth and Yankee Candle Company. However, it stands to benefit from the growth in the Chinese candle market. In 2011, China's domestic candle production reached US$915 million. While a significant portion of this production has traditionally been exported, domestic consumption for home use has increased. Chinese consumers are increasingly buying candles for the same reason as their Western counterparts – home fragrance and decorative purposes – as well as for their relaxation attributes.

Factors in Kingking's success

While there are more than 1500 candle and wax product manufacturers in China, Kingking is the only one to have achieved the level of success qualifying it to be a publicly listed company in China. What sets Kingking apart from its peer group is its founder's relentless pursuit of differentiation in the following areas:

Research and design

While most makers of similar products compete mainly on price by leveraging China's lower labor cost, Kingking stands out by making significant investments in research and design. Kingking employs a design staff located outside China, close to its major markets, where consumer research can be done in a timely fashion. Chen believes that being on the front end of new consumer tastes with regard to product type, product design, colour and scent is a key to winning – it is integral to being first or fastest to market with the most attractive products while maintaining a high profit margin. Unsurprisingly, Kingking has received 1200 patents for its designs.

■ Product breadth and life cycle

Most wax products tend to be decorative and one-time use items. Therefore, Chen believes the key to differentiation is being able to offer a wide range of products (in Kingking's case, 38 000) designed for specific occasions (holidays), themes (seasons) and placement (different locations throughout the living quarters), all with very short life cycles (90 days) to maintain a sense of newness.

■ Vertical integration

The main ingredient in wax products such as candles comes from oil residue. Early on, Chen realised that being a producer of a commodity product means low margins and potentially high volatility in raw material costs. To minimise this volatility, Chen began buying petroleum futures contracts to ensure a cushion against the oil market.

■ Building a brand

Most producers of similar products tend to be original product manufacturers that supply to other retailers, which in turn sell the producer's candles under their own brand. Under this arrangement, branding has little relevance or value. Chen recognised the importance of establishing his own brand in order to maximise revenue. Kingking's branding has been built on the foundation of product quality, speed to market, wide range of product offerings and rapid product life-cycles. Its emphasis on brand-building has resulted in Kingking receiving prestigious awards and recognition from the Chinese government, such as its designation as a 'China Top Brand' and 'China Export Top Brand'.

■ Key challenges

Developments in the Chinese and global macroeconomic environment have created new challenges for the company. These include:

- *Global market slowdown.* The great recession of 2008/2009 slowed down consumption in the United States and other developed markets, particularly the demand for discretionary items like candles, home fragrances, and home decorative items.
- *EU anti-dumping,* In February 2008, the EU commission initiated an anti-dumping investigation against Kingking. It should be noted that this type of investigation is common for many producers of various Chinese products, as China continues to gain prominence as a global hub for manufacturing.
- *Rise in raw material cost.* The spike in the price of oil in late 2007 to mid-2008, and again in 2011 to 2012, has had a huge and direct impact on Kingking's cost of goods

sold. In addition, volatility in oil prices over the past five years has created greater uncertainty in Kingking's business.

- *Rise in labor cost.* In January 2008, China introduced a new set of labour laws designed to enhance the rights of workers. The added protection and benefits represent an immediate rise in labour costs for China's manufacturing employers, including Kingking.
- *An appreciating RMB.* Since 2005, China's currency, the renminbi (RMB), has appreciated more than 20 per cent against the US dollar. Multiple external forces will likely lead to further appreciation of the RMB against the dollar, cutting further into a manufacturer's profit margin.
- *Higher taxes.* The corporate tax rate has increased from 12 per cent to 25 per cent, thereby increasing Kingking's cost of doing business.

Refocusing strategy

Chen knew that Kingking's future rested on the company's ability to refocus. To this end, he launched a new strategy that emphasised the following:

- *Lowering the company's dependence on exports by developing the domestic market.* China's robust economic development has created a large middle class, resulting in more eligible buyers for Kingking's products. Since switching to this strategy, Kingking has opened more than 100 company-owned and franchised stores in 36 locations in China, including the company's flagship store in Beijing's Wang-fu-jing.
- *Building the Kingking brand.* The retail stores have provided more visibility for Kingking's brand in China. In addition, the company has pursued a brand-extension strategy to other products such as essential oils and home fragrances. To protect its brand in international locations, Kingking has registered its brand in 26 countries.
- *Sharpening Kingking's manufacturing and export advantages.* To maintain its manufacturing and export advantages, Kingking pursued the strategy of backward vertical integration by acquiring two oilfields in Oklahoma and an even larger oilfield in Nueces County, Texas, for about US$200 million. Kingking also opened new manufacturing and processing bases in Busan, South Korea and Ho Chi Minh City, Vietnam.
- *Growth in international markets.* Kingking continues to set its sights on international market expansion and diversification by pursuing new markets and new customers abroad. In order to diversify its risks, it has maintained a policy of not having a single foreign customer account for more than 30 per cent of its sales volume.

Assignment for Kingking's management team

To help him think through how best to execute Kingking's new strategy, Chen assembled his top leadership team during the summer of 2012, and asked them to address the following key issues:

- How does the company establish a global brand and build a loyal customer following in China and abroad? Specifically, what new channels, particularly in e-commerce, should Kingking develop?
- How can Kingking continue to position itself as a reliable supplier to long-time customers like Walmart and Carrefour while establishing its own global brand and distribution network?
- In order to compete more effectively with Yankee Candle Company and Blyth in the United States and other developed markets, should Kingking establish retail stores in international locations?
- How should the company address the key difficulties in the global candle industry noted above, including escalating raw material and labour costs, anti-dumping allegations in the European Union and a strengthening renminbi (RMB)?

Chen was proud of what Kingking had accomplished during the past two decades. He thought that it was fortuitous that the company's leadership team was meeting in 2012 – The Golden Year of the Dragon – to address how the company could best pivot into its new global strategy.

▨ Discussion questions

7.1 Put yourself in the position of Kingking's management team. Address the questions listed at the conclusion of the case (Assignment for Kingking's management team).

7.2 Provide specific recommendations for each of these questions.

7.3 Critique Kingking's new global strategy. Is it sufficient to take the company to the next level of growth? Discuss.

7.4 Alternatively, should Kingking leverage its growing market capitalisation and the strengthening RMB to acquire or merge with another company in a developed country?

▨ Note and acknowledgement

This case is based primarily on the author's knowledge of the company and from personal interviews. Nisarg Desai assisted with the research for this case. An earlier version of this case study was presented at the University of Pennsylvania-Wharton School's China Conference. The authors gratefully acknowledge the support of the Institute for International Business, Center for International Business Education and Research (CIBER) and the Business School, University of Colorado Denver.

References

Blyth Inc. Brands 2012a, Annual Report, March.

——2012b, 'Who we are – our story', viewed 14 January 2013, <http://www.blyth.com/whoweare.asp>.

Baidu.com 2013, 'Company profile Qingdao Jin Wang Group', viewed 14 January 2013, <http://baike.baidu.com/view/490368.htm>.

Bloomberg LP 2013, 'Company Profile – Qingdao Kingking Applied Chemistry Co. Ltd', viewed 14 January 2013, <http://www.bloomberg.com/quote/002094:CH>.

Business Daily Update 2011, 'Market burns dimmer for candle makers', 23 December.

Kingking website, <http://www.chinakingking.com/en>.

National Candle Association 2013, 'Facts & Figures', viewed 14 January 2013, <http://www.candles.org/about_facts.html>.

Yankee Candle Company, Inc. 2013, 'The Yankee Candle Company – A True American Success Story', viewed 14 January 2013, <http://www.yankeecandle.com/about-yankee-candle/company-profile/t>.

YCC Holdings LLC, 2012, *Annual Report*, March.

8

Bangkok Dusit Medical Services Public Company Limited: Healthy international expansion

Pachsiry Chompukum and Chintana Bunbongkarn

In 1972, Dr Pongsak Viddayakorn bid farewell to government life in order to open a small medical institution in Bangkok. Dr Pongsak saw the opportunity to build a new private hospital to serve the growing number of patients in Thailand. Starting with five million baht of his own money and a one million baht construction loan, Dr Pongsak bought land to build Bangkok Hospital, a 50-bed hospital with two doctors, three dentists, ten nurses and 100 other staff members.

Bangkok Hospital has grown significantly over the past four decades. As Thailand's first private hospital, Bangkok Hospital capitalised on the country's population growth and increasing demand for private medical services. The hospital benefited from its excellent reputation as an organisation that employed a great team of medical experts who provided patients with high-quality and efficient health-care services. By 2011, Bangkok Hospital has become Bangkok Dusit Medical Services Public Company Limited (BDMS), one of Thailand's largest private hospital groups. The company's total assets had reached 32.2 million baht by December 2010. BDMS owns and manages five major hospital groups (Bangkok Hospitals, Samitivej Hospitals, BNH Hospital, Phayathai Hospitals and the Royal Hospitals), with 29 medical facilities and more than 5000 beds located in Thailand's popular tourist destinations such as Pattaya, Phuket and Samui, and in the neighbouring country of Cambodia.

BDMS is concentrated in Bangkok and various high-growth markets in the southern and eastern regions of Thailand. Committed to be a leading network health-care provider, BDMS serves the needs of Thai and foreign patients with high-quality, internationally accepted standards and value-for-money services, together with state-of-the art medical technology. The company's philosophy, vision and mission are summarised in Table 8.1, and reflect a commitment to high-quality health care, compassion for patients and leading-edge practice and technology.

The first location to which the hospital expanded was Pattaya. The hospital used the funds raised from its stock listing on Thailand's Stock Exchange to open more branches and access a wider range of customers. As shown in Figure 8.1, medical centres can be categorised by the standards of care provided – namely, primary care, secondary care, and tertiary care. Primary care centres provide general medical services such as clinics or small medical centres. Secondary care centers offer a higher

Table 8.1: BDMS's philosophy, vision and mission statements	
Philosophy	Bangkok Hospital is where advances in medicine meet with compassion.
Vision statement	Bangkok Hospital is a premier tertiary health-care provider, dedicated to international-quality, customer-focused care.
Mission statement	We are committed to being the leader in providing internationally accepted, efficient and ethical high-quality care through a dedicated health-care team, effective leadership and up-to-date technology.

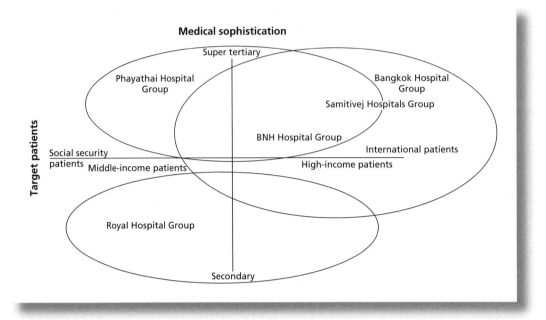

Figure 8.1: Diversification of patient mix

level of services to both in-patients and out-patients, as well as care for more complex illnesses. Tertiary care centres provide complete medical care and treatment for specific illnesses as well as complex diseases, with state-of-the-art medical equipment. BDMS covers all major medical services group. BDMS also merged with and invested in other private hospitals. As a result, BDMS has been able to serve a large group of patients, ranging from social security patients to international visitors.

■ Strategy and key success factors

To sustain its competitive advantage, BDMS differentiated its service offerings based on three key success factors that were derived from Dr Pongsak's vision: product leadership, customer intimacy and operational excellence (see Figure 8.2).

■ *Product leadership*

BDMS invested aggressively in specialty centres, built state-of-the-art laboratories and operating rooms, and hired nephrectomy doctors and neurosurgeons. The Cardiac Centre has brought the greatest recognition to BDMS. Other specialty centres, such as the Chest and Lung Disease Centre, were established later. Currently, there are 13 specialty centres and numerous clinics that provide an impressive range of specialist medical services in BDMS (see Appendix 1). Having established these specialty centres, BDMS further expanded its hospital branch network in order to reach more customers.

Product leadership

Product Leadership

Best product

Operational Excellence

Best total cost

Customer Intimacy

Best total solution

Operational excellence   Customer intimacy

Figure 8.2: BDMS's key success factors

■ *Operational excellence*

BDMS's emergence as the leading private hospital in Thailand is due largely to its excellent standards of professional governance. The hospital group is led by a board of directors instead of a family business administration, as is the case in many businesses in Thailand.

Dr Pongsak remarked that a strong board of directors was more objective, and could engage in vigorous debate and discussion on important matters of hospital governance without personally offending anyone. In his view:

> Freely voicing one's opinion is the best way for administration to generate great ideas. Great ideas do not come from one person alone but rather from many people. Fostering healthy argumentation is one of the important methods to carefully solicit opinions. With careful and healthy argumentation, operations can hardly go wrong and can easily succeed.

To effectively administer a multi-branch hospital, Dr Pongsak decentralised the administration. Each hospital and network has its own administrator, whose responsibility it is to execute on the company's strategy. Dr Pongsak explained:

> Everyone has limited capability. We need to know what our primary responsibility is. Our responsibility is to administer and manage the hospital. We set our work scope in that direction. We follow two principles: decentralisation and empowerment. We let individual leaders decide by themselves and we later take a look at their results.

Dr Pongsak also established a Shared Services Group to assist with administrative functions, such as purchasing, accounting, personnel training and marketing. The shared services model enables functional departments to run effectively and consistently, as well as benefit from scale economies.

Information technology and communications (ICT) has been a major driver in the success of Bangkok Hospital's administration. Everyone in the hospital, from doctors to staff members, relies on a computerised system to aid them with their communication and interaction with patients and other team members. Doctors' diagnosis and prescriptions are recorded and communicated via computerised information systems. In this way, information can be delivered from the diagnostic room, dispensing room, cashier and medical treatment services reliably, accurately and quickly, to satisfy client needs and expectations.

IT systems and user development are integrated and carried out concurrently. The board of directors, the management team and the medical team all participate in developing IT systems. Experts have been brought in to develop expand innovations and partnerships with doctors across the hospital to provide coordinated services. Teams of doctors have been involved with brainstorming ideas, since they are the end-users of the IT systems. Through a great deal of trial and error, as well as continuous updating, Bangkok Hospital has come up with back office and front office systems that efficiently and effectively meet the needs of its employees and patients, and these efficiencies contribute to the successful performance of entities in BDMC.

■ Customer intimacy

When patients are admitted to hospital, they do not only expect a high quality of medical care but also excellent service. In fact, private hospitals in Thailand compete for patients who pay premium prices by stressing their excellent service quality. BDMS has been known for its service excellence, a quality that provides a competitive advantage. The great majority of those who receive services at BDMS agree that the hospital's receptionists and staff are excellent, and as lively and friendly as their counterparts in the best five-star hotels in Bangkok. Additionally, the hospital promotes customer responsiveness. For example, it offers ambulatory services that are among the most advanced in the fields of medical evacuation and repatriation services throughout Indochina. Its trauma and ambulatory staff have extensive experience and are highly trained to deal with life-threatening situations. Utilising fleets of air, ground and water transportation vehicles that are well equipped with modern peripherals, BDMS has teams of doctors and nurses who are available 24 hours a day to assist in safely managing the movement of critical patients. Consequently, it can assure patients of the best total health-care solutions available.

■ Competitive human resource policy and systems

As of 31 December 2011, Bangkok Hospital had 2888 employees and 957 physicians, as shown in Table 8.2.

BDMS has stressed the importance of maintaining an exemplary human resource policy in order to uphold the hospital's exemplary service standards. As Dr Pongsak

No.	Type	Staff physicians and employees	Consulting physicians and part-time employees	Total
Table 8.2: Employee distribution table				
1.	Nurses	787	145	932
2.	Employees	1,621	335	1956
3.	Total employees	2,408	480	2888
4.	Physicians	345	612	957

Note: Staff Physicians refer to physicians who work 40 hours or more a week for the Company but are not considered employees of the company.

noted in his speech given on the day he received the Order of The Sacred Treasure, Gold Rays with Neck Ribbon, awarded by the Japanese Emperor:

> We need to maintain the level of the service standards that we have set and [keep] the great service mind ... I am only a representative of a thousand other working people in Bangkok Hospital who work hard as a team. This reward isn't all mine but rather everyone's.

Dr Pongsak explained that the company has set high standards for human resource management, starting from recruitment, training and development, and maintaining high-quality employees based on the following pillars:

- *Employee recruitment career improvement.* The company emphasises personnel development, commencing with the recruitment process. It specifies selective recruitment based on education level, work experience and expertise, and other requirements. BDMS uses a promote-from-within policy that considers internal applicants first before looking for people from outside to fill vacant positions. As a result, employees continuously enhance their chances for career development. Additionally, BDMS promotes diversity because it realises that patients have diverse backgrounds, and employs staff from all religious and cultural backgrounds.
- *Employee training program.* The company provides both internal training and supports external training for it staff. It encourages employee training and development in order to consistently and continuously improve and enrich workers' work and professional skills, so that they remain at the forefront of their profession.
- *Employee performance assessment systems.* The company uses a transparent and fair policy to evaluate employee performance and potential. The company evaluates employee capability, potential and capacity based on four dimensions – skill, knowledge, attributes and performance – and ensures that employees are made aware of the company's performance-assessment systems and processes.
- *Equal treatment of employees.* The company promotes equal treatment of everyone in the organisation, commencing with recruitment. Promotion is based primarily on merit and competence.
- *Feedback on employee satisfaction.* The company periodically surveys employees to get their feedback and levels of satisfaction and well-being, and utilises the

information from these surveys to inform and improve hospital services and administration.

- *Creating a better life quality for employees*. The company gives priority to the health and quality of life of employees by ensuring that they always work in proper hygienic conditions in the workplace. Employees are provided with annual health check-ups and high standards are maintained.

Pursuing foreign customers

The financial crisis that struck Asia in general, and Thailand in particular, in the late 1990s presented a major speed bump for Bangkok Hospital. Until then, Bangkok Hospital's business had grown continuously. However, at the height of the crisis in 1997–98, Bangkok Hospital's business slowed down because many customers who went to private hospitals deferred treatment of non-urgent illnesses, reduced the number of days spent recuperating at the hospital or chose hospitals that charged lower medical fees. To offset the sluggish demand in the local market, Bangkok Hospital set its sight on foreign customers. Dr Pongsak notes:

> There was not much motivation initially to pursue foreign customers. However, because of the crisis, it became necessary to obtain foreign customers. During the financial crisis in 1997, Thai people (became) 10 per cent poorer. The number of our patients decreased so we needed to find more foreign customers.

More than a decade after the Asian Financial Crisis, the number of foreign patients that BDMS and other hospitals in Thailand have been able to attract has increased considerably. Foreigners have shown great interest in coming to Thailand for medical care at private hospitals. One reason for BDMS and Thailand's success in luring foreign patients is its cost advantages (see Table 8.3). Most medical procedures in Thailand are about one-tenth the price they are in the United States.

Table 8.3: Comparison of medical costs in third quarter 2009 (US$)					
Medical costs for general surgery	India	Thailand	Singapore	UK	USA
Bypass	10 000	11 000	18 500	35 000	130 000
Valve replacement	10 000	10 000	12 500	54 000	160 000
Hip replacement arthroplasty	9 000	12 000	12 000	19 000	43 000
Knee arthroplasty	8 500	10 000	13 000	20 000	40 000
Fusion in spinal surgery	5 500	7 000	9 000	22 000	22 000

The Thai government has also decided to position Thailand as Asia's medical hub, and to encourage medical tourism into Thailand. In 2012, revenue from international patients contributed to roughly 30 per cent of total revenue, as shown in Figure 8.3. BDMS has decided to continue its program to pursue foreign customers

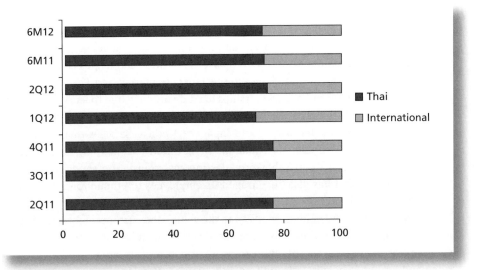

Figure 8.3: Revenue contribution by international patients

and plans to further increase the proportion of revenue generated from international patients to 40 percent. BDMS traditionally catered to foreign patients from the Middle East who came to Thailand for medical treatment. Patients from the United Arab Emirates (UAE) comprised its first largest group of foreign customers, followed by Qatar (ranked third) and Kuwait (ranked fourth). However, as BDMS looked into growing the number of foreign patients to serve, it considered expanding into a much broader market, including:

- tourists who became sick during their visit to Thailand
- foreigners who worked and lived in Thailand
- medical tourists who came for a short stay for cosmetic surgery (e.g. laser treatment, beauty treatment, lasik surgery) while enjoying a leisure stop in Thailand
- foreigners living in neighbouring countries
- foreign groups who chose to travel to Thailand to have medical treatment. While this category is considered to be the most profitable for the hospital, as these patients tend to have longer stays and more expensive procedures, it is also the most demanding and requires a major resource commitment on the part of Bangkok Hospital.

BDMS has also had considerable experience working with and servicing the Japanese market. Of all the groups travelling from other Asian countries, the Japanese travel and relocate to Thailand most frequently. Dr Pongsak explains:

> It was an unexpected development when the Japanese school that was initially located in front of Central Chidlom moved close to the Bangkok Hospital in 1977. The Japanese school manager was having problems with the Thai landlord, so we helped the school negotiate their contract. Soon we became better acquainted and later we were asked to provide physical check-ups for Japanese students in Thailand.

As so the Japanese market became an opportunity for development.

Cultural challenges

Catering to foreign patients posed additional cultural challenges for Bangkok Hospital's medical team and staff. Foremost among these challenges is the language issue. To address some of these issues in the Japanese market, ten Thai doctors were granted Japanese government scholarships to study in Japan and to learn to speak the Japanese language fluently. These doctors then returned to practise medicine in Thailand and have become part of the Japanese Medical Services that cater to the needs of Japanese patients in Thailand. In addition, BDMS has established an International Medical Centre that provides medical translation services in 24 languages. The hospital has also encouraged its employees to pursue foreign-language and cross-cultural training.

Understanding and being responsive to the values and customs of foreign clients is extremely important. For example, Japanese customers have high-quality standards for service, honesty, integrity and professional courtesy to patients. They are very demanding about hospital cleanliness and hygiene. Foreign customers also expect BDMS to localise some aspects of their service operations, such as employing chefs to prepare special Japanese dishes for Japanese patients.

Moreover, BDMS provides additional services, such as coordinating with the foreign patient's insurance provider so that those who are able to do so can use their medical insurance in Thailand. To facilitate this, BDMS has built partnerships with an extensive network of insurance providers worldwide. Finally, BDMS extends assistance to patients by appointing staff to escort and help facilitate their airport arrivals and departures, as well as clearance through customs. The patient service can be packaged to their needs.

Building international facilities

BDMS's first international investment was in Cambodia. Each year, more than a million tourists visit Angkor Wat in Cambodia. Before BDMS's decision to build a hospital in Cambodia, there was no private hospital in the area to serve these tourists. In fact, an earlier incident involving several tourists who became very ill, with some even dying because of improper treatment – a situation compounded by the lack of modern medical facilities – prompted BDMS's decision to establish a medical presence in Cambodia. Currently, BDMS has two hospitals in Cambodia and is building a third hospital with 1100 beds. The third hospital is also targeted to meet the medical needs of middle- and high-income Cambodians, who typically go to Vietnam for high-quality medical treatment. BDMS would like these patients to seek treatment in its hospitals in Cambodia instead and, in more serious cases, to be transferred to BDMS's hospitals in Thailand.

With the establishment of the ASEAN Economic Community (AEC), which encourages trade and investment between its members, BDMS is considering setting up a hospital in Myanmar in 2013, to take advantage of the changing environment in the country and its expanding economy. Among BDMS's patients from aboard, people from Myanmar comprise the second largest group after the United Arab Emirates. BDMS sees opportunities to grow in Myanmar, and has undertaken a preliminary research study to evaluate market demand.

BDMS has plans to increase the number of its hospitals to 50 by 2015. By then, BDMS will be the second largest hospital group in the Association of South-East Asian Nations (ASEAN) and the fourth largest in the world.

Appendix 1: BDMS centres and clinics

Centres	Clinics
Allergy Centre	
Anesthesiology Centre	
Anti-Aging Centre	• Aesthetic Anti-Aging Clinic • Anti-Aging Sport Medicine Clinic • Weight Management Clinic
Arthroscopy Surgery and Sports Medicine	
Aviation Medicine Centre	• Air Ambulance Get a Quote • Air Ambulance Insurance Coverage • Air Ambulance Services • Helicopter Air Ambulance • Lear Jet Air Ambulance • Our Activation Process
Bangkok Academy of Sports and Exercise Medicine (BASEM)	
Bangkok Hospital Emergency Services	• Helicopter Emergency Medical Services • Hydrolance Ambulance Services • Medical Escort Services
Bone and Joint Centre	• Arthroplasty (Joint Replacement) Clinic • Hand & Microsurgery Clinic • Spine Surgery Centre
Brain (Neuro) Centre	• Epilepsy Clinic • Neurosurgery Clinic
Cancer Centre	• Breast Cancer Clinic • Chemotherapy Centre • Head and Neck Cancer Clinic • Hematology Centre • Nuclear Medicine Centre • Oncologic Imaging Clinic • Surgical Oncology Clinic • Thalassemia Clinic
Chest and Lung Disease Centre	
Complementary and Alternative Medicine Centre	• Acupuncture and Moxibustions Clinic • Acupuncture and Tui-Na Clinic

(continued)

Centres	Clinics
Dental Centre	
Diabetes Mellitus and Endocrinology Centre	• Diabetes Clinic
Diagnosis and Imaging Centre	• Diagnostic Radiology Clinic • Neuroradiology Clinic • Vascular & Interventional Radiology Clinic
Digestive System and Liver (Gastroenterology) Centre	
Ear Nose and Throat (ENT) Centre	• Head-Neck Surgery Clinic • Paediatric ENT Clinic • Sleep Medicine Clinic
Eye Centre	
Health Check-up Centre	• General Practice Clinic
Heart (Cardiology) Centre	• Anticoagulation Clinic • Cardiac Anesthesiology Clinic • Cardiac Rehabilitation Clinic • Endovascular Centre • Heart Failure Clinic • Preventive Cardiology Clinic • Vascular Centre
Hyperbaric Oxygen Therapy Centre	
Gynecologic Oncology Centre	• Fertility Clinic • Maternal & Foetal Medicine (Pregnancy) Clinic • Obstetrics and Gynaecology Centre (Women's Health Centre) • Pathology Clinic • Paediatric Centre • Paediatric Surgery Clinic
Internal Medicine Centre Critical Care Medicine Centre	
International Medical Services (IMS)	• Arabic Medical Services (AMS) • Bangkok International Clinic – Khao San Road • Japanese Medical Services (JMS)
Kidney (Nephrology) Centre	
Mobile Cardiac Care Unit	• Motorlance
Plastic Surgery Centre	• Hair Restoration Clinic
Preventive Medicine & Medical Toxicology Centre	
Psychiatric Centre	
Rehabilitation Centre	
Skin (Dermatology) Centre	
Spine Centre	

Centres	Clinics
Surgery Centre	• Laparoscopic Surgery • Liver Transplantation • Parathyroid Surgery • Surgery Colorectal Clinic
Trauma & Emergency Services	
Travel Medicine Centre	
Urology Centre	

■ Appendix 2: Brief background of Dr Pongsak Viddayakorn

Dr Pongsak was born on 23 March 1934 in the eastern province of Trad. He graduated from the Faculty of Medicine, Siriraj Hospital, Mahidol University in 1960. He also received a Diploma in Tropical Medicine and Hygiene from Mahidol University and completed his postgraduate study at the University of Pennsylvania. Dr Pongsak commenced his career as a doctor at the Teachers Council of Thailand's infirmary, a place where he realised the value and the virtue of being a teacher. His personal qualities include honesty, humility, a willingness to compromise and perseverance. His colleague, Dr Kanokros, remarked that Dr Pongsak's achievements in life were based on his strong family values and his equally strong professional values. Thai cultural values also influence his personal and professional approaches.

In qualitative data collected, a Japanese patient who had been working in Thailand over a long period of time and had visited Bangkok Hospital regularly, commented on Dr Pongsak's ability to administer his work effectively and efficiently, at the same time upholding the dignity of human beings. She noted that, in addition to these administrative capabilities, 'He is still a doctor at heart.' Another foreign patient noted that the development of Bangkok Hospital had been brought about by Dr Pongsak's close attention to and awareness of all personnel and their advancement. Others noted his commitment to improved services through advanced technologies. However, they also observed that the technologies utilised at Bangkok Hospital served only as tools to increase services and administer the business successfully, noting that, 'The leadership of the executive matters most.'

Dr Pongsak's driving philosophy is that: 'Only big and strong organizations will be able to stand firm over a long period of time.' He developed and supported a mutual understanding that everyone is an owner, everyone is a host and everyone needs to take responsibility. Success will be achieved by all working together. Dr. Pongsak has received numerous honorary awards that reflect his achievements and outcomes, which have created a legend for private hospital development and compassionate health care in Thailand.

Source: Data from the authors.

▪ Discussion questions

8.1 Discuss the key factors that have contributed to the growth of Bangkok Hospital into one of Thailand's largest private medical groups.

8.2 Dr Pongsak has been recognised as an outstanding leader in health care in Thailand. Discuss his leadership style. Analyse the role that he played in influencing the organisational culture of Bangkok Hospital.

8.3 Discuss the major strategies utilised in the BDMS business model. Determine the impact of these strategies.

8.4 Identify and discuss the challenges that BDMS is likely to face in targeting:
   a. foreigners who work and live in Thailand
   b. foreigners who choose to travel to Thailand for medical treatment.

8.5 How can BDMS best deal with these challenges?

8.6 Explore the opportunities and threats that BDMS is likely to face as it expands into foreign locations such as Cambodia. Which countries should it target next and why?

▪ References and further reading

Anonymous 2012, 'Bangkok Hospital shows readiness for AEC in both capital and human resources and is ready to be number second in Asia', *Thansettakij*, 27–29 December, p. 22.

Anonymous 2012, 'BGH expands to "Cambodia–Myanmar" in the time of AEC, *Tan Hoon*, 24 December, p. 7.

Anonymous 2012, 'Interview with Wichai: BGH continue to invest in Myanmar', *Thansettakij*, 29 November–1 December, pp. 17–18.

Bangkok Dusit Medical Services Plc. 2010, *Annual Report*, viewed 8 August 2011, <http://bgh.listedcompany.com/misc/ar/ar2010.pdf>.

—— 2011, *Annual Report*, viewed 8 August 2011, <http://bgh.listedcompany.com/misc/ar/20120329-BGH-AR2011-EN.html>.

Viddayakorn, P 2011, Interview with the First Vice Chairman/ Executive Company Advisor, Bangkok Dusit Medical Services, 2 August.

Yuthana, P 2012, 'BGH plans to open Myanmar hospital', *Bangkok Post*, 22 December, p. B1.

The growth and internationalisation of Geely – the Chinese car manufacturer

Cindy Qin, Prem Ramburuth and Yue Wang

In March 2010, Chinese car maker Geely (a Chinese word meaning auspicious or lucky) signed a deal to buy Volvo from the US car giant Ford for US$1.8 billion. The acquisition is considered to be an example of China's growing influence in a range of industries on the international stage. It is fresh evidence of foreign direct investment (FDI) being made by Chinese car makers in a bid to gain access to European markets and Western technology. The Volvo deal placed Geely – which was barely known outside of China – in the spotlight. It also raised questions about just how ready Geely was to be a major player on the global stage. Did Geely have a clear and robust strategy for further development of its fledging international strategy? Was the purchase of an extremely well-established Western auto manufacturer by Geely – an emerging market automobile manufacturer – an act of egotism or a sound and strategic long-term investment? This case provides an insight into the global automobile market and China's growing interest, as well as an indication of Geely's growth and expansion, culminating in the takeover of Volvo.

■ Background: the automobile industry worldwide

The automobile industry is a large and critical sector of the global economy. Over the last few years, there have been dramatic changes affecting the industry. For example, significant changes are evident in the European Union and the United States, whose economies have suffered as a result of the global economic slowdown, leading to a decrease in car sales and a decline in the relative markets. In contrast to these declining trends in developed countries, emerging economies have become fast-growing markets for the automobile industry. China became the world's third largest car market in 2006, and then the largest in 2009; additionally, India recently posted its highest ever car sales figure – 195 million cars in 2011 (Gulati & Choudhury 2012). It is anticipated that the emerging markets will experience continued growth, with drivers including rising incomes, increasing availability of credit and falling car prices.

These emerging economies are also becoming the main players in car manufacturing. In 2005, a total of 46.86 million cars were produced worldwide. One-third of the cars were produced in the European Union, and 19.24 per cent were produced in Japan. In contrast, in 2011, production globally reached 58 million, of which 24 per cent (14.49 million cars) were produced in China. This made China's production for 2011 twice as large as Japan's, which first lost its title of the world's largest car manufacturer to China in 2009 (OICA n.d.).

Ongoing investment in new technologies will doubtless help the auto industry become even more competitive than it currently is. In 2011, five out of the top 20 research and development (R&D) spenders around the world were from the automotive sector. In particular, Toyota spent more on R&D than any other company in the world, largely to improve fuel efficiency and electronics (Jaruzelski, Loehr & Holman 2012; *Economist* 2012). Studies have also shown that profitability in the industry results not only from the *amount* of R&D spending, but also from *how* the money is spent, and whether it is utilised effectively – including effectiveness in defining new concepts and executing strategic plans (Booz Allen Market Services 2003; Booz & Co. 2010). While cars makers from advanced economies invest significantly in new technology, there seems to be persistent under-investment in R&D in emerging economies, such as those of India and China.

China's automobile industry

Nevertheless, the growth of the Chinese automobile industry – the origins of which were in the 1950s – is clearly evident. In 1965, the annual combined production volume of nine key Chinese manufactures (all state-owned) was less than 60 000 cars. After the initiation of its open door policy in 1978, China started to encourage FDI into the automobile industry and set up alliances and joint ventures with major foreign auto manufacturers, such as Volkswagen, General Motors, Toyota and Honda. Only state-owned enterprises were allowed to engage in automobile manufacturing and form joint ventures with international automobile manufacturers. Since the 1990s, with further advancement of the economic reform and open door policy, several new domestic enterprises have entered the Chinese automobile industry, including some privately owned companies, such as Geely Automobile. By the end of 1998, China's annual vehicle output had reached 1.6 million, making China the tenth largest auto producer in the world. Eleven years later, in 2009, China's annual automobile production capacity exceeded 10 million. It was at this point that China surpassed Japan for the first time as the largest automobile maker in the world. Approximately one-quarter of the cars in the world are now produced in China (see Figure 9.2).

Today, more cars are sold in China than in any other nation, and strong markets have emerged for cars at different price levels, from inexpensive sedans and vans to expensive Cadillacs and German luxury cars. While some developed countries, such as

Figure 9.1: Car production statistics between 2005 and 2011 *Data Source:* OICA (n.d.).

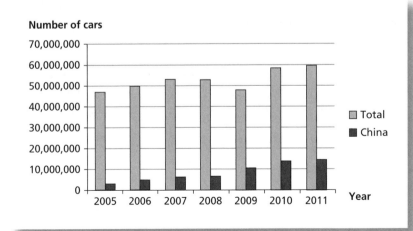

the United States, have experienced domestic market declines over the last few years, China has consistently registered high growth rates for its domestic automobile market.

The sale of automobiles within China has increased from 2.36 million in 2001 to 13.64 million in 2009, resulting in an astounding compound annual growth rate (CAGR) of 24 per cent. By the end of 2009, China had become the world's largest automobile market, and it continues to hold this position. This is a significant achievement, attained over a relatively short period of time, and it is the first time that China's automobile market has surpassed the market in the United States. In addition to locally manufactured cars, the Chinese market attracts a large number of imported cars, mainly from Europe, the United States, Japan and Korea. China's overall auto usage increased from five cars per 1000 persons and 2.6 cars per 100 households respectively in 2002 to 22 cars per 1000 persons and 8.3 cars per 100 households in 2009 (National Bureau of Statistics of China 2009). Although the vehicle penetration level has increased, it is still lower than in developed countries. As a result of its significant population of 1.3 billion, and its fast economic development, China's market size and growth potential make the country a game-changer in the international car market (US-China Economic and Security Review Commission 2006).

It has become evident, too, that the Chinese auto manufacturers now include both state-owned and privately owned enterprises. Since the 1980s, the majority of the state-owned enterprises have formed joint ventures with international auto manufacturers, with the joint ventures successfully becoming leaders in the automobile production market. Given that China's automobile industry was under the protection of high tariffs during the 1990s, the fast-growing automobile market has provided domestic auto manufacturers with great opportunities. Local governments have been supporting local automobile manufactures by providing financial assistance, reducing the local auto manufacturers' tax liability, reducing overhead costs – for example, through free use of industrial land – and so on. Consequently, some local automobile enterprises, especially locally state-owned car makers, have experienced rapid growth during this period. Since China entered the World Trade Organization (WTO) in 2001, central government control over local automobile enterprises has gradually loosened. The role of local government has also changed from direct intervention in the local automobile industry (mainly in support of local, state-owned enterprises) to support for all types of companies, including joint ventures and privately owned enterprises. Some local privately owned manufacturers quickly gained market share through the use of imitation and low-price strategies, without support from international enterprises. In 2010, among the top 10 automobile manufacturers in China, seven were joint ventures and two were privately owned enterprises, namely BYD and Geely. In 2011, Geely dropped out and BYD was the only privately owned automobile manufacturer in the top 10.

The Chinese government continues to play a central role in shaping the automobile industry. For example, Beijing launched a raft of policy measures that included automobile buying incentives to boost spending on cars; these incentives act to promote the continued growth of the automobile industry, and they resulted in continued growth during the global economic downturn. In terms of managing FDI, ownership policies mandate that foreign automobile manufactures enter into 50/50 joint ventures with local auto makers. The central government is strongly encouraging of R&D on alternative sources for power trains, including electric cars and gasoline–electric hybrids to help cope with energy shortages and rampant pollution.

During the last couple of years, on average, 10 per cent of automobile sales were allocated to R&D in China's automobile industry (National Bureau of Statistics of China 2009). Despite this investment in R&D, Chinese-owned brands are still under-developed, and face big challenges both domestically and internationally. Chinese auto makers appear to be heavily reliant on international suppliers for automobile parts; furthermore, many auto manufacturers in China suffer from a shortage of talent and a lack of experience in managing across borders.

Automobile manufacturers in China have, however, outpaced global automakers in developing cars specifically for emerging markets. As a result of China's automotive industry developing extensively through FDI in the form of alliances and joint ventures, international automobile manufacturers are unlikely to promote Chinese exports that compete with their own products in other markets (Tang 2009). Additionally, some Chinese self-owned brands seeking to enter industrialised countries are finding it next to impossible, partly because they are struggling to meet the safety and emission standards for these countries. Other emerging markets are therefore the main target of Chinese companies seeking to export cars.

Geely's venture into China's domestic markets

Geely Automobile Holdings Ltd is the tenth largest automobile manufacturer in China (Geely n.d.). Headquartered in Hangzhou, Zhejiang Province, Geely has six car-assembly plants and power train manufacturing plants in China, enabling a production capacity of approximately 300 000 cars per year.

Geely was founded in 1986 as a refrigerator maker, then switched to producing decorating materials. In 1992, Geely started to make motorcycle parts, followed by the manufacture of the entire motorcycle. By 1994, its motorcycles were being sold in 22 countries worldwide, an indication of its determination to succeed in whatever product it manufactured. Continuing its entrepreneurial spirit, in 1996 Geely bought the shareholdings of an automobile manufacturer in Sichuan province, a purchase that provided the company with an automobile manufacturing licence. In 1997, Geely officially launched its automobile manufacturing business for RMB 50 million (US$8 million). A year later, the first Geely car – the Geely Haoqing SRV – rolled off the production line. Geely's mission was to produce affordable cars that would become available to the ordinary citizens of China; consequently, most of the cars it produced were reasonably priced, around and even below RMB 40 000 (US$6000). Such prices were bound to attract local share.

As one of the first entrepreneurial, privately owned auto manufacturers, Geely experienced difficulties in attaining sufficient support from the local government of Zhejiang province, where it was located. This lack of local government support was clearly evident when Geely's founder and chairman, Li Shufu, invited local government officials to the launching ceremony of Geely's automobile business – only a few of them showed up. This lack of support was more than likely due to the fact that Geely was not yet one of the high-ranking local enterprises in the province at the time.

Geely operated in this 'awkward' situation until it was officially listed in China's automobile manufacturer index in 2001. This official recognition provided the company with excellent opportunities to compete against the more than 40 other private enterprises that reportedly wanted to enter the automobile industry. China's entry into the World Trade Organization (WTO) in the same year did not influence Geely much, given that China's car manufacturing sector – as a fledgling industry – was granted five to six years of protection. It was during these years that Geely became one of the fastest growing companies in the automobile industry in China.

The history and growth of Geely as a company is an interesting example of low-cost strategy and entrepreneurial leadership. The business venture commenced from humble beginnings as a family business, with its operating capital coming from Li Shufu's family and friends. In 2002, in a strategic move, Li Shufu invited a former accountant from the Zhejiang Provincial Local Tax Bureau, Xu Gang, to join Geely as the president. Using his networks, Xu set the framework for Geely to establish contacts and build relationships with many banks at the provincial level. Before long, Geely was able to raise a loan of RMB 100 million. In yet another strategic move, in the same year Geely signed a significant agreement with the China Everbright Bank, one of the largest banks in China.

Geely also sought to attract capital from overseas. In 2004, Geely purchased a shell company in Hong Kong, and had its Initial Public Offering (IPO) on the Hong Kong Stock Exchange in 2005. This brought Geely HK$2 billion by June 2007 – a development that was critical to Geely's growth and development. Being listed on the stock market in Hong Kong also attracted attention from well-known investment banks, which prepared Geely for its acquisition of Volvo.

Geely's transformation from a small family business to a public company listed on stock exchanges required dramatic and sweeping changes within the organisation. During the transition, two-thirds of the senior management was replaced, and 90 per cent of the old employees, including almost all of Li's family members and relatives, were forced out (Wu, Cao & Chen 2010). In a country like China, where *renqing* (mutual obligation) plays an important role in the culture, these changes could not be made by Li Shufu himself. Rather, the new senior executives were the implementers of the organisational transition process, and they managed the changes through processes in the human resources department of the company. The intention was to revitalise the workforce, and Geely has continued with its approach of attracting skilled automobile executives from established auto manufacturers or suppliers. Human talent is considered to be the most important resource by Li Shufu. Geely also has its own schools and colleges to educate and train people to meet the company's needs. In 2008, Geely donated RMB 12.5 million and established the Geely Future Talent Fund and the Li Shufu Education Fund, to ensure that it is continuously building its talent pool.

Geely's venture into international markets

Having established itself firmly in the local domestic market of China, Geely was ready to venture into feasible international markets. It began with exporting cars in 2003, and developed a strategy for a continuing growth in export numbers. In 2008, Geely sold over 220 000 cars, with 24.5 per cent of its cars being sold to 55 countries – mainly emerging nations around the world. Geely had tried to enter the developed markets in Europe and the United States. For example, earlier in 2005 it became the first Chinese automobile manufacturer to participate in the 61st Frankfurt Auto Show, held in Germany. A year later, Geely made history at the Detroit Auto Show by showcasing the first Chinese automobile at the biggest show in North America. Unfortunately, despite its intentions of asserting its presence and becoming known in the United States, its lack of international experience led to a rather ordinary, lacklustre display, featuring a small silver sedan that attracted criticism rather than admiration. The low-cost car was unsuccessful and uncompetitive on many fronts, and failed to meet the developed world's stringent safety and environmental regulations. It was mercilessly panned at the show.

Geely's senior management realised that it had to do better, and that focusing on low-cost cars would neither sustain the company in the long term – especially in the global automobile market – nor enable it to gain the international profile it desired. Geely kicked off a major transformation in 2007. A new mission was announced: 'Produce the safest, most environmentally friendly and most energy saving cars. And let Geely cars go all over the world.' (Geely n.d.) The transformation initiatives were carried out in an effort to get rid of Geely's image as a 'cheap' car manufacturer and to help the company become a technology-driven auto maker (Chen 2010). In 2007, Geely added another development to its strategy of innovation and entrepreneurship. The company entered a joint venture with Manganese Bronze Holdings, the established manufacturer of the London taxi. It strategically established Shanghai LTI Automobile Ltd as an arm of Geely, and commenced producing the iconic London taxi in China. Furthermore, in 2008 the company halted production of its three best-selling models, Haoqing, Meiri and Youliou, and planned to replace them gradually with better and more technologically sophisticated models in the form of the Free Cruiser, Kingkong and Prospect.

In the same year, at the biggest automobile show in China, Geely presented 23 new models in keeping with its strategy for change and ongoing innovation. All the new models employed new technologies and fell within the mid-range to high-end levels of car manufacturing. The shift in price is indicative of the shift in image building. For example, one of Geely's new high-end models cost RMB 3.6 million (US$580 000), which was several hundred times the price of Geely's old, inexpensive models. At the same time, Geely returned to the next international Detroit Auto Show in the United State, and presented two strongly competitive vehicles: the FC sedan featuring Geely's G-Power four-cylinder engine, and its newly revised version of the London taxi TX4. Even though Geely was still developing its overall strategy and schedule for entry into the US market, it was making progress in reaching US federal crash safety requirements and building a better perception of its product quality with reviewers.

In 2009, Geely made further strides forward in the international arena and bought Drivetrain Systems International Pty Ltd (DSI), a global transmission developer head-quartered in Australia. It then proceeded to build three DSI plants in China to produce gearboxes. Geely intended to equip all its passenger cars with automatic gearboxes made by DSI. In the same year, Geely also opened overseas car assembly plants in the Ukraine, Russia and Indonesia.

On another level, to attract international market share, Geely rolled out a major initiative to classify all of its new models under three major marketing brands – Gleagle, Emgrand and Englon – and segmented its advertising and sales channels by brands instead of the traditional approach of segmentation by models. It strategically removed the name 'Geely' from the nameplate of its three new brands in a move intended to avoid people connecting the new brands with Geely's existing reputation for low prices and poor quality. The revised branding strategy sought to put Geely in a stronger position to meet new market challenges and attract new customers. While features of the 'Gleagle' brand targeted fashionable young people, the 'Emgrand' and 'Englon' brands were defined as luxury and classic brands, and targeted buyers from middle- and upper-income groups. These brand-focused strategies prepared the way for Geely's next target – a world-class international brand. Hence it commenced its acquisition deal with Volvo.

Geely's takeover of Volvo

By August 2010, Geely was able to proudly announce that it had formally completed a deal to buy Sweden's prestigious Volvo Cars from the US auto giant Ford for US$1.8 billion. It simultaneously proceeded to raise an additional US$900 million to keep Volvo operating. The total cost of US$2.7 billion included US$2.1 billion in loans from the Bank of China, China Construction Bank, Export–Import Bank of China, Geely Automobile Holdings and the government of Gothenburg, where Volvo is headquartered. The move was welcomed not only by Geely but also by the Chinese government, with China's Minister of Industry and Technology, Li Yizhong, appearing at the signing ceremony in Gothenburg, sending a strong signal of support from the Chinese government. The message seemed to be that Geely was buying Volvo, but so too was China (*Economist* 2010).

Geely was determined that the Volvo brand and its reputation of prestige and quality would remain intact. It announced that Volvo would still be operated as a separate subsidiary, managed by Swedish personnel, and the Volvo China team – including its marketing and public relations staff – would operate independently of Geely. This distinctive approach is captured in the words of Geely's Chairman, Li Shufu, who noted that 'Geely is Geely, Volvo is Volvo' (ChinaBizGov 2012). On 15 July 2010, Li Shufu became chairman of the Volvo board; the then CEO, Stephen Odell, left Volvo and returned to Ford as CEO of Ford Europe. Before he left Volvo, he told the media: 'Volvo is well positioned for the future with an exciting range of products that remain true to its core values: safety, quality, environmental responsibility and modern Scandinavian design.' (Ford 2010). A few weeks later, Stefan Jacoby – the previous head of Volkswagen's operations in the United States – was appointed the new president and CEO of Volvo Cars and a new board of directors was elected. A Volvo–Geely Dialogue and Cooperation Committee (DCC) was set up to steer the communications and joint efforts of both parties (*Global Times* 2010).

Volvo's main production sites will continue to be in Sweden and Belgium, but Geely plans to open two factories and an engine-assembly plant in China. Li Shufu has claimed that the corporate synergy could help Volvo nearly double its sales to 600 000 vehicles by 2015. Geely-Volvo is considering selling Volvo cars manufactured in China into the US markets, which could help reduce exchange-rate risks for Volvo, and make it one of the first companies to bring Chinese-made vehicles into the United States.

However, as in all acquisitions in international business (Datta 1991), bringing together two very different organisations can be problematic. In this instance, three months after Geely's official takeover of Volvo, Li Shufu admitted that there were severe conflicts between the Geely management team and the Volvo management team, mainly due to strategic differences. For Li Shufu, selling big and luxurious cars was the only way the Swedish brand could make up for lost time in the Chinese market. 'The fancier the better,' he said. 'Few have an eye for Volvo's Scandinavian no-frills style, to be honest.' (Yan & Pollard 2011). Yet Volvo's management advocated – at least initially – that Volvo stick to its tradition of focus on core mid-size models, where safety and fuel-efficiency are important.

Li Shufu responded by saying that Jacoby needed to understand China better. He told the media that many of China's new rich 'behave outrageously, showing off their wealth', and are willing to buy upscale car brands. He also inferred that it was like producing cigarettes, noting that 'smoking is bad for your health, but tobacco companies make and sell cigarettes. The same is true with Volvo.' (Shirouzu 2011)

In May 2011, four months after the establishment of a new Volvo China headquarters in Shanghai, Volvo's new S60 model – targeting the world's largest vehicle market – was launched in China. It was considered the blueprint for Volvo's expansion into luxury cars (Shirouzu 2011), and also seen as a sign of the smoothing over of the significant misalignment between the Geely and Volvo management teams (Yan & Pollard 2011). Whether Geely and Volvo can overcome their differences and steer Volvo towards success in the long term is still uncertain, but what is clear is that there are broad implications for China's global expansion. Chinese companies have poured tens of billions of dollars into foreign acquisitions in recent years, such as Lenovo's purchase of IBM's personal computer business and TCL's acquisition with Thomson, but have done so with little success. Although in a different industry, Geely and Volvo are facing similar challenges to those faced by other Chinese companies and their partners when involved in international acquisitions. Not only are there differences in strategy, but there are also cultural conflicts, and differences in management style and values (Krolicki, Pollard & Yan 2010).

There is one factor that is clear, though. Geely's takeover of Volvo did not stop it from the global expansion of its own brands. More recently, in 2011, Geely entered into the Australia markets with a Geely MK city sedan selling for around A$11 990 (US$12 350), which is believed to be one of Australia's cheapest cars. Another model, the Geely Panda, will be launched in Australia very soon – probably at an even lower price. Interestingly, the company decided to return to using the 'Geely' nameplates on these two models, two years after they were removed from the new brands launched in 2009. It was thought to be important to market and continuously strengthen the 'Geely' brand in the international arena – a sign of a successful auto brand from China!

■ Appendix 1: Volvo

Volvo was a Swedish car maker officially founded in 1927, when its first car rolled out of the factory in Gothenburg. Sweden's Volvo is the epitome of good middle-class taste. Volvo's very safe and practical cars were, in better days, the default choice on many a suburban driveway in the United States and Europe. Volvo was the first car manufacturer in the world to equip its cars with three-point safety belts as a standard fitting (1959). Volvo passed the two million car production mark in the 1970s. In 1976, the US traffic safety administration (NHTSA) purchased a number of Volvo 240s, which were used to set the safety standards against which all new cars on the US market were tested. Volvo cars became more powerful, faster and safer in the 1980s. The 1990s marked the biggest technical transition for Volvo. In 2007, the ReCharge plug-in hybrid concept was unveiled, signalling a new emphasis on environmental solutions. In 2008, Volvo introduced two mid-size models with extremely economical and clean diesel engines (Volvo, n.d.a). Table 9.1 presents the sales figures for Volvo between 2000 and 2011.

Volvo Car Corporation was sold to the Ford Motor Company in 1999 for US$6.45 billion. Before being taken over by Geely in 2010, the last time that Volvo had shown an annual profit was in 2005. In 2010, the president and CEO of Volvo Car, Stefan Jacoby, announced that Volvo had witnessed a turn-around in the car market and had returned to profitability. Volvo's retail sales for 2010 increased by 11.6 per cent to 373 525 units, compared with 334 808 units in 2009. In China, 2010 sales improved against 2009 sales by 36.2 per cent, and in the Nordic region they grew by 29 per cent. Corresponding European sales grew by 10.4 per cent, and market share improved by 0.14 per cent to 1.2 per cent. However, during this period of global growth, Volvo sales volumes in the United States decreased by 12.2 per cent to 53 952 units, compared with 61 246 in 2009 (Volvo, n.d.b).

Table 9.1: Volvo sales figures, 2000–11	
Year	No. of cars (thousands)
2011	449
2010	373
2009	334
2008	374
2007	458
2006	428
2005	444
2004	456
2003	415
2002	407*
2001	412
2000	409

* As of 2002, sales are defined as cars delivered to end-customers.
Source: Volvo (n.d.b).

◼ Appendix 2: Li Shufu vs Stefan Jacoby

'Mr Jacoby and Mr Li are a study in contrasts.' (Shirouzu 2011)

Geely's founder and chairman, Li Shufu, is being heralded as the equivalent of Henry Ford in China. He was born into a farmer's family in a poor village in Taizhou, Zhejiang province. Using the 120 Chinese yuan (US$15) he got from his father, he started a photography business after finishing high school. He also tried producing and selling silver and gold using a chemical separation, an 'innovation' that came from his experience while processing photos. The story of Geely Corporation began one day when Li Shufu saw four shoemakers producing refrigerator parts. He started to make refrigerator parts at home by himself, and before long set up a factory with his brothers to manufacture the entire refrigerator. After that, he dabbled in various business areas, such as producing decoration materials and brokering real estate. Not all of these attempts were successful. His failure in the real estate business, which he rarely mentions, made him believe he was not a good player in capital markets. Yet he was still extremely ambitious in pursuing his automobile manufacturing dream. His vision was one of China walking down a new Silk Road with Geely leading the way.

Volvo's CEO, 53-year-old Stefan Jacoby, is a reserved German with a sports streak: 'I am an athlete at heart and have always been inspired by the challenge of climbing Mount Everest.' (Mbuya 2008) Jacoby earned a MBA degree at the University of

Cologne in 1985 before starting a lengthy career at Volkswagen AG, where he was a Secretary General, Executive Vice President for the Asia-Pacific Region, Executive Vice President for Marketing and Sales, and finally accepted the position of CEO and president of the Volkswagen Group of America in 2007. As a VW golden boy in the United States, he had engineered both the building of a $1 billion plant in Chattanooga and an ambitious recovery plan for Volvo (Motavalli 2010). Jacoby's jumping to Volvo in 2010 was a surprise to both those inside and outside of Volkswagen.

Discussion questions

9.1   What is Geely's business strategy? Do you think Geely's choice to discontinue the production of cheap cars in favour of concentrating on the high-end market is risky?

9.2   What kind of foreign entry mode did Geely use in this case study? What are the advantages and disadvantages of using this (these) entry mode/modes?

9.3   What factors motivated each company during Geely's takeover of Volvo? What benefits can both Geely and Volvo expect to gain?

9.4   What do you think will be the main issues faced by Geely after its purchase of Volvo? Is Geely ready for further expansion and takeovers?

References

Booz & Co. 2010, 'Corporate R&D spending declined during 2009 downturn, finds Booz & Company Global Innovation Study, 3 November, viewed 20 November 2012, <http://www.booz.com/global/home/press/article/48789421>.

Booz Allen Markets Services 2003, 'R&D spending in the German automotive industry', 13 November, viewed 20 November 2012, <http://www.boozallen.com/consulting/industries_article/981897?preview=1&psid=0&ph=c0a9>.

Chen, X 2010, 'Shedding its skin', *Global Times*, 31 December, viewed 20 November 2012, <http://auto.globaltimes.cn/automakers/geely/2011–03/607631.html>.

ChinaBizGov 2012, 'Volvo is Geely and Geely is Volvo', viewed 20 November 2012, <http://chinabizgov.blogspot.com/2012/02/volvo-is-geely-and-geely-is-volvo.html>.

Datta, DK 1991, 'Organizational fit and acquisition performance: effects of post-acquisition integration', *Strategic Management Journal*, vol. 12, no. 4, pp. 281–97.

Economist 2010, 'Geely buys Volvo, status symbol: an obscure Chinese carmaker buys a famous but ailing Swedish one', 31 March, viewed 20 November 2012, <http://www.economist.com/node/15825810>.

—— 2012, 'R&D spending', 30 October, viewed 20 November 2012, <http://www.economist.com/blogs/graphicdetail/2012/10/focus-7>.

Ford 2010, 'Ford motor company completes sale of Volvo to Geely', viewed 2 August 2010, <http://media.ford.com/article_display.cfm?article_id=33059>.

Geely n.d., 'Mission, vision and value', viewed 2 August 2010, <http://global.geely.com/general/MissionVisionAndValue.html>.

Global Times 2010, 'Volvo, Geely set up Dialogue & Cooperation Committee', viewed 20 November 2012, <http://www.globaltimes.cn/feature-template/2010-01/501888.html>.

Gulati, N & Choudhury, S 2012, 'India 2011 car sales growth slows to 4.3%', *The Wall Street Journal*, 11 January, viewed 20 November 2012, <http://online.wsj.com/article/SB10001424052970204257504577152331478380006.html>.

Jaruzelski, B, Loehr, J & Holman, R 2012, 'The 2012 Global Innovation 1000 Study: making ideas work', Booz & Co, viewed 30 December 2012, <http://www.booz.com/global/home/what_we_think/global-innovation-1000>.

Krolicki, K, Pollard, N & Yan, Y 2010, 'Special report – saving Volvo: Geely buys brand and management test', Reuters, 22 July, viewed 20 November 2012, <http://www.iii.co.uk/news/?type=reutersnews&articleid=TRE66L2EP&feed=Bus&action=article>.

Mbuya, J 2008, Stefan Jacoby, *Washington Post*, 16 June, viewed 20 November 2012, <http://www.washingtonpost.com/wp-dyn/content/article/2008/06/15/AR2008061501732.html>

Motavalli, J 2010, 'Stefan Jacoby, leaving VW for Volvo, may have felt passed over', 28 June, *CBS News*, viewed 20 November 2012, <http://www.bnet.com/blog/electric-cars/stefan-jacoby-leaving-vw-for-volvo-may-have-felt-passed-over/1838#ixzz1PyZipZnF>.

National Bureau of Statistics of China 2009, Various statistics, viewed 26 April 2011, <http://www.stats.gov.cn/tjsj>.

OICA n.d., Production Statistics, OICA, viewed 26 April 2011, <http://oica.net/category/production-statistics>.

Shirouzu, N 2011, 'Chinese begin Volvo overhaul', *Wall Street Journal*, 7 June, viewed 20 November 2012, <http://online.wsj.com/article/SB10001424052702304563104576363041069364856.html>.

Tang, R 2009, *The rise of China's auto industry and its impact on the U.S. motor vehicle industry*, working paper, Congressional Research Service, viewed 20 November 2012, <http://www.fas.org/sgp/crs/row/R40924.pdf>.

US–China Economic and Security Review Commission 2006, *Report to Congress of the US–China Economic and Security Review Commission*, viewed 20 November 2012, <www.uscc.gov/annual_report/2006/annual_report_full_06.pdf>.

Volvo n.d.a, '2000–2008: A historical review', media release, viewed 20 November 2012, <https://www.media.volvocars.com/media/articles/html/10675_1_5.aspx>.

——n.d.b, 'Sales volume', media release, viewed 20 November 2012, <https://www.media.volvocars.com/global/enhanced/en-gb/About/Sales/Archive.aspx>.

Wu, A, Cao, S & Chen, S 2010, 'Geely's wild growth' (吉利的野蛮生长), *Caijing Magazine*, 4 January, viewed 20 November 2012, <http://magazine.caijing.com.cn/2010–01–03/110351047.html>.

Yan, F & Pollard, N 2011, 'Analysis: Volvo China union bearing fruit after rocky honeymoon', Reuters, 12 May, viewed 20 November 2012, <http://www.reuters.com/article/2011/05/12/us-volvo-china-idUSTRE74B0PK20110512>.

10

Parking Creators International

Massoud Saghafi

Background

Mr Rahman Jr looked from his office window down to the factory floor. Sparks from the welding and grinding machines were flying everywhere, lighting the factory up like fireworks on the fourth of July. The place buzzed with workers hammering, punching, welding, painting, assembling and packaging finished parking lifts to be shipped to Hong Kong. 'It was not always like this,' he thought. 'I remember not too long ago when I was the one building the lifts from start to finish. Now we can crank out ten lifts in a day. I just wish we could sell that many.' Demand had slowed and Mr Rahman Jr expressed deep concern about the survival of his company and the need to establish a permanent network of distributors overseas.

A humble start

Mr Habib Rahman Jr was the President of Parking Creators International (PCI). Located near Los Angeles, California, the company had production facilities that occupied 1860 square metres of factory space, in which it created its main product: hydraulically operated automobile lifts. Founded by his father, Mr Rahman Sr, five years earlier, under the name of Halabi Welding, the company had begun as a simple welding operation that produced railings, fences and metal cuttings.

Halabi Welding was born, and Mr Rahman Sr was awarded several contracts by National Steel, where he had been employed. Even though he had neither the production facility nor the labour force to do the work at that time, Mr Rahman Sr seized the opportunity to start his own business. He asked his son to find a suitable location and to set up a workshop within the next few months. When the reality of high rent and equipment prices set in, the Rahmans resorted to the next best alternative: they began operations from the garage of their home, while continuing to look for a more suitable facility. During their search, they came upon a company that manufactured steel products and had, in the past, produced auto lifts. It continued to receive demands for auto lifts, but no longer produced or knew much about the product.

The Rahmans capitalised on the opportunity. They struck a deal to use one of the company's idle shops, which was equipped with the necessary heavy machinery to begin the auto lifts operation. Mr Rahman Sr utilised his experience in machine design and welding to begin production himself. Two months and five employees later, Halabi Welding was manufacturing more than 50 units per month. By industry standards, this output was unusually high, with the standard time to make a lift being 30 hours. There were only five people involved in the production at the company, working 40 hours per week.

A new beginning

A year after Halabi Welding was established, sales turned sluggish. Looking to increase business, Mr Rahman Jr pursued an inquiry he had received a few months back. In July, a distributor, Parking Solutions, had approached him with an offer to market the lifts. As Halabi Welding was operating at full capacity at the time of the initial offer, Mr Rahman Jr had declined, concerned about meeting the additional demand as the business had no feasible way of quickly expanding the existing production facility. Now that sales were down, Mr Rahman Jr believed a deal could be worked out. Fortunately, the distributor was still interested. An agreement was reached in which Halabi Welding would manufacture a line exclusively for Parking Solutions.

Things went well for a year. Then one of the company's major distributors suddenly stopped placing orders with Halabi Welding, resulting in Halabi being left with over 150 units in excess inventory valued at over US$400 000. It was forced to lay off all but two employees. For the next five months, the focus was on survival, with the Rahmans working hard to keep their business going. After reducing inventory and obtaining new orders, operations resumed and the Rahmans were optimistic again. However, it was not meant to be – the landowner of the facility they were leasing was in bankruptcy and the bank repossessed the land. Halabi Welding had to move. As the company was still recovering from its struggle to survive, it had no reserves available to face this emergency. The only alternative was to relocate to a smaller facility where there was no room for the heavier machinery that contributed to faster production. The move to a smaller location in Los Angeles was completed in July of the same year, and scaled-down operations resumed once more.

In late July, as a contingency against any future problems in production or sales, Mr Rahman Jr looked into establishing another small facility to diversify the company's steel output with equipment that could to make the lifts as well as other products. This new entity became Parking Creators International (PCI), and its new location became the production site for both new and existing products. When the sales of lifts picked up again, PCI was able to assume production and cater for the excess demand. The Rahmans breathed a sigh of relief.

It was at this stage that the Rahmans' partner in Halabi Welding decided to sever their relationship. PCI became the Rahman's saviour. A deal was struck: the Rahmans would give up their interest in Halabi Welding but would retain the manufacturing equipment from that operation. In addition, they would keep all dealer and distributor agreements from their Halabi Welding operations in the United States and overseas, with the exception of a dealer agreement in Japan. PCI would move out of the premises. This prompted the move to a larger facility, which PCI shared with its main distributor, Parking Solutions.

▒ Product line

An auto lift is a four-post steel structure with a hydraulically operated centre platform. A vehicle is driven on to the platform and an electrical switch is activated to lift the vehicle. Another vehicle can then be parked underneath, which effectively doubles the parking capacity. PCI offers 11 different models with lifting capacities from 4000 pounds (1815 kilograms) to 7000 pounds (3175 kilograms), which range in price from $2550 to $4995. The motor for the lift is made by Webster and carries a one-year warranty. Webster is highly regarded, with readily available replacement parts and service centres globally. Through DuPont, PCI has developed a finishing paint that renders steel resistant to rust.[1] This was especially valuable in the Asian countries, where weather erodes unprotected steel. The finish was produced exclusively for PCI.

Every lift produced was fitted together prior to shipping to ensure easy installation and proper functioning. This was a part of the company's quality control and was labour intensive, taking an average of two hours to perform. However, this process was necessary to ward off any problems that could cause lifts to be returned. After-sale service was an essential part of PCI's strategy. The distributors were equipped and supplied with the necessary replacement parts. Generally, the most in-demand service was the annual replacement of the bushings on the hydraulic cylinder. The process was simple and the parts were inexpensive.

Competition

Competition for the PCI Auto lift Division stemmed mainly from three companies in the immediate target market, and was defined as any company that made at least one model comparable with a PCI model.

Domestic competition

- *Autolifters of America*. This company boasted that it was the top lift company in the United States. However, with only 400 feet of production lines, this was not quite true. Other competitors were much bigger and had larger sales. Autolifters did, however, offer a model closely paralleling PCI's PC 6.0. It had the same lifting capacity and similar features, although the designs were completely different, with PCI's unit being designed for easier installation and heavier use. The comparably equipped PC 6.0 was $200 less expensive than Autolifters' lift. PCI rated the threat of this company low to medium.
- *Backyard Buddy*. Located in Niles, Ohio, this company occupied the same-sized manufacturing space as PCI's 1860 square metres. It manufactured one product that was in competition with the PC 4.5. Its competitive strategy was based on price. Backyard Buddy offered a complete stripped-down model for $2495. This model was not patented, and PCI had offered the same model in the past, fully equipped, for $2995. (PCI had taken this model out of production until it could further improve the safety locking mechanism.) PCI believed that Backyard Buddy was misguiding its customers, since a stripped-down model was not very useful for the average customer.[2] When all the options were added to the stripped-down model of the Backyard Buddy, the price went up to $3200. PCI rated the threat of this company in the near future as low.

■ *International competition*

- *Park Plus Corporation*. Founded in 1969, Park Plus was considered the global market leader, with manufacturing facilities throughout the United States and 30 distribution networks covering the globe. Its domain was South Africa, Canada, Brazil, Argentina, Columbia, England, Finland, Germany, Spain, France, Turkey, Saudi Arabia, India, China, Japan, Taiwan, Hong Kong, Australia, Hawai'i and the United States. Its main line was the Space Maker, which included units that were close to PCI products. The DP001 and DP002 were close competitors to the PC 5.0 and PC 6.0. However, the price difference was about $500 on each unit in favour of PCI.

  Park Plus Corporation was aware of the existence of PCI. Its distributor in the West had originally offered Mr Rahman Sr the opportunity to manufacture a parking lift for it. However, the offer was turned down because of the main condition that PCI become a wholly owned subsidiary of Park Plus. PCI rated the threat of this company as extremely high because of its dominant presence in international markets that were vital to PCI's survival and growth.

■ Distribution

■ *Domestic*

PCI had three distributors in the United States, all in California. One was in San Francisco and the other two were in Los Angeles. Domestic distributors received the products they ordered approximately two weeks after placing an order. Generally, they paid for the product when it was finished, but prior to shipping. All lifts were sold ex-factory (PCI). The distributor, whose profits depended on the monthly quantity and type of machines ordered, then arranged for shipping to the ultimate customer.

Parking Solutions in Los Angeles accounted for over 90 per cent of PCI's domestic sales. The company's territory was undefined, enabling it to sell domestically and/or internationally. However, all of its sales were domestic. Its main marketing strategy was to place ads in specialty magazines such as *Car Collector*, *Autoweek*, *Hemmings* and *Motorcycle Collector*, and then – using leads generated from these ads – develop a list of potential customers for future approach and sales. However, Parking Solutions' overall sales had dropped dramatically in recent years, not because of lower demand but due to poor follow-up on the sales leads generated by the ads. The employees were generally unmotivated and displayed a 'who cares?' attitude towards finalising sales. Parking Solutions had even informed PCI of the company's plans to shut down its entire operations and exit the distribution industry.

■ *International*

On the international front, PCI had distributors in Hong Kong, Taiwan, Greece, Germany and Saudi Arabia, and interests from companies in other countries. These independent distributors had played an instrumental role in keeping PCI alive. If it had not been for their orders, PCI would have shut down a long time ago. However, the international orders were inconsistent and usually came in small quantities. All international sales were Free On Board (FOB) from Los Angeles/Long Beach, paid in US$. Purchases were paid in advance with a letter of credit and the buyer arranged for shipping out of the United States. The distributor for Hong Kong and Taiwan made up the largest bulk of purchases, ordering about 20 machines every six months and enjoying exclusive territory in the region. Other international distributors working with PCI were still in the process of developing demand in their perspective regions.

In addition, PCI had received new inquiries from other international distributors and dealers, particularly from an Italian company, which had learned about its products from the US *Commercial News* magazine. PCI was very interested in establishing relations with this Italian distributor. However, further research was necessary before more steps could be taken.

■ Financial summary

PCI is a family-owned, small and debt-free business. It is able to obtain a line of credit from banks or suppliers quite easily, but has not yet exercised that option. Mr Rahman Jr commented:

> In a growing business like mine, I cannot afford to take a loan. When demand was increasing, I thought about borrowing in order to expand. In retrospect, if I had done so, I would be out of business today because I had an extended period of slow sales. I faced many uncertainties in the beginning, and taking on a loan would have added to the confusion. I paid for what I bought upfront, so that no one could control my operations.

PCI's debt-free status is a reflection of the owner's beliefs that debt is bad and the only form of ownership is full and unleveraged. Mr Rahman had often shied away from opportunities, mainly because the company had not had the cash on hand required to enter into a new project and he had been unwilling to borrow. PCI operates under a small budget with a total assets size of only $360 000, total current assets of $53 000, revenue of $152 000 and net profit of $12 000 on a $36 000 gross profit.

Other financial information for PCI is provided in Table 10.1.

Table 10.1: PCI financial information

Total current assets: $53 000
Total assets: $360 000
Revenue: $152 000
Gross profit: $32 000
Net income before taxes: $16,000

Past mistakes and outlook

From Mr Rahman Jr's perspective, the future looked uncertain:

> Looking back now, I realise that I was not entirely in control of the company. My main distributor was, and I was at his mercy. There were no real sales forecasts. When he placed an order, I made money. If he didn't buy, I didn't sell. I am changing my thinking, however. I am looking into hiring a marketing expert and establishing a solid network of dealers and distributors domestically and internationally. I believe we have an excellent product, an above-industry average warranty and good after-sales support and service. What we need is to establish a presence where the market potential exists, such as South-East Asia and Europe.

The company stumbled on to the international stage by chance. Several orders from South-East Asian companies had alerted Mr Rahman Jr to the product's international appeal. Upon further exploration, he discovered that international demand was high. There were several paths along which PCI could proceed. PCI's top priorities were accessing international distribution channels and meeting the price demanded in those markets.

Opportunities

The Japanese option

The Japanese market had the largest international potential, due in part to a law enacted in Japan in the 1990s: to purchase a car in many parts of Japan, one must present proof of possessing a parking space. If parking proof were not provided, cars could not leave the showrooms. A car parking lift could solve this problem. The Chinese government later adopted a similar law in several major metropolitan areas of China. All Japanese and foreign car manufacturers selling in Japan had been forced to respond to the challenge. Wholesale prices for car lifts were generally 20–30 per cent lower for the Japanese than for domestic market, but the distributor profit margin was the same. PCI had established a connection with Toyota in the Japanese market, but had lost this connection due to negligence on the part of the Halabi Welding representative when PCI broke off from Halabi Welding. Nevertheless, Toyota and other Japanese companies were still showing interest in PCI's product line.

Establish own networks

Lifts were shipped to customers in sections, and could be assembled in two to three hours. The majority of customers were not technically oriented, however, and required installation service. This constraint lent itself to the need for regional distributors who were capable of installing the lifts. Since the defect rate was very low, service was not essential after the product was installed. PCI relied on its main distributor in California, Parking Solutions, which controlled its distribution network across the United States. The network was very small and ineffective, which caused many customers to decline the purchase of lifts. Parking Solutions only had alliances with one distributor outside the United States. To overcome this ineffective system, one solution for PCI was to establish its own network of distribution outlets. The bulk of PCI's sales came from New York, Florida, Ohio, Michigan, California, Hong Kong and Taiwan. PCI would need to establish a service/sales centre in each of those areas.

According to Parking Solutions, the minimum estimated cost to start and run a service office was as shown in Table 10.2.

Table 10.2: Cost of starting and running a service office	
Domestic operations:	
Rent, utilities and phone	$24 000 per annum
Staff	$38 400 (two employees @40 hrs/week @$10/hr)
Equipment and supplies	$10 000
Total	**$72 400**
International operations:	
Rent, utilities and phone	$4,000 a year
Staff	$11 520 (two employees @40 hrs/week @$3/hr)
Equipment and supplies	$10 000
Total	**$25 520**

The total cost of a distribution network of five domestic and two international offices was therefore $411 040.

■ The Saudi proposal

A large Saudi car dealer had proposed a joint venture: 51 per cent Saudis, 49 per cent PCI. The car dealer would provide all the capital needed to construct a production plant around the Jeddah area. In return, PCI would transfer its manufacturing and technology to Saudi Arabia, train local employees, and oversee productions and operations. The proposed plant would have a 250-lift per month initial capacity, based on a 35-hour weekly work schedule. The Saudi potential partner also offered a guaranteed distribution access through his dealer network across the entire Persian Gulf region.

The main advantage of a Saudi plant was operating cost reduction, which would enable the company to enter international markets at an even more competitive price. The labour cost cut would be substantial. It was estimated that by manufacturing in Saudi Arabia, the labour savings would range between $272 and $400 per machine. Such savings would be an added competitive advantage in expanding not only into Saudi Arabia, but also in other regions like the Middle East, South-East Asia, Europe and Africa. Competitors would be hurt by such drastic price reductions, since their cost structures were much higher than PCI would be able to offer.

Other savings from a plant in Saudi Arabia would be in the form of administrative and factory overheads, income taxes and raw materials. Such costs were expected to

Table 10.3: Monthly wage rates in Saudi Arabia

Position	Number	Salary/employee per month	Total
Engineers	3	$600	$1 800
Office staff	6	$400	$2 400
General labor	48	$400	$19 200
Total	**57**		**$23 400**

be lower in Saudi Arabia than in the United States due to higher wages, tax structure and raw material prices in the United States. Labour in Saudi is imported from low-wage neighbouring countries such as India, Pakistan and Sri Lanka. Table 10.3 depicts the monthly wage rates in Saudi Arabia for PCI.

These are also fixed costs for PCI in Saudi Arabia compared with the United States, as illustrated in Table 10.4.

Table 10.4: Comparison of Saudi and US costs

Total units	US cost	Saudi cost	Cost savings	Savings per unit produced
100	$195 736	$168 536	$27 200	$272
150	$293 604	$241 104	$52 500	$350
200	$391 472	$313 672	$77 800	$389
250	$489 340	$386 240	$103 100	$412

■ The Italian prospect

Several inquiries had been made by Italian companies, expressing an interest in importing the lifts due to the scarcity of parking spaces. Italy had experienced a tremendous increase in the number of vehicles: 24 million cars for an almost constant 30 000 public car parking spaces. Based on an Italian study of 23 European cities, there was an average of one parking space for every 130 people in the European Union. In Italy, the average was even lower. It was estimated that the Milan, Turin and Naples had more than 4400 vehicles per square metre of parking. Table 10.5 shows the ratios of inhabitants to parking spaces in the largest Italian cities according to market research.

Table 10.5: Ratios of inhabitants to parking spaces in Italian cities

City	Milan	Genoa	Turin	Rome	Naples
Ratio	300:1	700:1	750:1	870:1	1460:1

Transportation policies in Italy had long neglected parking, and had favoured the construction of roads and highways. Driving down a footpath crowded with pedestrians to reach a potential parking space was a common practice. The government passed a law that sought to address the parking issue by attempting to shift parking to large Italian towns in order to reduce traffic and pollution, and set new quotas for parking spaces in new and old buildings. The idea behind the law was to stimulate the construction of public and private car spaces. It made funds available to various city councils for borrowing the equivalent of $1.3 billion at low interest rates. However, the money appropriated was never disbursed and the parking problem continues to worsen.

Parking habits

Although there was a shortage of parking spaces, many public parking lots remained under-utilised. One explanation seemed to be that drivers preferred to park illegally but free rather than pay a high price for a parking space. The chance of getting fined was low and people were willing to risk it. To address this problem, the government had raised fines, increased the number of parking patrols and even introduced a tax on street parking. This would force drivers to use parking lots and increase the demand for multi-storey car parks and mechanised parking systems. Mechanised car parking systems showed promise because of their low cost, low management requirements and easy setup. Many old buildings had courtyards that could easily be fitted with a parking lift. The economies seemed compelling: the average annual cost of a parking space outside the centre of Milan was about $3000. Moving closer to the centre of the city, the price increased to $5000.

Competition in the Italian market

There were already some Italian companies and multinationals in the market. Although the exact figure was not known, the number was relatively low compared with the potential demand. It seemed that there was an opportunity for an imaginative high-tech parking system that would allow more cars to fit in the same limited space. In fact, the

Table 10.6: Italian market share profit projections				
At market share of:	5%	10%	15%	20%
Units sold	2739	5479	8218	10958
US revenue	$7 122 453	$14 244 906	$21 367 359	$28 489 812
US gross profit	$1 780 613	$3 561 227	$5 341 840	$7 122 453
U.S. gross margin	33%	33%	33%	33%
Saudi revenue	$6 147 225	$12 294 450	$18 441 674	$24 588 899
Saudi gross profit	$1 805 268	$3 610 536	$5 415 804	$7 221 072
Saudi gross margin	42%	42%	42%	42%

All sales are assumed at a wholesale price of $2600 if manufactured in the United States and $2244 if manufactured in Saudi Arabia. The revenues are based on a market potential of 54 788 units given in the table.

Italian Association for Parking (ASSOPARCHEGGI) was anxious to secure contracts with American companies providing high-tech parking solutions. Table 10.6 shows projected revenues and gross margins from sales in Italy if produced in and exported from the United States or from Saudi Arabia at various market shares for PCI.

Acknowledgement

I would like to thank SDSU CIBER for financial support to edit this manuscript.

Discussion questions

10.1 Analyse PCI's current position, its leadership and management structure, resources, vision and strategies that have led to successes and failures.

10.2 Compare and contrast the domestic and international options.

10.3 Should PCI go international? Does it have what it takes to succeed internationally? Justify your response/s to these questions.

10.4 If PCI decides to go international, which option would you recommend: Italy, Japan or Saudi Arabia? Give reasons for your recommendation/s.

Notes

1 The paint, Osha Blue, includes a rust treatment compound, a primer, and a finish gloss combined into one. It prevents weather conditions from eroding the steel. Since all three compounds are built into one, the time for finishing the product is reduced. The Osha Blue compound is also quick-dry.
2 Backyard Buddy's stripped-down model does not come with an attached motor. The power supply is a 12 Volt DC car battery that must be purchased separately, at an additional cost of $350. PCI's lifts include an AC motor.

References and further reading

Backyard Buddy n.d., viewed 18 January 2013, http://www.backyardbuddy.com>.

Driving in Japan: tolls, driving laws, traffic, parking, navigation systems, viewed 18 January 2013, <http://factsanddetails.com/japan.php?Itemid=851&catid=23&subcatid=153>.

Parking a Car in Italy: Sidewalks & Crosswalks n.d., viewed 18 January 2013, <http://www.italylogue.com/about-italy/parking-a-car-in-italy-sidewalks-crosswalks.html>.

Spacemaker Group n.d., viewed 18 January 2013, <http://www.parkplusinc.com>.

Tasty Southern Seeds

Jessica Smart and André M Everett

'Tasty Southern Seeds' is a small business based in Central Otago, in New Zealand's South Island. Bianca founded the business in 2004, looking for a lifestyle change. Having been a nurse for the previous 30 years, Bianca decided to reduce her working hours to part time (one or two days per week) and became a late-blooming entrepreneur. The business grew steadily (but not without challenges), and within four years Bianca was making a net profit greater than her after-tax wages. Locals were her initial customers, but tourists – especially foreign visitors – rapidly became the majority. Eight years after establishing Tasty Southern Seeds, Bianca faced a series of interlinked questions: Should she give up her 'day job' and focus exclusively on Tasty Southern Seeds? Should she sell the business under the assumption that because of her age she would be slowing down soon and could not devote enough energy to keeping it growing? Or – her personal preference – should she expand into overseas markets through either exporting or franchising?

As a nurse with an interest in diets, Bianca knew the health benefits of various foods, and had created her own personal mix of sesame, sunflower and pumpkin seeds. Experimenting for over 20 years, she also developed a variety of seasoning mixes, with garlic and chilli being her favourites. Friends, family and visitors all appreciated sampling her seed mixtures at her home, and it was regularly suggested that she should sell her seeds at the local farmers' market. She decided to test the saleability of her mixture at the annual arts and crafts festival in early 2004, selling her sample of 20 packs more quickly than she had thought possible. Tasty Southern Seeds was born – although the name wasn't created until a few weekends later, when she arranged a stand at the weekly farmers' market. Eight years later, the stand continues to attract regular customers, but the vast majority of sales occur in increasingly widespread and diverse locations outside Bianca's home town – hence her interest in exploring overseas expansion, or alternatively letting her business fly under someone else's ownership.

▪ The product

Although mixing and flavouring seeds sounds like a simple task, making a profit from it is deceptively complex. Only after 20 years of experimenting did Bianca feel sufficiently confident to attempt to sell her seed mixtures – and the subsequent eight years have seen substantial customer feedback result in constant improvements and extensions to the range. All seeds are not equal, so sourcing matters; likewise, marketing and distribution impact on sales. Underlying these are the taste and vision of the entrepreneur. To continue the success of her business, Bianca combined her experience and intuition with formal advice and careful strategic planning.

The initial mixture blended three seeds and a selection of seasonings; subsequent additions to the product range included other seed mixtures, different flavours, several sizes and – in some markets – freshly baked seed snack bars (or 'slices', in local terminology). Most of the mixtures are roasted – typically for about three hours – although some include only raw seeds. Although the precise ratios of the contents of each mixture are Bianca's secret, reverse engineering the composition would not be difficult. Discerning the various seasoning blends and roasting/cooling times would be a bit more complex. Nonetheless, it would be quite feasible for others to recreate the products. That is where Bianca's emphasis on a recognised brand name, high-quality ingredients from credible sources, quality control and carefully targeted marketing should pay dividends.

◼ The ingredients

Bianca refers to the components of her original mix – sesame, sunflower and pumpkin seeds – as her 'Big Three'. Over time, many other seeds and some nuts (technically also seeds) have reduced the 'Big Three' to less than a quarter of her total purchase volume, but they remain her personal favourites. The second most popular mixture, based on another recipe she had developed over the years, is nicknamed LSA for its three key ingredients – linseed, sunflower seeds and almonds. Each mixture features a selection of seeds in different proportions, with a range of flavourings and preparation processes.

The quality and freshness of the ingredients are critical. From the outset, Bianca was exceptionally choosey, only purchasing the best ingredients available. All inputs were purchased locally, although the majority were imported by local vendors or their wholesalers. As the business formalised and grew, Bianca initiated direct purchases from importers and wholesalers in New Zealand, in order to simultaneously lower her costs and to have more influence on the quality and timing of her inputs. However, her dependence on imported raw materials sourced through wholesalers highlighted a key vulnerability in her supply chain when, on several occasions, particular ingredients weren't available according to her schedule or quality requirements. Negative consequences in terms of product stockouts[1] resulted for both the sales volume and the reputation of Tasty Southern Seeds, but fortunately for Bianca her customers remained loyal (and new ones constantly arrived in the form of incoming tourists).

In one particularly memorable instance, when Bianca had not yet learned to order sufficiently large quantities in advance, a three- to four-month national stockout of savoury yeast flakes in 2005 led her to substitute brewer's yeast. The resulting change in the taste of the flavoured roasted seed mixtures was highly noticeable, leading to customer complaints and declining sales of the products that used the yeast flakes as a key component of their distinctive flavour. Through a combination of intense negotiations and judicious use of personal contacts, Bianca managed to regain suitable supplies, but not without considerable stress and learning an important lesson.

Other external forces also impact on Tasty Southern Seeds in unpredictable ways. For example, in 2006 the Ministry of Agriculture and Forestry (MAF) in New Zealand responded to biosecurity concerns by changing the phytosanitary restrictions on the importation of sunflower seeds. The initial result was that all imported sunflower seeds were heat treated, rendering them nearly black and unpalatable to consumers, or irradiated, resulting in their being legally acceptable only for animal or bird feed. On checking the actual government rules, Bianca quickly determined that this was an area for specialists, and she clearly should not even attempt to either circumvent the rules or try to directly import any seeds herself.

Given that sunflower seeds were one of her dominant 'Big Three' ingredients, this could have pushed her out of business. Instead, she focused on diversification (away from sunflower seeds and from heavy reliance on just three seeds), and bided her time, as it wasn't just her business that had been affected by the unavailability of suitable sunflower seeds. MAF further refined the rules, determining that specific inspections for weed seeds and certain pests could be conducted by certified authorities overseas (typically in the country of production, which in this case would be primarily Canada, China and the United States). Shipments accompanied by suitable certificates would be exempted from heat treatment (Ministry of Primary Industries 2012;[2] see also FSANZ 2012).

Production and investment

When it looked as though potential sales would exceed the capacity of her small home kitchen, very early in the commercial existence of Tasty Southern Seeds, Bianca opted for a financially logical choice and hired the local community hall, with its large, licensed kitchen facilities, for the meagre sum of NZ$12 (about US$8 at that time) per day. This option proved very cheap, allowing her to price her mixtures below what a commercial food preparation company would be able to charge, but it caused other difficulties in terms of coordination, transportation of equipment and ingredients, and the inability to produce small batches (such as custom orders) on short notice.

The decision to personally invest in a proper, licensed commercial kitchen in her own house – by converting a spare garage – proved to be a turning point in the business, the moment at which she could have opted to either remain a 'hobbyist' and maintain existing sales volume, or become a fully fledged entrepreneur at the helm of a real business aspiring to substantial growth. The hefty price tag of NZ$27 000 included not just new equipment but multiple inspections to ensure that the facilities met government health and safety requirements. Current demand is just approaching the capacity of the kitchen, installed six years ago, as it was substantially under-utilised for the first few years (Bianca retained her part-time nursing job to ensure sufficient income and 'just in case' something unexpected happened to her seeds business). When demand exceeds her own time availability, she employs a friend on a casual basis to help increase production. However, any further substantial growth will require further investment in both facilities and regular staff – perhaps starting part time but likely to become full time – and then multiple employees in a relatively short timeframe.

Sales and marketing

With the exceptions of a few minor setbacks, due primarily to the lack of availability of specific ingredients and the occasional intervention of matters such as the Global Financial Crisis (GFC), which reduced tourist flows, Tasty Southern Seeds has experienced fairly steady sales growth. Regardless of any other factors, the business has remained highly profitable on a cash-flow basis, which is the way Bianca prefers to work – with revenues being nearly double costs in every year for direct sales. Sales grew rapidly until the GFC set in, rising from about NZ$12 000 in the first financial year (2004–05) to just over NZ$100 000 in 2007–08. Although New Zealand wasn't strongly affected by the financial issues faced elsewhere, tourist numbers and revenues decreased throughout the country, resulting in slowed growth for the seeds business, which averaged only 10 per cent per annum until the boom returned in the 2011–12 year, when sales rose sharply from NZ$138 000 to NZ$193 000. The NZ$27 000 cost of the commercial kitchen – initially a major investment and commitment for Bianca – now appears paltry beside the NZ$74 000 before-tax profit from the most recent year alone.

However, as Bianca explains it, she is not in the business for the money – that is not her focus, although some attention to the financial details is obviously necessary. Her interest lies more in spreading her seed mixtures into new, appreciative markets (preferably ones that will return a profit, of course!). Every sale to date has turned a profit, beginning with the initial farmers' market and continuing through to her current drive to increase wholesaling to other retailers. Although the profit margin for wholesaling is half that of her direct retail business, her mixtures are now available at 27 outlets on South Island, including seven large urban supermarkets. In the 2011–12 year, wholesale surpassed direct retail sales for the first time (NZ$101 000 vs NZ$92 000, providing NZ$25 000 and NZ$49 000 profit respectively). She still prefers to personally operate the stall at the weekly farmers' market, as personal interaction with customers provides direct feedback she feels she can trust, unlike some of the less-informed second-hand comments she occasionally receives through the buyers from the other retailers.

The North Island provides the most obvious expansion potential, with the largest markets in New Zealand (Auckland and Wellington), as well as four-fifths of the total population, located there. Direct retail sales to the North Island via mail order have been growing, but remain lower than she expected. Bianca believes there are two possible reasons for this: the lack of any form of advertising (purely word-of-mouth and North Island residents returning home from vacations on the South Island) and maybe some viable competitors, although she remains confident that her product would win any direct comparison on taste and quality (although probably not on price). She has contemplated some serious market investigation of the North Island's potential, but has neither the expertise nor the time to 'do it right', so has decided it can wait.

Pricing

Pricing turned out to be an issue in a way Bianca had not expected. Although happy to provide her seed mixtures at even a marginal profit, she set initial prices high enough to 'meet the market' – where supply equals demand, according to basic economic theory. She figured that was why she was able to sell out on most weekends at the farmers' market. Based on the recommendation of a friend (also inevitably a seed mixture consumer), Bianca attended a marketing seminar for entrepreneurs hosted by the local university in early 2008. At the free one-hour follow-up consultation, led by postgraduate marketing students, she was amazed to hear that her seed mixtures could be treated as a semi-luxury product, and priced accordingly. The quality of the product warranted both better packaging and a higher price, according to the consulting advice. Providing more detailed nutrition information and focusing marketing on the health benefits was part of the recommended 'upgrade' for Tasty Southern Seeds.

Sceptical at first, Bianca tried this strategy – and was surprised at the results. Predictably, some long-time customers objected to the price increase and a few bought fewer seeds (or none), but most accepted that a premium product deserved a premium price (nicer packaging may have helped convey that impression as well). Tourists did not seem affected by the increase, as they were unaware of the previous lower pricing. Mail orders took a brief decline but recovered within a couple of months. Wholesale actually picked up, as the enhanced packaging attracted additional customers as well as prolonged shelf life, important for a product that Bianca continued to insist must be fresh to be as good as it could be. Overall, sales rose and profits rose sharply – albeit with a lag due to the price increase coinciding with the peak of the GFC.

The future

Foreign tourists – particularly Australian, British, Canadian, German and Norwegian visitors – are among Tasty Southern Seeds' biggest fans. Due to import restrictions on food products, Bianca cannot satisfy their demand through international mail order – and a few have even reported that their seed mixtures were confiscated by over-zealous agriculture quarantine officials at their home airports. Providing suitable certification for her products would be expensive, unless the volume sold overseas were to increase significantly.

That idea led Bianca to investigate the business' export potential – with one key advantage over simply expanding to North Island: the government was willing to provide support, in terms of motivation, contacts, business planning assistance and even some travel grants (under certain conditions) through its export development agency, New Zealand Trade and Enterprise (NZTE). Bianca's initial thoughts, based on reading case studies on the NZTE website (NZTE 2013) and speaking with a local representative, were that being a semi-luxury product would help, while exporting products containing mostly imported ingredients could be a disadvantage with regard to import tariffs in some countries. Clearly, specialist advice would be needed – but NZTE promised to provide that, at no cost.

So what would it be – an Australian 'vacation' to explore export potential, or setting up an international licensee or franchisee in Australia? Or maybe setting up in Britain – or both? Those were the two countries whose visitors to her farmers' market stand were most eager to buy Tasty Southern Seeds products at home. Or should she consider local expansion to New Zealand's North Island? Or establish some subsidiary kitchen(s) somewhere, or keep all production literally at home? If everything went according to plan, she would be utterly exhausted – the business clearly had the potential to expand beyond her capabilities to manage it appropriately. She would have to think about managing expansion of the business or seeking outside assistance, but she could not imagine the business she had created being outside her control. Yet, at age 61, retirement and taking a break were sounding increasingly attractive. She contemplated her options . . .

Discussion questions

11.1   As her business analyst, advise Bianca on her decision to internationalise. What would be the opportunities and threats for her business if she were to expand internationally?

11.2   Bianca has indicated that she wants to internationalise into Australia and feels that NZTE is encouraging her decision. Has she made the right business decision? Advise her on her choice of country.

11.3   If Bianca wants to export her products to other countries, where would you advise her to export to and why? How feasible or difficult would it be for Tasty Southern Seeds to establish a version of its product in foreign markets that would be appealing in terms of price, localised flavours, marketing strategy, freshness and availability?

11.4   Advise Bianca on options other than internationalising that might help her to grow and expand Tasty Southern Seeds.

11.5   Using any of the common models showing usual patterns of internationalisation, plot Tasty Southern Seeds on the various dimensions for its current and intended short-term international operations.

Notes

1   A situation in which the demand or requirement for an item cannot be fulfilled from the current inventory.
2   The rules have since changed again, but only slightly; for further information, visit the website of MAF, as of 2012 integrated into the Ministry for Primary Industries (MPI), and search for the standards such as 'Importation into New Zealand of Stored Plan Products Intended for Human Consumption' and 'Importation of Grains/Seeds for Consumption, Feed or Processing Plant Health Requirements'.

References

FSANZ 2012, *Imported food*, Food Standards Australia and New Zealand, Canberra and Wellington, viewed 20 February 2013, <http://www.foodstandards.govt.nz/consumer information/importedfoods.cfm>.

Ministry of Primary Industries 2012, *Importation into New Zealand of Stored Plant Products Intended for Human Consumption*, viewed 20 February 2013, <http://www.biosecurity. govt.nz/imports/plants/standards/bnz-npp-human.htm>.

New Zealand Trade and Enterprise (NZTE) 2013, home page, viewed 20 February 2013, <http://www.nzte.govt.nz/Pages/default.aspx>.

Introducing innovations in education: The Ateneo Graduate School of Business

12

Asuncion Sebastian

Changing trends in business education have made it necessary for business schools across the world to rethink their programs and curricula, their student composition and their ability to innovate and retain competitiveness, as well as their openness to internationalisation. This case study focuses on a business school in the Philippines that sought to reposition itself, and in particular its MBA programs, in a highly competitive and globalised business education sector.

The Ateneo Graduate School of Business

Founded in 1859 in the City of Manila, the Ateneo de Manila University (ADMU) started when it entrusted its administration of the Escuela Municipal de Manila to the Spanish Jesuit priests. The Jesuits expanded the school's curriculum, introduced new and dynamic degree programs and renamed it the 'Ateneo Municipal de Manila'. Further developments led to the establishment of the Graduate School of Ateneo de Manila in 1948, with initial offerings being the Master of Arts programs in education and English. Other fields of study were gradually added, and in 1964, the Master of Business Administration (MBA) was introduced. In 1966, after a number of reorganisations, the Ateneo Graduate School of Business (AGSB) was established.

The AGSB's vision statement reflected its intent:

> To be a leading management educational institution in the Asia-Pacific region for the business practitioner seeking to become a professional and ethical business leader committed to nation building.

Its mission, based on the Jesuit institutions' tradition of service and academic excellence, was to develop leaders and managers characterised first and foremost by integrity, expertise and service. It was also committed to use facilitative learning methodologies that integrated technical, technological, political and ethical dimensions, in both theory and practice. Finally, the school aimed at harnessing the resources of its various stakeholders in addressing the changes and challenges in its domestic and global environments.

The emphasis on educating leaders and responding to changes in the environment ensured that by the early 1990s, the AGSB offered three MBA programs: the MBA Standard, the MBA for Middle Managers and the MBA in Health. In 1993, Father Bienvenido Nebres, then appointed president of the ADMU, introduced further key initiatives to include basic education development, public health development, housing and social development, as well as leadership and good governance (Valarao 2008). In the same year, Alfredo RA Bengzon, then Dean of the AGSB, brought changes and innovations that led the school in new directions. Under his leadership, the school embarked on two defined tracks:

1. the program track, which aimed at making the school more responsive to the market by launching program innovations and interactive methodologies in program delivery, and
2. the branding track, which aimed at enhancing the profile of the AGSB, its identity and character as sources of inspiration, its mission, and aspirations for moving forward.

The year 1993 marked the start of AGSB's 'revitalisation years' (*Frontline* 2007, pp. 53–4).

The MBAs in the 1990s

The AGSB had to consider its path of 'revitalisation' if it were to fulfil its aspirations to produce effective leaders and managers, and be part of business schools' advancement in Asia. With business trends rapidly moving towards globalisation in the early 1990s, business schools – particularly those in the West – focused on training and developing 'global managers' for the international business arena. Strategies included updating their curricula, making them more relevant to the global workplace, and establishing global networks and partnerships with universities and corporations in other parts of the world. They also diversified their faculty and student population to develop a global learning environment on their campuses. They increased and intensified student-immersion initiatives, student-exchange programs and internship programs to provide global exposure for their students (Masilungan et al. 1994).

Teaching methods also evolved, with a shift from traditional methods to more interactive approaches to teaching and learning. In addition to case-based teaching, business schools started using group discussions, simulation exercises, group projects and presentations, and technology to spur interactivity among students. The 1990s saw the emergence of new technologies that have continued to develop and increase their impact on program design, course delivery and online interactions. Business schools' engagement and partnering with the corporate sector, and developing better understanding with the business world's requirements in relation to education and training, also became a feature of the changing education environment (Masilungan et al. 1994).

Despite AGSB's revitalisation initiatives, the school continued to face the challenge of developing its strategies to ensure that it kept up with the developments and changes that were occurring, maintained pace with universities and business schools in the Asian region and successfully achieved its education agenda.

Serendipity in the AGSB

An opportunity for the AGBS came when its President, Father Nebres, read an article in the *Wall Street Journal* about the recognition it gave to the Regis University (RU), a Jesuit University in the United States, in July 1991 for its 'innovative approach to delivering high quality education' (Adultlearn 2008). The article also recognised the Chancellor of RU, Father David M Clarke, for bringing a 'customer service' orientation to higher education. RU was well established and had been serving its community for 130 years. It offered a wide-ranging portfolio of successful programs to service educational needs at all levels of study – undergraduate and graduate degrees, non-credit programs, academic certificates, corporate education programs and many others, including adult students and working professionals under the College for Professional

Studies. It made available flexible, convenient options to accommodate the students' educational goals, learning preferences and lifestyles. Depending on their preferences, students could attend classroom-based courses, work independently outside the classroom or take courses online. Classes were small, averaging 15 students per course (Adultlearn 2008).

Given the common Jesuit backgrounds of the RU and AGBS, their service orientation to education and training, and the close similarities of their markets, Father Nebres considered adopting the Regis system in 1995 and exploring the potential for partnership between the two schools to further intensify AGSB's revitalisation program. Serendipitously, a few months later, Father Nebres met Dr Ira Plotkin from RU, and they exchanged visits to observe their respective teaching methodologies. The visits were followed by training for the AGSB delegates to better appreciate the RU methodologies and use of technology. In 1997, a licensing agreement was signed between ADMU and RU, allowing the AGSB to adopt the RU system in its MBA program. It was at a period when the school's management realised that its existing programs would not be sustainable in the long run. AGSB management thought that introducing the new program would indeed be strategic for the AGSB.

Features of the Regis-MBA program

The Regis-MBA program was designed to

> arm the executives and business leaders with the theories, skills, and values that are necessary for today's dynamic environment. It recognised the program participants as workplace-based and experience-driven learners and delivers the course in appropriate learning technologies. (Ateneo Graduate School of Business 2008)

The introduction of the RU technology required AGSB to shift its teaching style for this particular MBA program from lecturing to facilitating – from pedagogy to andragogy[1] – as the new method was based primarily on adult learning principles. Under the new program, each course had more distinctive and more clearly defined objectives. The students were required to engage in extensive reading and research so that classroom hours were optimised for discussion. The program was shortened from the 15-week term of the standard MBA to an eight-week term, with longer class sessions of four hours instead of the standard MBA class of three hours. This intensive mode was expected to fast-track completion of the program. Immediate feedback to students was deemed crucial so that examinations were held more frequently, and consultation time with the faculty – whether face to face or via the internet – was set aside. To better care for the students and to make the teachers' load more manageable, class sizes were limited to 25 students, smaller than the regular MBA's 40 students.

The Regis-MBA Program was positioned as a 'premium product' in that students had to pay more (approximately Php 17 000 per subject, or US$395) than they would pay for a standard MBA (Php 11 000, or US$255), or for the MBA for Middle Managers (Php 15 000, or US$349). The Regis-MBA Program was AGSB's answer to the executive MBA or accelerated MBA that was emerging in the market at the time. Although its target enrolees were similar to those of the MBA for Middle Managers, in that they were required to already hold managerial positions and have at least five years of work experience, the Regis-MBA primarily catered to those with the competence to meet its more rigorous requirements over a shorter period of time.

◼ Breaking barriers

Change is often accompanied by some level of resistance. 'A diluted MBA' was the Ateneo community's general perception of the new Regis-MBA program, considering its shorter completion time when compared with the standard and middle managers' programs. There were those from the Ateneo de Manila University (ADMU) who questioned the Business School's (AGSB's) move to create the new MBA. Others doubted whether Filipino students would be able to cope with the demands of the Regis-MBA, given that approaches to learning were different in the Philippines. The possible 'cannibal-isation' of the standard and middle managers programs was also raised.

The strongest resistance came from the AGSB faculty members who had to work on the new curriculum, and adjust or change their teaching styles, engaging in various facilitation techniques rather than traditional lectures, or having to undergo an assess-ment to determine their capacity to teach using the new technologies. The new program also called for more papers to be read, more examinations to be marked and more time spent engaging with students.

To overcome these obstacles, the Regis-MBA team implemented a communication strategy to convince all stakeholders about the rationale behind the new program, the effectiveness of its design and the value of it being an accelerated program. The team also argued that if the AGSB did not offer such a program, then a competitor might eventually do so. It further maintained that, while the standard and middle managers programs might lose some students to Regis-MBA, AGSB would nonetheless stand to gain – not only from such students but also from the new market that the Regis-MBA would attract.

The Regis-MBA team adopted further strategies to gain the confidence of all, especially the teaching faculty. It invited RU professors to provide AGSB faculty with seminars and workshops on the use of facilitation techniques, and to equip them with the teaching skills that the new program required. Those who successfully completed the training then shared what they had learned with the others, thus arousing the curiosity of the other faculty members. The faculty staff were also given monetary incentives to teach in the Regis-MBA program.

Following appropriate marketing of the new program and an initial enrolment of 33 students, the Regis-MBA program was finally launched in May 1998. From that point, enrolments steadily increased, with classes in the program reaching full enrolments by the second year. Despite the rigour and intensity of the courses, the enrolments were sustained as students got to finish their MBA in a year and a half. Some took two years because of the demands of their workloads. Evidently, the shorter version of the MBA had found its niche. However, it led to a drop in enrolment in the standard MBA program; hence the Regis-MBA team focused on propelling the growth of the school at several levels. In October 1998, for example – just a few months after the Regis-MBA started – the AGSB opened a satellite office in Sta Rosa, Laguna, specifically for this new program. In 1999, another branch was established in Subic and one opened in Cebu in 2002. The areas for expansion were strategically chosen: Sta Rosa for its technology and science parks and its proximity to Cavite, which had industrial parks; Subic for its free port; and Cebu because it is one of the main business centres in the southern Philippines.

It took two years to get buy-in from the entire organisation, over which time the incentives to faculty gradually were removed. The new program was of significant financial benefit to the school, as it improved the cash flow and created more surpluses because of its shorter but more frequent cycle within a given school year. Marketing also became easier for the school when it reached its third year, as the Regis-MBA program increasingly gained acceptance and popularity in the community (Vinuya 2008).

A review of the Regis-MBA program

The AGSB evaluated the effectiveness of its programs based on feedback from students, alumni, employers and market information. A study conducted from 2008 to 2010 with a sample of 180 students (90 each from the standard program and the Regis program) showed no significant difference in the performance of the students in two of the courses undertaken. However, there were significant differences between the groups in a third course (Strategic Management), with the Regis-MBA students averaging 5.06 (very satisfactory) on the measure, while students from the standard MBA averaged 4.39 (satisfactory) (Constantino et al. 2011).

Yet another indicator of success – given that the teaching style was more dynamic and richer in the Regis-MBA than in the other programs – was that the number of faculty members who wanted to teach in the Regis-MBA had grown. These observations led to the adoption of the RU technology in the MBA for Middle Managers and the standard MBA programs. Professor Ante, a Regis-MBA faculty member, observed that:

> The students in the Regis-MBA are much more focused, experienced, interactive … they ask a lot of questions. On the other hand, those in the standard program are young. As a teacher you really have to draw them out during class discussions. Thus it is more challenging to teach in the Regis-MBA; you have to go to class prepared. (Ante 2008)

A decade after its launch, the Regis-MBA program accounted for approximately 33 per cent of the AGSB population. Looking back, Dean Buenviaje (2008) reflects:

> If we had not launched Regis, we would not now have the innovative learning technology suited to adult learners and, consequently, the additional 500 students we now have under the program.

The global challenge

After celebrating the 10-year success of the Regis-MBA program, another challenge confronted the school: how could it enhance the program and develop its market

Table 12.1: MBA programs of selected schools in Asia, 2009						
Name of institution	One-year full-time MBA	Two-year full-time MBA	Part-time MBA	Executive MBA	Dual/double MBA	Distance learning
Asia-Pacific Management Institute, Singapore						x
British Council, India						x
Chinese University, Hong Kong	x		x			
De La Salle Professional School, Philippines			x		x	x
European University, Malaysia	x		x	x		
European University, Singapore	x		x	x		
Hong Kong University – with Columbia Business School and London Business School	x		x	x		
Indian Institute of Commerce and Trade		x		x		x
Indian Institute of Management	x	x				x
Insead, Singapore	x			x		
James Cook University, Singapore		x		x		
Nanyang Technological University, Singapore	x			x	x	
Narsee Monjee Insitutte of Management Studies, India		x	x			
National University of Singapore		x		x		
PSB Academy, Singapore	x		x			
SP Jain Institute of Management and Research, India	x	x		x		
SP Jain Institute of Management and Research, Singapore	x			x		
Shanghai Jiao Tong University, China		x	x	x		
Singapore Institute of Management				x		
Singapore Management University	x					
Symbiosis Institute of Business Management, India		x		x		
Universiti of Malaysia		x	x			
Universiti Utara, Malaysia		x	x			
University of Colombo, Sri Lanka		x				
Waseda University, Japan	x	x			x	

Data culled from the school profiles at Find MBA (2009).

further? As institutions in Asia globalised their MBAs, AGSB discussed its options for expanding their market to include the rest of South-East Asia and launching an online or distance MBA. The proposition was attractive, but AGSB was also aware of the strong competition from many US and European institutions offering MBA degrees in Asia.

Many business schools in the region have continued to 'globalise' their MBAs by increasing the enrolment of foreign students, employing faculty members from various parts of the world and/or forging relationships with Western business schools. The leading MBA schools in the region have boasted of 75–85 per cent foreign student composition (Lee 2009).

To remain competitive and attract students, as well as provide relevant education for changing times, greater diversification was introduced into the MBA program portfolio. Students were provided with wider program options, from general management programs to specialty niches, executive development courses and online instruction (Lee 2009). Most business schools in Asia also started offering more than one type of MBA. Table 12.1 shows the MBA offerings of selected schools in Asia, some of which were in partnership with European and American educational institutions.

Some people argued that a quality gap prevailed between the education delivered in Asia and that in the home-base country, while some pointed out the Asian universities' lack of Western-educated faculty ('US MBA Programs' 2007). On the other hand, it was observed that the reputable business schools in the Asian region were comparable with those in other parts of the world in terms of teaching quality, the research capability of faculty and their infrastructure. Advocates also maintained that the programs offered great value for money to students in that, at far lower rates, the programs provided education of a similar quality to those available in Western schools (Lee 2009).

AGSB's Regis-MBA program enrolees continued to grow – albeit at a decreasing rate. From 450 students in 2008, its enrolment grew by almost 50 per cent to 670 in 2010. However, its growth slowed down to 700 enrolees in 2011 and 790 in 2012. Foreign students – mainly from China, Korea, Taiwan, Malaysia and Indonesia – consistently constituted around 10 per cent of the student population. Closest to the popular East-West MBA partnership program that the AGSB developed was awarding its Regis-MBA graduates double recognition beginning in 2010: a Diploma from the ADMU and a Certificate of Recognition from the RU. Yet, despite the number of innovations it had adopted through the years, the AGSB was once again confronted by the seemingly perennial challenge of keeping up with its changing environment while successfully achieving its education agenda.

Discussion questions

12.1   What opportunities/threats were present in AGSB's environment in the 1990s and how did AGSB respond to them?

12.2   What challenges did AGSB encounter after the new program was launched? How did it overcome them?

12.3   What opportunities/threats were present in AGSB's environment in the 2000s and how could the school respond to them?

12.4   If you were to formulate an entry strategy for the Regis-MBA program into the Asian market, what factors would you consider?

Note

1   Developed by adult learning theorists Malcolm Knowles, KP Corss, and Carl Rogers, andragogy assumed that learners were self-directed; that their readiness to learn was developed from life experiences and that these experiences were in themselves resources for learning; that the learners' orientation was task or problem centred; and that the learners' motivation was basically intrinsic rewards (*Frontline* 2007, p. 9).

References

Adultlearn 2008, 'Regis University: traditional or online education in the Jesuit tradition', viewed 12 November 2008, <http://www.adultlearn.com/regis-university.htm#bus>.

Ante, R 2008, Interview with Asuncion M Sebastian, 11 December, Makati City.

Ateneo Graduate School of Business 2008, Ateneo-Regis MBA Program brochure.

Buenviaje, AL 2008, Interview with Asuncion M Sebastian, 9 October, Makati City.

Clarke, Rev. David M, Chancellor of Regis University 2009, viewed 26 May 2009, <http://www.cic.edu/projects_services/archives/pconsultants_resumes/dclarke.pdf>.

Constantino, WM, Palo, RR, Ibarle, YF & Reyes, KU 2011, *Accelerated learning in business education*, Ateneo Graduate School of Business, Makati City.

Find MBA 2009, website, viewed 5 February 2009, <http://www.find-mba.com/asia>.

Frontline 2007, Ateneo Professional Schools, June.

Lee, YM 2009, 'MBA in East Asia', Hobsons MBA Central, viewed 9 February 2009, <http://www.mba.gradview.com/advice/mbaglobal_eastasia>.

Masilungan, EO, Sebastian, AM, Salim, JE & Azanza, RJ 1994, *Management education trends and competition among graduate schools of business*, Asian Institute of Management, Makati City.

'Primus inter pares: a brief history of the Ateneo Graduate School of Business 2007, *Frontline*, vol. 3, no. 1, n.p.

'US MBA programs in Asia draw students from West' 2007, EFinancialCareers, viewed 5 February 2009, <http://www.efinancialcareers.com>.

Valarao, C 2008, 'Vocation, the value of Ben Nebres to Philippine education', *Educator*, July–August, n.p.

Vinuya, B 2008, Interview with Asuncion M Sebastian, 3 November, Makati City.

Part III

Managing People in International Business

13 John Parker's expatriate experiences in China

Cindy Qin, Prem Ramburuth and Yue Wang

John Parker

Sitting in his office on the 14th floor in Beijing's CBD, John Parker was reflecting on his experience during the last year and wondering where things had gone wrong. He had been a successful manager in DigiMat, a United States-based company with subsidiaries in Asia and Europe, and one year earlier he had been assigned as the Asia Pacific Sales Director. His job required him to spend about half of his time based in China, with the rest of it to be spent mainly between Singapore and Australia. With his 15 years of experience in the IT industry, an MBA and a sound educational background, and his outstanding performance as a manager in North America, he had a great deal of confidence when he first took on his new assignment. He had been looking forward to moving to China, a country with a unique cultural environment that he had long admired but had never visited.

Back in the United States, before his departure, the headquarters had given him a two day cross-cultural training session to prepare him for his new venture. The session provided him with a brief introduction to Asian culture and showed him how to best handle the expected culture shocks that accompany working in a different environment. The training had reminded him of the cross-cultural management course that he completed during his MBA program a few years before; he still remembered the concepts provided by Hofstede's (1991) cultural dimensions and Hall's (1976) cultural context theories. This culture-related knowledge, together with his strong industry and management background, boosted his confidence, and John believed that he was totally ready for the new job. It would be an exciting experience, he told himself, before he headed to China.

John was pretty happy during the first couple of weeks after his arrival in Beijing. Things appeared to be going well, and he seemed to be making very good progress. John found that everyone in the office was very friendly and cooperative. On his first day, his local team in the Beijing office threw him a welcome party, which served as an opportunity for him to have a short, casual meeting with the local employees. People were standing in one corner of the office, listening to his brief self-introduction and short speech, aimed at boosting team morale. He hoped that the speech would make him more 'approachable' and that it would help develop a harmonious relationship with his Chinese subordinates. John had tried to make his first speech in China very casual and friendly. Following his introduction and speech, the local employees volunteered a few friendly questions, and his humorous answers made everybody laugh. John felt that he had achieved what he set out to do: the meeting was harmonious, and it seemed that everybody liked their new boss.

John was a little surprised at first, because he had not expected to receive so many questions following his speech. All of the training that he had undertaken, and the stories he was told, had led him to believe that Chinese people were rather silent during meetings. In fact, when he prepared for his first speech to his Chinese subordinates, he had actually thought very hard about how he would handle the anticipated lack of response. His training also indicated that language would present itself as a big issue when doing business in China. But that too seemed like it would not be a major problem, which he thought was excellent. He even telephoned one of his friends in the United States and told him that, 'People in my office speak very good English, and this will make my job much easier than I had thought.'

But before long he started to sense a change, and was puzzled as to why things were turning out differently. Everyone was still polite and friendly, and his team members often took him out to lunch and on some occasions even to dinner. They had shown him around the area and introduced him to different types of food and local activities. John knew that everyone in his local team was working hard to achieve their work goals. But he felt that there were times – such as when he and the team discussed how they might best reach a potentially attractive account, or close a business deal, or keep high-end existing customers – that the local team proposed approaches that were totally different from what he had expected. It seemed that this was happening most when it came to DigiMat's major accounts.

John wondered whether this difference in accounts and customer management was because of differences in the professional training backgrounds between himself and his staff. He decided that he would introduce his team to the knowledge and systems in which he was so thoroughly trained back in the United States. He organised sales skills training and made it a requirement for everyone in his team to participate. John took on the role of trainer and set out to share his experience with senior team members, using examples from real cases with which he had dealt in North America. He found that in his training room there were small and active sub-group discussions that frequently switched to Chinese; however, as soon as the discussion was pulled back so that the whole class could join in (including John), people became silent. He was puzzled about this reluctance to share information, noting that this was very different from his first experience of interactions with the group. He tried to interpret their facial expressions to try to work out what was going on, but failed. In an effort to get a discussion going, he addressed one of the team members and asked why the team was not participating actively in the training. The answer he received was:

> The situation here in China is totally different. You cannot handle customers in the same way as you did in North America. We have actually had some similar training before. I believe the skills we are discussing here are helpful ... but in the context of China, these skills are not enough, and sometimes they even don't work here.

John felt both disappointed and frustrated. He believed that his expertise was not recognised and appreciated by his team in China. Even worse, John was starting to feel that his team was excluding him and leaving him out of important conversations. The team members were happy to discuss their goals with him, but they tried to avoid talking about their customers in detail. In order to manage the team more efficiently, and to grasp information at first hand, John arranged a weekly meeting with his team where he requested that everyone report to him on the progress they had made with their customers and their accomplishments during the previous week. John also wanted them to start sharing information with other team members. However,

John still had a strong feeling that his team members were continuing to work in their own way, and this worried him deeply.

Compared with working in China, John had felt much more comfortable when he was working in Australia and Singapore. Although he had felt that there were strong cultural differences between the United States and these two countries, he had also felt that his teams in these two countries were more open than the team with which he was currently working in China. His subordinates in Australia and Singapore seemed to be happier to have discussions with him about the customers with whom they were working, and he was more familiar with the way in which they handled their customers. But China really was a different case! John did not know whether their sales practices were really under his control or influence. He knew that DigiMat's headquarters had very high expectations of the subsidiary companies in emerging economies, including China, and his team had been assigned very challenging goals based on these expectations. John felt that, given the situation, he could not afford to take the risk of losing control of his team.

John decided that he could use his prior knowledge and skills (which had brought him great success) to help change the situation, and hoped that by doing so he would get the team back under his control. Even before he came to China, he had strongly believed that he had substantial skills and experience that he would be able to bring to the new position. John believed that developed countries, such as the United States, had accumulated in-depth knowledge and practical experience which had contributed to developing mature systems for conducting business successfully. He felt that the advanced levels of knowledge and experience should be transferable, and could be applied effectively in emerging economies. John had once made the following argument with one of his colleagues when trying to convince them about the benefits of Western business practices:

> Doing business the Western way is highly efficient and superior compared to other ways. Don't you know why scandals, such as paying bribes, happen in developing countries more often than they do in developed countries? Have you ever thought about why so many elites from Asian countries study business and take their MBA courses in Western countries?

John believed that if he could transfer his knowledge to his team in China and influence them effectively, then they would be able to engage in doing business in the 'right way'. In order to understand further just how knowledge is transferred, and how best to facilitate the transfer with the company, John sought to explore and read about popular knowledge-transfer models (e.g. Gupta & Govindarajan 2000; Kogut & Zander 1992) and related books (such as Nonaka 1994).

John concluded that the introduction of a knowledge-management system would be an effective tool, and that its use would facilitate the knowledge-sharing process. In fact, DigiMat had made a significant investment in launching its Enterprise Resource Planning (ERP) system within the company globally, and he felt that if the knowledge management capabilities in their current ERP system were utilised, they would have a positive effect on the knowledge-transfer process. On his arrival in China, John had noticed that the system was not being used effectively by his team, and upon inquiring why this was so, he was told:

The ERP system was designed according to the standardised business process in Western countries. Here in China, we feel it is very hard to use it – especially for sales – as there are many things either too contextually embedded or too sensitive for inputting into the system as account data.

John was not convinced by this response. He insisted that everyone in his team should use the ERP system, as he believed it was the most efficient way for his team members to manage their cases, while also allowing him to monitor their progress. He waited to see the outcome of his efforts to bring about change. Much to his disappointment, after he had advocated the change for almost six months, the system was still rarely used.

John's failed efforts seemed to make an already unacceptable situation even worse. He now felt like an outsider to his team in China. His team respected him as their boss, but it seemed that they did not trust his capabilities to engage in business in China. They always seemed to have different ideas about how they should be approaching customers and closing deals. When John first arrived, his Chinese subordinates had tried to persuade him that China's cultural, political and business environment was different from that of Western countries, and that business had to be done in a different way. But John believed that 'business was business', and he wondered why people in China did not do business in the professional way with which he was familiar. In a vigorous discussion with Lei, one of his team members, the argument went as follows:

John: I am not Chinese, but I know *guanxi*. It is a word that is known worldwide. Nowadays, almost everyone who is interested in China knows it. It is not difficult to understand, and in Western countries we need to network too.

Lei: Yes, I am sure you know *guanxi*, and its importance in doing business in China. But you may not know how to *build guanxi* in China. It is not just having one or two dinners together, or giving someone one or two gifts. Building *guanxi* is very complicated; you have to develop the relationship so that people owe you something.

John: What do you mean by saying 'people owe you something'?

Lei: It is really difficult to explain – I don't know how to put it into words. You know there is a Chinese saying: 'The thing cannot be explained but be perceived' – *Zhi ke yi hui, bu neng yan chuan*? You have to stay in China for a few years to understand it.

John did not mind having to spend a few years in China in order to fully understand the complexities of the country's culture, but at the same time he could not afford to take the risk of spending another year facing the same situation of being excluded and managing issues of non-cooperation at work.

▪ Jeremy Lin

In a different room on the same floor, Jeremy Lin, the director of DigiMat's R&D centre in China, was having a conversation with one of his subordinates, Sean Zhao.

Sean: I believe we should set up our own process and change the model here. It goes without saying that the standardised procedure and model that have been used in our headquarters are mature and have proved to be effective. But, given the situation here, I would suggest that we change the process and modify the model.

Jeremy: If the model has proven to be effective, we should follow it, but tell me more about your thoughts first. Why do you think we need to modify the process?

Jeremy and John had known each other for eight years, since they had both started working in DigiMat's US headquarters. Jeremy's background was different from John's; John grew up in the United States, whereas Jeremy was born and grew up in Taiwan. Jeremy had completed his undergraduate degree in Taiwan, and then completed his PhD in the United States. Jeremy had worked at DigiMat's R&D centre in the United States until three years previously, when he moved to China to take up the position of director at the R&D centre. Having lived and worked in both Asian and Western cultures, Jeremy was aware of the need to understand the norms and values of other cultures, and the need to accommodate host culture norms and values where necessary. Needless to say, Jeremy's Chinese background made his work in China somewhat easier compared with John's background and experiences.

Furthermore, Jeremy's team trusted him – which was somewhat different from John's team. Jeremy's team members shared their ideas with him, and they asked for his advice and support in complex and confusing situations. They also liked to participate in discussions with Jeremy about non-work-related Western concepts which might be unfamiliar to them. For example, a concept that they had recently been discussing with Jeremy recently was self-governance. Like John, Jeremy liked to share his knowledge and experience with his team, the only difference being that Jeremy's team seemed to respond to this more positively than John's team.

Jeremy knew that members of the younger generation in mainland China were eager to be successful in the workplace, and that they were embracing many fresh ideas and concepts that had originated from the West. Jeremy's experience in both cultures helped him to find a more convincing way to explain Western concepts to his Chinese team members and also helped him understand his Chinese subordinates better. The team's morale was high, and this had enabled positive performance in the workplace from Jeremy's team. This was evidenced by the fact that it was the third year in a row that Jeremy's team had won the 'excellence at work' prize – a prestigious award presented by DigiMat's headquarters in the United States.

John had often expressed his frustrations to Jeremy:

> You are so lucky! You look Chinese and you speak Chinese. Your team naturally considers you to be a member of their group and they trust you. For me it is different. I look Western and I speak a foreign language, and I seem to think differently! My team does not believe that I belong with them.

But Jeremy did not agree with John. He told John that his predecessor, Bob, who was from Europe, had successfully managed the same team. He even believed that the friendly and open atmosphere within the team, to some extent, could be attributed to Bob's previous successful leadership. Jeremy remembered how one of his team members, Sean, had described John's predecessor when John first came on board. In Sean's words:

> Our ex-boss, Bob, was a very smart person. He was open-minded. You know, those people from headquarters don't understand how we do things in China. They always ask us to do things their way, but that doesn't work here. Bob was good, he listened to us, he trusted us. When he believed that we had enough reason to, he would let us do things our own way. He even said he was glad to learn something about business processes in China from us, which encouraged us a lot.

■ Bob Martin

John vaguely remembered Bob, whom he had briefly met on several occasions back at the US headquarters. Back then, John had only just started his job with DigiMat as Sales Manager for North America. Shortly thereafter, Bob quit and moved on to head a Chinese-based subsidiary of a European company. With Jeremy's help, John met up with Bob in a cafe. John was keen to explore the secrets of Bob's success, and sought his advice. Taking a sip of coffee, Bob started talking:

> People are people. They are the same around the world. Respect them and trust them. Treat your team like they are your family and friends and they will give the same respect and trust back to you.
>
> People always think that language is a big issue here in China. But I believe that Chinese employees possess the essential skills and abilities, even though their English language and communication may not be perfect. As long as they are willing to share their ideas, they will find an excellent way to express themselves. And, in turn, the sharing of their ideas improves their language skills significantly.
>
> Chinese people sometimes make others feel as though they are not willing to express themselves, or to share their ideas. But that is not because they want to protect their knowledge, or that they do not intend to share their knowledge with others. Chinese employees are afraid of losing face; they are worried about saying something wrong or saying it in the wrong way. But do you know what? If you are afraid of losing face, you will never learn! Without asking any questions or seeking clarifications, you may make even bigger mistakes and actually risk losing even more face than by asking the questions in the first place. People learn from their failures, and they realise that it is important to seek clarification and ask questions when they are communicating with each other. Chinese employees are only just getting used to asking questions and making comments during presentations and discussions.
>
> Back at DigiMat, I spent lot of time building good relationships and developing trust with subordinates so that I could encourage them to be more open. There might be other ways to let them be open with you, but I am quite confident that relationship and trust are very important. I even tried to learn some Chinese. But I tell you, learning Chinese is not an easy task. The four tones, the three- and four-character idioms just drove me crazy. I told myself I could never learn how to speak Chinese, but I didn't totally give up. I think my efforts to learn Chinese also had an impact on the willingness of my Chinese staff to cooperate with me. It helped. Believe it or not, I feel that I learnt lots of things back then, not only a bit of the Chinese language, but I also learnt some Chinese wisdom.

I understand the Chinese culture much better now, and this gives me a great deal of advantage when I'm working and doing business here.

And more interestingly, I have seen the cultural shift that is going on in China too. It is exciting to be a part of the transition. Six years ago, when I did presentations in China, the audience would always listen quietly to my talks. Even when you asked the Chinese audience, at the end of the presentation, if they had any questions, what you often got was silence. Nowadays – and you have probably realised this too – it has changed somewhat. Chinese people are becoming more assertive. They like taking risks. I don't know if this is the result of globalisation or cultural conversion and the influence of Western countries. But I tell you, Chinese culture has changed a lot, from my perspective.

Discussion questions

13.1 What are the main conflicts between John and his team in China? What do you consider to be the causes of the conflicts? Do you agree with Bob's comments that, 'People are people. They are the same around the world'?

13.2 John asserts that Jeremy manages his team successfully only because of his cultural background and language skills. Do you agree? How do John and Bob differ in their management styles and interactions with their respective teams?

13.3 Using Hofstede's dimensions (or any other cultural framework that you may have studied), explain the characteristics of Chinese culture that you can identify in this case. How do the cultural differences between China and the United States impact on John's and his Chinese colleagues' attitudes and behaviours in knowledge-sharing?

13.4 Do you think cultural difference is an obstacle in knowledge transfer? Do you agree with John that the local employees (in China) do not know how to cooperate?

References

Gupta, AK & Govindarajan, V 2000, 'Knowledge flows within multinational corporations', *Strategic Management Journal*, no. 21, pp. 473–96.

Hall, ET 1976, *Beyond culture*, Doubleday, New York.

Hofstede, G 1991, *Cultures and organizations: software of the mind*, McGraw-Hill, London.

Kogut, B & Zander, U 1992, 'Knowledge of the firm, combination capabilities, and the replication of technology', *Organization Science*, vol. 3, no. 3, pp. 383–97.

Nonaka, I 1994, 'A dynamic theory of organizational knowledge creation', *Organization Science*, vol. 5, no. 1, pp. 14–37.

Dilemmas in working across cultures: Arun in a conundrum

Amanda Budde-Sung

Arun Gupta was born in northern India and trained in the United Kingdom as a professional accountant. He enjoyed his life in the United Kingdom, and opted to remain there to further his career after he had finished his studies. While the United Kingdom was different from India in many ways, he felt he had adjusted well to his host country. He attributed part of his success in cross-cultural adaptation to his background, as he had had been exposed to an essentially British system of education in India.

After many years of experience in his field in the United Kingdom, he decided he was ready to venture further abroad and seek work opportunities in an accounting company in another country. With the increased globalisation of business, accountants with significant international experience are highly valued, and can often command higher salaries within their organisations. Arun began considering worldwide options for a location in which he could continue to develop his professional skills while enhancing his CV with international experience. After talking to friends and colleagues, he began to focus his search on South Korea. Arun had a personal interest in Korean culture: his girlfriend was of Korean ancestry, having immigrated to the United Kingdom with her parents when she was a young child, and her family had introduced him to some of the highlights of Korean culture – including Korean food, which he had come to enjoy. He had even taken a Korean cooking class in London to learn how to make his favourite dish, *bibimbap* (a signature dish in the Korean cuisine). His girlfriend was keen to move to Korea with him, both to reconnect with her culture and to seek further career opportunities. There were good employment prospects for a fully bilingual English/Korean businessperson in Asia, and the financial crisis in Europe was limiting career advancement opportunities for both of them in the United Kingdom. A move to Korea seemed like a great idea for both of them, personally as well as professionally.

With Arun and his girlfriend convinced that a move to Korea would be a good opportunity for both of them, he began to look more seriously at job opportunities. Finally, he identified a suitable professional accounting position with a seemingly attractive compensation package that was advertised by a large Korean company in Busan, South Korea. Busan, South Korea's second largest city, offered a lifestyle that both Arun and his girlfriend thought would suit them perfectly. Arun liked nature and outdoor activities, while his girlfriend loved museums and shopping in big cities. Busan, with its beaches, mountain hikes and hot springs, combined with its museums and the world's largest department store, Shinsegae, was an ideal location for them.

He contacted the company, and after a few exploratory conversations formally expressed his interest and submitted an application online. He had a few more discussions with the Korean company, and was pleasantly surprised when he was offered the position of an accountant with the company. Negotiations for salary, work conditions and other benefits ensued. These negotiations were conducted entirely via email between Arun and Mr Kim, the director of the department. Arun was impressed by the smoothness of the initial stages of the job application process. However, this soon changed when, after several months of emailing back and forth, there was little success in reaching a resolution to the negotiations. Arun was keen to commence working in Korea, and thought it was time to act. He bought an air ticket and flew to Busan to settle the matter in a more expedient fashion.

On his flight to Busan, Arun reflected on his discussions with the company and the negotiations in which he had engaged thus far. He was basically happy with the offer of the conditions of employment and future prospects with the company. The position with a prestigious Korean multinational company, with a great deal of room for career advancement, was just what he was looking for. The starting salary was acceptable, and some of the benefits that went with the job were very attractive. However, there were aspects of the position and work conditions that Arun wanted clarified before he formally accepted the job. These areas included official work responsibilities associated with the role, expectations in relation to working hours, progressive salary rises and incentives, and a performance bonus structure. Arun wanted to have these issues clarified in writing before he officially accepted the position. All of the issues seemed fairly minor, but he had heard stories from friends about cultural differences in work expectations between the United Kingdom and Korea, and he thought it best to make sure that everyone was in agreement on these issues before he took the job. Past experience had made him cautious, and had taught him to get everything specified in writing to avoid problems or misunderstandings in the future. At times, he did wonder whether he was being too cautious, and should instead just 'let things unfold' and deal with them later, but decided against this approach, based on his limited understanding of potential cultural differences.

When Arun arrived in Busan, he headed straight for the office of the Korean company that was hiring him. He was surprised to find that the position being offered was different from what he had come to expect as the industry norm. There seemed to be significant differences between his expectations and those of Mr Kim, and Mr Kim's boss, Mr Lee. They had not taken into consideration the requests and revisions he had included in his negotiation emails, and there were differences in what they envisaged the job would involve in relation to specific matters including the job title, level of seniority and job responsibilities. Furthermore – and much to his disappointment – there was no contract for him to sign.

Arun was quite confused and wondered what he should do. The job he was now apparently being offered was significantly lower in status and included duties that he felt were more appropriate for a junior-level employee, rather than an employee with multiple degrees and over ten years of experience in the industry. He asked about the differences and expressed his dismay at the change from what had been discussed in the emails to what was actually being offered. He was annoyed, too, at having travelled all the way to Busan to find such a disappointing situation.

Tension began to grow. Mr Kim appeared to be offended by Arun's questions, as he was the senior member of the hiring committee and he made the decisions. He also did not approve of Arun's tone and expressed the opinion that the position being offered was appropriately suited to Arun's skill set and level of ability. This suggestion offended Arun further, and he elaborated on his substantial experience in the industry and his exceptional track record. Mr Kim indirectly suggested that Arun's record could not be as impressive as it seemed, given his relative youth. After all, Mr Kim, suggested, Arun was just 34 years old, and Mr Kim was not convinced by Arun's claims of wide experience. Mr Lee, who was Mr Kim's boss, and whose approval would be needed to officially hire the person whom the selection committee recommended, appeared to agree. He frequently interrupted Arun, communicating directly with Mr Kim in Korean. Arun could not help but feel very much an outsider when the two of them broke into sidebar conversations in Korean. He also worried about what was being said; he had noticed Mr Lee shaking his head when Mr Kim was questioning Arun's professional experience.

When Arun insisted to both Mr Kim and Mr Lee that his professional record outline in his CV was certainly not fabricated, and that his age had nothing to do with his skills and abilities, Mr Lee intervened and began speaking to Arun in English. He made it very clear that he did not approve of Arun's attitude and line of response, even to the point of raising his voice and informing Arun that he did not believe that he would fit in with this organisation if there was no trust and respect between them. When Arun questioned why Mr Lee did not think he would fit into the organisation, Mr Lee began telling a story about a Korean folk tale involving an aggressive tiger who was ungrateful to the man who had saved his life.

At this point, Arun – despite being angry – paused and thought for a moment. When he was a little boy in India, his grandmother had often scolded him in the form of a (seemingly unrelated) story. Arun had hated listening to long stories that had nothing to do with him, but as he grew up he had come to understand that his grandmother was using the stories to indirectly teach him about appropriate behaviour. What was the point of Mr Lee's story about the tiger? It seemed that Mr Lee was suggesting that he had been too forward, too aggressive, and had not shown proper gratitude to the company for considering his application. Arun realised that he had to demonstrate that he was fit for the job, that he would be able to show respect for his employers and that he was able to adapt to both the local and organisational culture. He immediately apologised for sounding ungrateful, and again expressed his eagerness to join the company. He explained that he accepted that there could have been some misunderstanding and that he would like to discuss the matter of his position more. Mr Kim agreed that there seemed to be some misunderstanding, but noted that in his opinion the misunderstanding had been on the part of Arun. While Arun would have liked to have protested and stated that the misunderstanding was the responsibility of both parties, he decided not to do so as it might be seen as an angry or ungrateful response. Perhaps it was safer not to challenge the position of the boss in Korea.

Trying to salvage the meeting, Arun decided to be less confrontational and focus on establishing a positive relationship and building trust. He agreed that they needed to establish a basis of trust in order to successfully move forward. He began to explain his other reasons for wanting the position. He told them of his strong interest in Korean culture and in Busan in particular. He told them about his Korean girlfriend and of his close relationship with her family, his love of Korean food and the similarities between Korean food and the traditional food that his grandmother in India used to make at home. His Korean connection helped ease the tension, and conversation appeared to improve, as did the overall atmosphere.

He went on to say that he would love to take the position, and suggested that they may be able to approach the situation from a win–win perspective. He subtly pointed out that he had the professional skills that they were seeking and from which the company would benefit. Mr Lee and Mr Kim both nodded, and Mr Kim then proceeded to the usual interview-style questions. He asked Arun when he would be able to begin his work there. Arun replied that he had not yet quit his job back in the United Kingdom, as he could not quit his current job without a signed contract for the new job. Mr Lee and Mr Kim were both shocked that he had not already submitted his resignation at his current job, and were further dismayed to find that it would be a minimum of three months before Arun would be available to begin working in Busan. To Arun, it seemed only logical that he should not quit his current job before being guaranteed another job. To Mr Lee and Mr Kim, the matter of an unsigned contract was an inconsequential detail, a mere 'loose end' to be tied up at the last minute.

The atmosphere of the meeting once again took a turn for the worse, as Mr Kim suggested that Arun had not trusted them in their offer. Arun refrained from pointing out that they had not had any contract for him to sign when he arrived, so from his perspective there had been nothing to trust or to distrust. Knowing that an outburst like that would ruin the meeting, he instead took a deep breath and drank a large gulp of the tea that a secretary had brought them in the meeting room. He decided to change topics, saying that he was really looking forward to meeting his new colleagues.

At the mention of the colleagues, Mr Lee and Mr Kim told Arun that he would have to really work hard to 'repair his relationship with the department staff'. Arun was confused and asked what they meant. Mr Kim explained that many members of the department staff were unhappy with the tone of his emails in the negotiations. Arun had expected those exchanges to be confidential – he had no idea that his emails were made public to everyone in the organisation. Not only did his soon-to-be colleagues know the details of the contract negotiations, they also knew what salary level Arun had been offered and other details of the job offer. Arun noted his displeasure at having had his emails shared with the entire company, and said that the company would be hiring him for his skills, not for his ability to focus on unnecessary politicking. Mr Kim and Mr Lee again spoke to each other in Korean, and Mr Kim turned to Arun and told him that all great accomplishments in the company – in fact, in the society – had been group efforts. At that point, Arun decided that it was best that he keep his job in the United Kingdom and continue to look for international positions elsewhere. He did not know whether this lack of basic respect for confidentiality was an organisational situation or a cultural expectation, but he had had enough. Mr Lee and Mr Kim were right – Arun would not fit very well into this company if the norm was to indirectly accuse job applicants of fabricating the experience on their CVs and violating expectations of confidentiality, and his individual skills meant far less than his ability to effectively join a clique. He felt he had narrowly escaped a bad situation, and was grateful that he still had his job in the United Kingdom to which to return.

As the meeting ended, Arun said that he regretted the miscommunications, but was happy to have had the chance to talk face to face. Mr Lee expressed remorse, and noted that Arun 'should have communicated more with him' in order to avoid having to have come all the way to Busan. Arun forced a smile and suggested that, in the future, perhaps they would meet again at an international industry conference. The men shook hands and Arun left. Mr Kim commented to Mr Lee that Arun had not seemed like a very good fit with the organisation. He did not seem like a team player, based upon his email communications and the interview. He had not asked about the team with which he would be working in any of his negotiation communications. He had not bothered to contact any of the other staff with whom he would have been working in the department. The employees who would have been Arun's colleagues (whom he had not met, but who knew about him from reading the negotiation email exchange) suspected that he was an overly direct, demanding foreigner, and were offended that he had not communicated with each of them in a personal, friendlier manner. He had not studied the hierarchy of the company. He did not seem to know who was in which position, and where he would have stood in the company hierarchy.

To Mr Lee and Mr Kim, Arun seemed to display an overly individualistic personality style, evidenced first by his arriving in Busan uninvited, when they had not expected him, and second by his expectation that he should not have to work his way up in seniority and rank, the way other employees had to. His tone in addressing both of them indicated that he believed they were equals, when in fact they outranked Arun by several levels. Mr Kim had been in the position for which they were interviewing Arun 20 years earlier, and believed that he knew better than Arun what the position required and how best to approach it. Mr Lee was a close family friend of the company's president, and had been with the company since shortly after the company's founding 40 years earlier. The men agreed that there was no place in the company for a young man who did not know how to properly respect authority or how to work within a team.

The night after the disastrous meeting, as Arun prepared to depart on his flight back to the United Kingdom, he reflected on his experience. He tried to figure out just what had gone wrong. Clearly, there were cultural differences between the Koreans he had met and himself. But he had managed cultural differences before when he settled in the United Kingdom and travelled to different parts of the world, and his girlfriend was Korean. So what went wrong in this experience? What did he not understand? Also, what did Mr Kim and Mr Lee fail to understand about him, his expectations and his behaviour? He thought he had been very reasonable in his demands, and wondered whether he would ever make the effort to seek employment with a Korean company again, given the differences he had experienced.

Discussion questions

14.1   To what extent does culture impact on this situation?

14.2   What advice would you have given to Arun before he began the negotiation process with the Korean company?

14.3   What advice would you have given to Mr Lee and Mr Kim before they began their negotiation process with Arun?

14.4   Is there any way in which this situation might be salvaged? Discuss possible strategies and their impact.

References and further reading

Hofstede, G 2001, *Culture's consequences: comparing values, behaviors, institutions, and organizations across nations*, Sage, Thousand Oaks, CA.

—— 2012, 'The Hofstede Centre', viewed 20 November 2012, <http://geert-hofstede.com/geert-hofstede.html>.

House, RJ, Hanges, PJ, Javidan, M, Dorfman, PW & Gupta, V (eds) 2004, *Culture, leadership, and organizations: the GLOBE Study of 62 Societies*, Sage, Thousand Oaks, CA.

Javidan, M, Dorfman, PW, de Luque, MS & House, RJ 2006, 'In the eye of the beholder: Cross-cultural lessons in leadership from Project GLOBE', *Academy of Management Perspectives*, vol. 20, no. 1, pp. 67–90.

15 Working in Chinese firms

Haina Zhang and André M Everett

China's remarkable growth is seen as an economic miracle – one that is having an increasing impact on the world. Like most things in China, working in Chinese firms differs in many significant ways from working elsewhere. This case focuses on the real-life experiences of employees working in two authentic companies that represent the two dominant forms of business ownership in China: privately owned enterprises (POEs) and state-owned enterprises (SOEs). Differences between working in the two types of companies are highlighted, particularly in the areas of career development, working environment and internal communication – all important areas that impact on the lives of employees. Understanding how Chinese business leaders and supervisors interact with their employees can inform Western business performance in China, as well as in international dealings with Chinese firms.

This case compares the experiences of Mr Qing, Ms King and Mr Wong, who worked for the Heilongjiang Yanglin Soybean Group (a POE), and Mr Su, Mr Gong and Mr Tian, who worked for Harbin No. 1 Tool Manufacture Ltd (an SOE).[1]

Company profiles

Heilongjiang Yanglin Soybean Group (POE)

Heilongjiang Yanglin Soybean Group ('Yanglin'), established in 1996, has become the second biggest privately owned cooking oil group in the Heilongjiang province of China, occupying a leading position in the national market. The core business of this enterprise is processing non-transgenic soybeans, but it also has extensive business involvement in grain marketing, rice processing, agricultural research, livestock and poultry breeding, hotel services, tourism resorts, logistics and other fields. It has 10 subsidiaries, with 1128 employees in total. The five existing soybean-processing production lines have an annual capacity of 1.8 million tonnes of soybeans, while the world-class refined rice production line annually processes 40 000 tonnes of rice.

The main products of this factory are premium-quality soybeans, refined rice, generic soybeans, soybean oils for cooking and other uses, soybean meal, microcapsules of soybean powder, protein concentrate, lecithin and defatted soybean meal. The majority of these products are sold throughout China, with some exported to Japan, South Korea, Russia, Indonesia and other neighbouring countries. The 'Yanglin Soybean' brand has been honoured as a 'China Top Brand' by the national government. A series of Yanglin products have gained organic food certification and non-genetically modified (non-GM) certification through the China Green Food Development Centre. The organisational structure of this company places the president at the top, followed by the top management team (the directors of finance, human resources, information technology, administration and business development), and then about 50 middle-level managers in these departments, all of whom work in the headquarters of the Yanglin Group. In this case study, Mr Qing worked as a junior manager in the IT Department, Ms King was a senior accountant in the

Accounting Department and Mr Wong worked as a director of the Strategy Development Department. Their respective supervisors are senior level managers or above.

■ *Harbin No. 1 Tool Manufacture Ltd (SOE)*

Harbin No. 1 Tool Manufacture Ltd was restructured in 2006, based on the Harbin No. 1 Tool Corporation whose history can be traced back to 1951, the dawn of the era of state-owned enterprises in communist China. As the earliest factory to be established in the Chinese tool industry, over a period of more than half a century of development, the company has grown into the largest sophisticated tools and computer numeric control (CNC) tools producer and research base in China. Its total asset value is RMB 410 million, and it has 1900 employees. The company is mainly engaged in research and development (R&D), manufacturing, sales and service for all kinds of tools needed in automobile manufacturing, equipment manufacturing, machine tools, energy, aerospace and other industries. The main products are sophisticated tools, cutting tools and non-standardised tools. It has a strong technology and product R&D capability, with its own technology centre – the only national-level enterprise technology centre for tools in China. It is the recognised leader in developing and producing China's core technology for sophis-ticated and cutting tools, leading the direction of tool manufacturing development. Its products, with awards at the provincial and national levels, sell to 30 out of China's 31 provinces and municipalities, taking approximately 35 per cent of the domestic market. The products are also exported to Europe, the Americas, South-East Asia, and other countries and regions. The organisational structure consists of the president at the top, followed by the top management team composed of the senior managers of each department as high-level leaders, and then junior managers as middle- or low-level leaders. The total managerial staff number around 130. In this case, Mr Su was a junior staff member in the Corporate Culture Department, Mr Gong worked as a middle-level manager in Sales Department and Mr Tian was a senior manager in the company. Their respective supervisors are senior level managers or above.

■ Career development

■ *Heilongjiang Yanglin Soybean Group (POE)*

Mr Qing is a middle-aged man who has been working in the Information Technology (IT) Department of Heilongjiang Yanglin Soybean Group for nine years, since graduating from a well-established university with a good academic record and outstanding IT skills. With the number of certificates he had earned, and with his growing expertise, he was able to acquire this position through a competitive recruitment process. He is hard-working and keen to learn, but sometimes feels frustrated with the need to continuously update software and deal with problems with new hardware. He sometimes complains about the lack of support from the training programs that the company should have offered:

> They [management] only want to hire 'talents' who can work for them directly and efficiently after recruitment, without providing any ongoing training for the new hires. I can understand that this policy is due to concerns about costs, but personally I think that it is difficult for individuals to grow quickly in this environment.

Fortunately, his direct supervisor, Mr Wu, is supportive and keen to assist his employees. Since the city where Yanglin Group is located is small and undeveloped, compared with the capital city of the province (Harbin), each time Mr Wu goes on a business trip to the capital he offers to buy some useful books or software for Mr Qing. Sometimes he seems more concerned about Mr Qing's career than Mr Qing himself. Mr Wu often buys these resources out of his personal funds to help Mr Qing catch up with advanced knowledge, resulting in better performance and thus gaining promotion more quickly. However, Mr Qing finds it difficult to accept all of these favours from Mr Wu, and repeatedly suggests that the company should reimburse Mr Wu for these expenses as the company will eventually benefit from what he learns.

The generosity of Mr Wu is an example of the traditional culture of humanism in Chinese society, in which acting in such a concerned and self-sacrificing way is a normative impulse born out of the realisation that, by building up those around you, you simultaneously build up an internal dynamic of personal development of *lian* ('face') from giving and the social aspect of 'face' by showing such concern. Mr Qing, who is well aware of these aspects of Chinese culture, is anxious to avoid a feeling of obligation, and a sense that Mr Wu may have other motives – for example, creating a dependency that he can later exploit. Both of these dynamics are at play here.

■ *Harbin No. 1 Tool Manufacture Ltd (SOE)*

Employees at Harbin No. 1 Tool Manufacture Ltd receive support that is different from the POEs in this case. Mr Su, a young graduate from university, has just started his career in the Corporate Culture Department in this company. Raised in a traditional village and educated in a small city, Mr Su experienced culture shock when he first began his job in the capital city of Harbin, with its population of over 10 million. He clearly remembers his feelings of frustration when he first came to this city and began in his new role two years previously:

> I felt totally lost when I came here. Everything was so new to me and the life pace was so fast. Before I came here, I held strong hope to start my new life in such a modern city, full of energy. But all of a sudden, I felt like I was losing all my confidence. At that time, I even thought about giving up and going back to my countryside.

Mr Yang, the director of the Corporate Culture Department and Mr Su's supervisor, offered kind and significant support to Mr Su at this crucial moment of his life. Mr Yang picked him up at the railway station on his arrival, and invited him to stay at his home for several days while showing him around the city and hunting for a flat.

After helping Mr Su to move into his new flat, he also gave him some household items, such as quilts and pots, in order to ensure that this young man could live comfortably at the lowest cost.

Due to his family background and introverted personality characteristics, Mr Su had major difficulties socialising with his colleagues. He felt inferior to his peers and believed he was being discriminated against by them. Mr Yang was very patient with Mr Su's adaptation, and gave him substantial encouragement through personal talks after work. He helped Mr Su to realise his strengths and shared many of his working experiences with him. From the detailed feedback that Mr Yang provided about his work, Mr Su gradually picked up key aspects of his work and has now become a qualified staff member of the department. When thinking about the past, Mr Su gratefully said:

> I think if I had been in other companies, I would have already been abandoned due to my adaptation problems and slow start. I really appreciate this company and my supervisor. He is one of the most influential persons in my life . . . very helpful in my growth in this company, especially when I lacked experience both at work and in my social life. Without his help, I couldn't begin my career in such a big modern city so smoothly and successfully.

Although we see evidence of personal support from the managers at both the Yanglin Group (POE) and Harbin No. 1 Tool Manufacture Ltd (SOE), the corporate culture in the SOE seems to suggest more supportive behaviour, with the manager in the SOE demonstrating stronger obligation to offer his support to subordinates, especially new arrivals. In contrast, support from the manager in the POE seems to be based on an individual's preferred behaviour, rather than contextual or corporate demands. Clearly, the differing induction practices suggest differences in the organisational culture between the POE and the SOE.

■ Work environment

■ *Heilongjiang Yanglin Soybean Group (POE)*

As a well-developed POE, Yanglin has established strict business regulations in relation to the work environment, and expects its employees to act strictly in accordance with its policy. Ms King, a senior accountant, has been working for Yanglin Group for the past six years. She once worked for a state-owned company, and shifted to Yanglin after that SOE went bankrupt. She felt at ease when she worked for her previous company, living and working at a slow and relaxed pace. But here, in the POE, every day she feels the stress of the job, the high expectations and the compelling need to constantly catch up with new knowledge. She never imagined that, at her age and level of seniority, she would still need to learn how to use new statistical software to do her job more efficiently. She did acknowledge that she had grown quickly in the role – especially in relation to the development of new skills and knowledge – since commencing at Yanglin. But she had also developed a strong sense of the fact that, if she did not keep pace with her younger colleagues, she could not keep the job at Yanglin, even though she was senior and had ample work experience in her field.

Recently, Ms King felt distracted from her work for personal reasons and was afraid that this might impact on her work – and it did. An important aspect of Chinese culture is good education, but she found out that her son had failed his school examinations at the end of the semester. She saw her son's failure as partly her own failure in encouraging him in his education, and in her communication with him. She struggled with understanding how to rectify this parental failure and was concerned about how to improve her son's academic performance. This concern led to her being preoccupied, and to making mistakes at work. Her supervisor, Ms Hua, a high-ranking accountant with a strong reputation for performance in the industry, noticed Ms King's distraction and called her to her office. After acknowledging Ms King's difficulties, she proceeded to share her experiences of how she had guided her own son's education. Since Ms Hua's son had been very successful in his studies at school, Ms King appreciated the advice from Ms Hua and felt that this sharing was very valuable to her approach to her own son's education in the future. She also appreciated her supervisor's understanding and kindness, and the fact that Ms Hua had not linked the conversation to her errors at work. It seems, however, that Ms Hua's approach was rather more indirect. Just when she thought the discussion was over and prepared to leave the office, Ms Hua said:

> I understood your situation but as a professional, I think you still shouldn't let your family affairs interfere with your work. Your bonus for this month will be reduced by half a per cent. I hope you can solve your family issues soon. In the meantime, you have to concentrate on work during office hours, and I don't want to see any more mistakes in your work.

Ms King left her supervisor's office with feelings of confusion. This would not have happened in the previous state-owned company for which she had worked. On the one hand, she felt let down and vulnerable, but on the other hand she felt that she may have deserved the reprimand and reduction in her bonus for having let her personal affairs impact on her professional performance.

■ Harbin No. 1 Tool Manufacture Ltd (SOE)

At Harbin No. 1 Tool Manufacture Ltd, the work culture and environment were somewhat different. In comparison to the stress to which the employees at the Yanglin Group were exposed, employees in the SOE felt more relaxed and cared for. Mr Gong (aged 45) has been working at Harbin No. 1 Tool Manufacture Ltd for 25 years, since he obtained his father's allocation in this company after his father retired (in the past, employment in popular state-owned enterprises was limited and jobs became almost hereditary). He devoted his life career to this company. Almost 10 years ago, the company went through a very tough period due to severe competition in the market, and restructured. At that time, rather than changing his job to a POE for a higher income (as some other employees did), Mr Gong preferred to stay at Harbin No. 1 Tool Manufacture Ltd, even though his salary dropped to one-third of the amount he had earned before. Apart from loyalty to, and special emotional ties with, this company, the easy and relaxed working environment was one of the key reasons for him remaining in this SOE. He liked the collaborative work environment, and strongly believed that relationships among colleagues should be cooperative rather than competitive. He also believed that the work climate and culture should be people-centred rather than task-oriented. At Harbin No. 1 Tool Manufacture Ltd, he could share a wide range of topics and interests from work issues to family life with his colleagues, and even with his supervisors. He had a good sense of humour, and enjoyed playing jokes or saying amusing things when socialising with others, sometimes during office hours. He had never ever been criticised for his behaviour at work, and was happy in his workplace.

Mr Gong had other positive and supportive experiences at Harbin No. 1 Tool Manufacture Ltd. At one stage, he worked in the Sales Department, when the company first started selling machine tools in Shanghai, and the senior leaders planned to send him to Shanghai, far away from Harbin. This was just after he had married; he found it difficult to accept this arrangement, and was unhappy with the situation. This impacted on his work – his usually high levels of performance and enthusiasm dropped dramatically. To his surprise, when his supervisor learned about his situation, he intervened and did his best to negotiate with the senior managers to delay Mr Gong's posting to Shanghai for six months. Mr Gong still remembers this event and the example of the management's support of its employees:

> I have never thought that the managers could be that considerate. I knew I shouldn't have demonstrated negative emotions at work at that time and should have followed the organisation's work arrangements. But I think I was very young and may have lacked maturity in making decisions. I thought I might lose the job. I was deeply grateful when I was told that the company had replaced me with someone else for that position. When I filled the same position in Shanghai half a year later, I worked very hard. I think I'm highly motivated by wanting to reciprocate to the company and to my supervisor.

Because there is no obvious pressure, as a middle-level manager of Harbin No. 1 Tool Manufacture Ltd, Mr Gong is never strict with his subordinates, who consider him very easy-going. He hesitates to impose any severe punishment: if his employees are late for work in the morning, as long as they are able to explain the causes to him (such as a traffic jam), he never enters these matters formally into their performance records. If there are no urgent tasks for the day, he might dismiss his workers so that they can go home earlier, to allow them to enjoy family life rather than staying in the office. Given that he favours such an approach, he feels that he is much better off working for an SOE rather than a POE, where things may not be so relaxed or easy. He also knows that if he were working for a POE, he would not have received the same consideration for his personal circumstances. He is extremely happy where he is!

■ Internal communication

■ *Heilongjiang Yanglin Soybean Group (POE)*

Mr Wong has been working for Yanglin for four years, after retiring from the local government where he had worked as a civil servant. As director of the Strategy

Development Department, he is responsible for designing strategies to cope with government policies affecting the industry of the company he has recently joined. He has noted the significant differences between the communication style he experienced in his previous role with the local government and that in his current role at Yanglin. As a senior person working directly with the CEO of Yanglin, Mr Yun, he has not received any direct criticism from his boss, but he is always nervous about his work performance since noticing how others suffer from severe and direct criticism due to their poor job performance. At the same time, he notes the open compliments often given to outstanding performers in the company. To him, either criticism or praise in public are inappropriate and make him feel uncomfortable. He regards public criticism as demeaning to the employees under attack, causing them loss of 'face'. He also finds public praise inappropriate, as he believes it encourages employees to compete against one another, which he feels is not consistent with Chinese culture and the practice of working collaboratively. He is still struggling to accept these behaviours as common practices in the organisation.

Mr Wong prefers to point out the errors of his subordinates subtly through personal talks, rather than through direct, public criticism. Similarly, he prefers to provide positive feedback and recognition to those who have performed well at work in private. He consequently finds that his communication style is somewhat in conflict with the culture of the company. He has been warned by his boss to change his style of evaluation of his subordinates' work, and to be more open and direct with his criticism. He also senses that some younger employees – particularly those who have achieved high levels of work performance – are dissatisfied when their performance is not complimented or recognised in public, as is the practice in other departments. Mr Wong ponders on how different the practices are from his previous local government culture and work environment.

In addition, Mr Wong feels confused about the way in which meetings are held in the company, and wonders about the growing influence of Western practices. The meetings in this company are very quick and efficient, with little opportunity for lengthy discussions – something with which he was familiar when he worked in the local government. Furthermore, Mr Wong is rather shocked by the openness of discussions at meetings. Despite his seniority, his ideas and proposals have often been directly challenged by his younger subordinates. Although he realises that, in a rational way, he should accept that this is the culture here, and that what employees are objecting to relates to work issues rather than to himself as a person, he still struggles emotionally to accept these practices. Consequently, he works harder before department meetings to ensure that his proposals do not display weaknesses. He tries to work out challenges facing him:

> I know I shouldn't feel uneasy and they didn't intend to offend my authority but I do feel that I lose 'face' if my points aren't accepted at the meeting. Maybe my approach is out of date in expecting that they should give me 'face' rather than only think of ideas when they illustrate points at the meeting . . . I have to accept this way of communication and adapt myself better to this environment despite all the emotional difficulties.

■ *Harbin No. 1 Tool Manufacture Ltd (SOE)*

Things are different at Harbin No. 1 Tool Manufacture Ltd. Mr Tian, as a senior manager in this company, has devoted his whole career to it and witnessed its growth over 30 years. He is a serious person who rarely smiles at work. However, this neither means that he is very strict with his followers nor that the climate of the department he leads is dull or gloomy. On the contrary, everyone is cooperative and the relationships are generally harmonious. He seldom praises an individual in public, no matter how important the contributions that person has made to the department. Instead, he gives the credit to the whole team for their combined effort and successful work. He spends personal time, including out of office hours, to help solve his subordinates' problems or correct their mistakes, rather than criticising them in public:

> I want to give 'face' to, and protect 'face' for, everyone so I wouldn't like to criticise anyone in public. I see such behaviours as damaging to one's psychological capital and personal growth. Usually, I invite those to dinner who didn't perform well or made mistakes at work, and guide and correct them in a relaxed atmosphere. I think this method can ultimately achieve good effects . . . I also think it's not so good to avoid giving positive recognition to individuals who really make significant contributions to the department, but I have no alternative approach to offer. I don't want them to suffer from their colleagues' jealousy, which sometimes destroys relationships . . . You know, as human relationships are so complicated, I really don't want them to have enemies just because of several complimentary sentences from me. I think my approach is all right as long as their good performance can be realised by me through personal talks.

No one in the department complains that their good performance is not recognised by their manager. Instead, they all agree with his approach and accept that workplace harmony should be a primary concern. They even joke that anyone who is invited to have dinner with Mr Tian should be concerned, as the invitation indicates that he or she must have done something wrong! Consequently, by ensuring that he always upholds the practice of giving 'face' to his colleagues and his subordinates, Mr Tian, himself never suffers from losing 'face' in public. No one really challenges Mr Tian's opinions at department meetings, and under most circumstances he is in full charge of the meetings, delivering the working plans, asking for advice and ending meetings easily with no dissenting voices.

■ Conclusion

The contrast between the Heilongjiang Yanglin Soybean Group (POE) and Harbin No. 1 Tool Manufacture Company provides researched evidence of the differences in ownership types, corporate culture and management styles between these two companies. In each company, there is a different way of leading, motivating and communicating with staff. In the Heilongjiang Yanglin Soybean Company (a POE), time is money, decisions need to be made swiftly and the discussions prior to making decisions need to be open and frank so that mistakes are avoided. This cuts across many of the cultural norms that have been accepted as part of life in China. Some may suggest that open and frank discussion is a very necessary part of modern company culture.

However, examples from the Harbin No. 1 Tool Manufacture Company show that this is not always the case. The profiled manager believes that people are motivated by the quality of the relationships they have with their staff. As described above, managers work hard at being competent and caring leaders, who are able to give recognition to high-performing staff without alienating the others and causing loss of face. In private conversations, employees are congratulated for a job well done, rather than receiving public recognition that may make staff members feel good but risks them being seen as motivated by the desire to achieve greater personal recognition. Working cooperatively in a supportive team environment is encouraged.

The discussion of key practices in the two companies – a POE and an SOE – in China indicates a clear contrast between the more Western style of management adopted by a POE that encourages competition, and the more traditional Chinese approach to management found in an SOE that encourages cooperation and respect for leaders.

■ Discussion questions

15.1 Identify and discuss some of the key features of organisational culture for these two companies. Imagine yourself as one of the leaders of a company. What type of organisational culture would you like to establish and why?

15.2 Identify the major differences in communication styles in these two companies. Which communication style would you prefer to utilise and why? What should you take into account in order to communicate effectively with your subordinates/colleagues?

15.3 Summarise similarities and differences in the leadership styles used in these two companies. Identify some commonalities that Chinese leaders share in their leadership practices, based on these examples (or other experience).

15.4 Research and discuss the two dominant ownership types of enterprises in China – POEs and SOEs – to further understand their management practices.

■ Note

1   The names of the companies are authentic, but the names of the employees have been altered for privacy reasons.

16

Losing touch with the context: The story of Ravinaki Resort in Fiji

Sally Anne Gaunt and Dan V Caprar

The sun was setting opposite Ravinaki Resort on the island of Batiki situated in the centre of Fiji's volcanic Lomaiviti Island group. Caroline Childs and her husband, Gerald, had just arrived from Sydney and were soaking up the atmosphere after a day and a half of travelling.

Caroline was no stranger to Fiji, or to Ravinaki Resort. Eight years previously (in 2001), she had been the water sports manager at Ravinaki. The resort is home to an impressive marine ecosystem cherished by scuba divers and snorkellers. It also offered game fishing, seasonal surfing and kayaking. It was Caroline's responsibility to ensure that tourists were able to take full advantage of the many wonders that the nearby reef offered, as well as ensuring the safety of visitors and staff while out on the water. Caroline had loved her time at Lomaiviti, and she wanted to show her husband the delights of Ravinaki – albeit now under new management.

■ The Ravinaki Resort and its founders

Ravinaki was the only resort on the island of Batiki. It was set up in 2000 by James Brennan and his wife, Sarah, who started working on the island as part of a marine-based NGO project. James, a marine biologist from the United States, was responsible, along with a number of other marine biologists, for evaluating the health of the local Batiki reefs. Sarah, originally from England, had a background in hospitality, and was responsible for the project's overall management, including catering, logistics and sanitation. They were well suited to their roles, but also developed other interests in the area. Given his background, James had been particularly impressed with the pristine coral reefs that surrounded the island of Batiki. The couple had dreamed of being able to combine their careers so they could both stay in the tropical paradise of Batiki, so when the NGO project ended in 1999, James and Sarah seized the opportunity to open Batiki's first and only resort. They decided to target the more intrepid tourist who would not mind making the day-and-a-half trip from the closest international airport in Fiji's capital, Suva, to reach their unspoilt paradise island. Moreover, due to both James and Sarah's limited financial resources and the environmental issues presented by the island and its community, Ravinaki was unable to offer the luxury accommodation found in Fiji's high-traffic tourist destinations. Therefore, it had been important that, while emphasising the delights of Ravinaki's unspoilt marine life, the resort's marketing material also managed guests' expectations, pointing out that Ravinaki was an 'eco resort' with no air-conditioning and limited electricity usage.

■ The Ravinaki Resort under new management

On her return to the resort, Caroline was curious about her experience as a tourist in a place she knew so well. Gerald, Caroline's husband, was awe-struck by the spectacular sunsets and the beauty of the surroundings, and could see why Caroline had loved her time working in Fiji. While admiring the spectacular sunset, the couple started chatting with Ross Griffiths, the resort's new owner, and Gerald commented on the half-finished deck at the entrance to the resort. Ross sighed and told Gerald how disappointed he was at the slow progress being made by the contracted Fijian workers, most of them coming from the local villages. 'They go at two speeds, dead slow and stop. I don't know when we are ever going to get it finished,' said Ross. This struck Caroline as a very inappropriate conversation to be having with a guest. Ross continued to complain:

> I've brought over an ex-colleague of mine who is a civil engineer, he's been helping me upgrade the resort, but he's really struggling with these Fijian workers. Mike and I write detailed instructions for the foreman but half the time I don't know why we bother as the instructions are never followed. I now have Mike watch over these Fijian guys so he can spot when they're about to make a mistake. And everything takes so much time to achieve – we miss deadline after deadline, it's really frustrating. We have tried increasing their pay and offering individual targets with an accompanying bonus in the hope that they achieve them. We even offered promotion prospects, but none of these incentives work.

As she listened to the conversation, Caroline began to feel a wave of unease. The Fijians Ross was describing had been her colleagues, who were part of the effective and fun working team that had made her time at Ravinaki so rewarding. After the conversation ended, Caroline began to wonder what had happened. When did her former Fijian colleagues become problem workers? And why was working with them such a struggle? When Caroline had been working at the resort, the former owners, James and Sarah, were well respected by their Fijian staff. James had always allowed for 'Fiji time', and did not expect projects to be completed as quickly as in other contexts; there had rarely been a problem with the staff meeting James' expectations. Caroline wondered whether Ross was not being realistic in his expectations or whether the workers simply did not respect him enough to work towards his expectations.

Ross had visited Fiji for the first time five years ago, in 2004. At the time, he owned a chain of electrical stores and was based in Toronto. It was Ross's first trip outside North America and he fell in love with the Fiji island lifestyle. He had stayed on the Yasawa islands in Fiji's north, and decided that he would sell up his business in Canada and buy a resort in Fiji. This coincided with James and Sarah's decision to return to the United Kingdom for family reasons. Ross felt Ravinaki had plenty of potential, especially as the currently challenging logistics involved in getting to Batiki were likely to improve, given continued improvements in Fiji's infrastructure. Therefore, there was the potential for more flights between Levuka, the closest airport to Batiki, and the international airport based just outside Fiji's capital, Suva. Ross was unimpressed by the basic accommodation and immediately upgraded the resort's rooms by including air-conditioning from 6.00 p.m. onwards. He also doubled the rates of the rooms with ocean views. Prices continued to increase as he made further upgrades to the resort, which clearly created a shift in the type of clients the resort could attract.

■ Staff and culture at Ravinaki Resort over time

After the conversation with Ross about his perception of the local workers, Caroline could not help but feel uncomfortable. However, she was determined to enjoy her holiday. The next morning, when Caroline and her husband arrived for breakfast, Caroline was delighted to see that Malcolm, a previous colleague who had been in charge of food and beverages, was still working at the resort. Malcolm came from Viti Levu, Fiji's main and largest island, and had worked in a couple of other large resorts in Fiji's popular Denarau region. During Caroline's time at the resort, James and Sarah had actively recruited as many Fijian staff as possible, including in management positions. However, it had proved extremely difficult to promote employees recruited from the three most local villages. Lomaiviti's remoteness meant that the communities still strongly adhered to a structured hierarchy, where the ruling chief of each Fijian village had ultimate power, and employees felt uncomfortable giving directions to other staff from the same village, especially if they had strong connections to the chief and his family. The Ravinaki resort owners soon realised that one way to combat this was to recruit well-trained Fijian staff from the international resorts found in the high tourist traffic regions of Fiji, such as the Coral Coast and the Mamanuca Islands. These staff members could demand a higher salary, but the advantage was that they generally worked well with the local Fijian employees and caused relatively little friction. Malcolm was one such employee.

Caroline, being from Australia, was an exception to James and Sarah's recruitment strategy. It was nearly impossible to find a Fijian to manage the water sports division, as the manager needed to be a qualified diving instructor, which required a certain level of education and training. Of course, there were many Fijians with the necessary level of education to become a diving instructor, but they lacked the professional training. Few would choose a profession in water sports, opting instead for careers in recognised professions such as banking, nursing or IT. Caroline had been selected on the basis of both her qualifications and experience. She held a Professional Association of Diving Instructors (PADI) certificate, had been working on an NGO project in the Mamanuca Islands, and had other similar positions in a number of South-East Asian countries. She had developed an admiration for the country and its people.

While Caroline had been at the resort, Malcolm had always been a favourite with the guests. People loved his friendly and amusing style. However, having known him so well in her previous role, she soon sensed that Malcolm's enthusiasm for his job had waned. Furthermore, as she looked around, she realised that many of Malcolm's previous team members were no longer around. Caroline also observed that many of the new staff members now employed were quite obviously not Fijian.

After breakfast, Caroline chatted with Malcolm, and asked him how he liked working with the new Canadian owners. Malcolm looked towards the floor and shook his head. 'I'm no longer manager of food and beverage,' he said. Apparently, there was a need to upgrade the restaurant to cater for a more upmarket clientele, so the management brought in a new chef from Brazil:

Fernando is a brilliant chef but he has upset everyone. Nothing we do is good enough. He is always shouting at us. He says we don't even know the basics of cooking. But you know that this is not true, it's just that we have not been taught in the same way as he has. He gives us an order but doesn't tell us how to do things, and then yells at us when we don't do things the way he wants them done. It's as if he thinks we're telepathic and can read his mind, but we cannot. Everyone is unhappy and looking for new jobs.

Malcolm left to get back to the kitchen, concerned that if he stayed any longer he would be reprimanded by Fernando for loitering.

Caroline sighed, and could not help but reflect on how Ravinaki had changed from being a well-run and successful resort eight years previously to the current situation where even the guests seemed less relaxed, as if they could sense the stern atmosphere of discontent. When she had been recruited, her new employers (James and Sarah Brennan) had told her that this was a 'hands-on' organisation: 'We can't afford to carry anyone and everyone needs to be flexible and at times share in the mundane tasks such as carrying and fetching supplies.' James would often say, 'You have to lead from the front, and do your fair share of the physical work.' Caroline distinctly remembered that every time supplies needed to be unloaded after their weekly arrival from Suva, it was always James who, despite being the owner, had been at the front of the unloading chain. It was James who set the pace to ensure everything was unloaded as quickly as possible, and it was Sarah who spent time in the kitchen, both helping the staff and advising on the menu and food preparation. Caroline herself had always made sure she actively helped to pack the boat each morning, which included loading diving equipment and tanks.

After the conversation with Malcolm, Caroline and her husband ambled down to the water sports centre to decide when they would venture out to the reef. The manager was Ross's nephew, Sam, who was 25 years old. This was his first time overseas. He started the procedure for the day, making sure that all the guests signed the various forms required by the resort before they could set out for the day's activities. Caroline looked at the list of diving and snorkelling locations and quickly realised that some of the most popular sites during her time at Ravinaki were no longer available. She asked Sam why this was the case. 'Oh, we are in the process of suing some of the local chiefs because they have told us that we cannot go to these spots unless we pay them for the privilege,' he said. 'My uncle says that he does not do business in this way and has brought in a lawyer. In the meantime, it's too problematic to go there.' He then added: 'I'm relieved, quite frankly, as some of the sites are quite treacherous and I'm still trying to become familiar with the place.' Caroline asked Sam why he didn't use the local Fijian guides who knew these waters so well. 'My Uncle says the guests prefer to deal with expats when it comes to water activities, as they feel safer,' came the reply. Caroline found this to be a very strange decision, as she would never have dreamt of taking guests out without the expert experience of the local Fijian guides who knew the reefs so well. She certainly couldn't recall any guest complaining about this before. She also thought it was absurd to try to sue a local Lomaiviti chief, and could not see what this would ever achieve. Lomaiviti's remoteness meant the local chiefs had tremendous power. When Caroline had been at Ravinaki, she and the resort owners had spent many evenings drinking kava with the chiefs to ensure relationships were strong.

■ Lessons of the past and struggles of the present at Ravinaki Resort

After the conversation with Sam, Caroline stared at the ocean and once again found herself reflecting on James and Sarah's approach to dealing with the local employees. James and Sarah motivated the staff by maintaining good relationships. They had found that trying to engage the staff from the local villages with individual rewards and bonuses was pointless: employees were uncomfortable with competitiveness within their close-knit communities. Recognising this, under James and Sarah, Ravinaki set simple group targets, such as increasing the number of people going on snorkelling tours or increasing the guest list overall. If these targets were achieved, Ravinaki would pay for development projects in the villages, such as the upgrade of the school, church or community centre. Ravinaki was careful when implementing these incentives, as it was easy for money to disappear, leaving a project unfinished. Ultimately, Ravinaki's directors would buy the materials and expertise rather than giving bulk sums of money. Such projects were not only a more successful way of incentivising Ravinaki's local staff, but also helped cement relationships with the local chiefs. Without the cooperation of the local communities, especially the chiefs, the functional running of the resort would have become very challenging. If the chiefs where unhappy with the resort, the employees from these local villages would have torn loyalties and often the loyalty to the chief would come before their job at Ravinaki. Caroline felt that suing a local chief was burning a bridge with a vital resort stakeholder, and wondered how the relationship could ever be restored. Even if the resort won – and, given the legal context of Fiji, there could be no forgone conclusion – it would be impossible to monitor the outcome.

Caroline found herself reflecting on other aspects of her former time as a staff member at Ravinaki. It was evident that the resort was now far from full and, although guests were paying more for their accommodation, the number of visitors taking diving, kayaking and snorkelling tours had dropped significantly. During her time at the resort, Caroline had actively encouraged guests who did not dive to try a 'Discover Scuba' session, which often led them to want to take a full diving course. According to the records, there had not been one 'Discover Scuba' offered in the last 12 months. Caroline was astonished to see such a decline in what had once been an important revenue stream.

■ The future of Ravinaki Resort: What next?

It seemed to Caroline that increasing guest numbers and guest spending while at the resort were fundamental to the future survival of Ravinaki, and Caroline was concerned that both these vital elements were diminishing rapidly. She felt it was

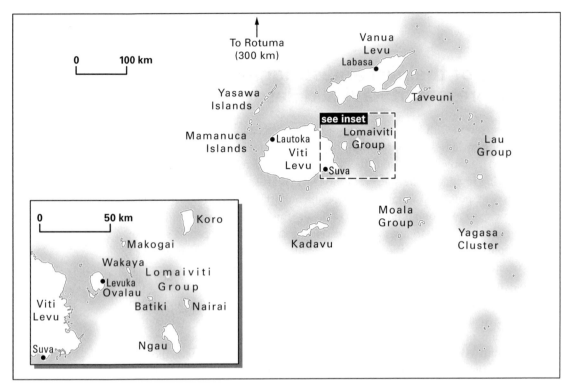

Figure 16.1: Map of Fiji
and Lomaiviti Group area

important not to romanticise her previous experience, as there had been problems, but the solutions had been found through dialogue, relationships and negotiation, and not through suing – especially given Fiji's rather fragile legal system. She was wondering why the new management made such choices that were clearly not helpful (and destroying the good standing of the resort within the community). She understood that the resort was keen to attract a more lucrative upmarket clientele, with the potential for greater profitability, and therefore it needed to change. However, she was struggling with the decisions the new owners were making and was wondering what could be done in order to address the current situation.

▪ Discussion questions

16.1   What are the key differences in the leadership of the resort under previous and current ownership? How is this impacting on the motivation of the employees and the business in general?

16.2   Who are the key stakeholders of Ravinaki Resort? Compare approaches undertaken by the previous and current owners in managing relationships with these key stakeholders. How important an issue is this in doing business across cultures?

16.3 What is your opinion of the practice of making payments to local chiefs in order to obtain access to certain reef spots? What are the implications of making, or not making, such payments?

16.4 What recommendations would you make to the owner of the resort in order to address the current situation at Ravinaki Resort? Draft strategies that you think might turn the business around so it is again a success.

▪ References and further reading

Chen, M & Miller, D 2011, 'The relational perspective as a business mindset: managerial implications for East and West', *Academy of Management Perspectives*, vol. 25, no. 3, pp. 6–18.

de Vries, RE, Pathak, RD & Paquin, AR 2011, The paradox of power sharing: participative charismatic leaders have subordinates with more instead of less need for leadership, *European Journal of Work & Organizational Psychology*, vol. 20, no. 6, pp. 779–804.

Earley, P & Mosakowski, E 2004, 'Cultural intelligence', *Harvard Business Review*, vol. 82, no. 10, pp. 139–46.

Farrelly, T 2011, 'Indigenous and democratic decision-making: issues from community-based ecotourism in the Bouma National Heritage Park, Fiji', *Journal of Sustainable Tourism*, vol. 19, no. 7, pp. 817–35.

Javidan, M, Dorfman, PW, De Luque, M & House, RJ 2006, 'In the eye of the beholder: cross cultural lessons in leadership from Project GLOBE', *Academy of Management Perspectives*, vol. 20, no. 1, pp. 67–90.

Sanchez, JI, Spector, PE & Cooper, CL 2000, 'Adapting to a boundaryless world: a developmental expatriate model', *Academy of Management Executive*, vol. 14, no. 2, pp. 96–106.

17

Foxconn: The complexity of quality control in a Chinese context

Shih-wei Hsu, Maris Farquharson and Anders Örtenblad

During the past decade, Apple (Inc.) has achieved spectacular success in the consumer electronics industry and was awarded the 'World's Most Admired Company' from 2008 to 2012 (*Fortune* 2012). However, this triumph was somewhat over-shadowed by a series of worker suicides that occurred in one of Apple's main contract manu-facturers, Foxconn International Holdings Ltd, in China. This case study is based on our interviews with five managers and one production line leader in Hon Hai Precision Industry Co Ltd, the parent company of Foxconn, between October and December 2010.

Foxconn is a subsidiary of Hon Hai Precision Industry Co Ltd (hereafter Hon Hai), a Taiwanese company and one of the largest electronic manufacturers in the world. Hon Hai was ranked 132nd among the Global Fortune 500 Companies in 2009 and 109th in 2010. Hon Hai was founded in 1974, and Foxconn Technology Group was adopted as its trading name. In 1988, Foxconn established its first multinational manufacturing base in mainland China. The company opened a factory in Shenzhen, an industrial city in south China. By 2010, Foxconn had 13 factories in nine cities in China (Lau 2010); the largest (and oldest) is located in the Longhua Science & Technology Park in Shenzhen. This factory is also known as the 'Foxconn City', or 'iPod City', or more locally as the 'Foxconn Campus'. There are more than 230 000 workers in this walled campus (Duhigg & Bradsher 2012), along with restaurants, shops, worker dormitories and a bank. Foxconn is particularly famous for assembling electronic goods such as Apple's iPhones and iPods.

■ The 'problem': A general view

In 2010, Foxconn faced an international media backlash and became the target of escalating criticism as a result of a series of worker suicides. Sixteen workers jumped from high buildings, resulting in 14 deaths. Many believed that the main reason behind the suicides was low wages, and that Foxconn's workers had to work overtime to earn extra money since their basic salary barely covered actual living expenses. Other reasons offered included workers' loneliness, Taiwanese managers' discriminatory action against local Chinese workers and local workers' discrimination against migrant workers from other provinces. However, some reports revealed that Foxconn's wage was com-paratively high in terms of the industrial average, and therefore low wages may not have been the main reason behind the suicides. For example, the Shenzhen Municipal Trade Union and Shenzhen University conducted research on local salary levels. Based on a survey of 5000 young migrant workers in Shenzhen city during April and June 2010, the respondents' average wage was reported to be RMB 1838.60 (US$267) per month (Chan & Pun 2010). This was well above the local average minimum wage.

Might other factors explain the workers' suicides? For some, Foxconn manage-ment practices seemed to revive memories (or fears) of Taylorism, which was widely practised around the beginning of the twentieth century. In general, it is believed that Foxconn's scientific management style caused unbearable levels of work stress for workers; this caused depression, which in turn led to the suicides. It is claimed that a scientific approach to management results in the deskilling of workers and the dehumanisation of the workplace. The Foxconn factories represented a typical case of scientific management – workers spent hours on assembly lines, performed repetitive tasks and were allowed no human interaction, with even conversation between workers often forbidden (Maisto 2010). Commentators such as Tam (2010) suggested that Foxconn needed to adopt a more humanistic approach to management. For example, it was recommended that sociological and psychological support could be made available to workers, and that motivational programs could be introduced to increase job satisfaction and enrichment.

Upon closer examination, however, there seemed to be some initiatives to support workers – initiatives that provided a somewhat different perspective when it came to the work context at Foxconn. Foxconn had, for example, put into place a number of motivation initiatives in order to increase job satisfaction and enrichment. The company had implemented a highly sophisticated pay system and performance-related bonuses, resulting in workers at Foxconn receiving a higher than average wage. In addition to the highly flexible pay system and reward schemes, the company also sought to create a 'humanised' workplace by providing various recreational facilities to motivate staff. Facilities included 'an Olympic-sized swimming pool on the campus, as well as badminton courts and ping pong tables' (Maisto 2010). The trade union was also active in promoting 'fun' activities. Motivation strategies appeared to play an important role in Foxconn's management practices, based on the logic that managers should motivate workers because happier workers would lead to better performance (as advocated by motivation theories). Indeed, Terry Guo, the CEO of Foxconn, could be viewed as a competent motivational CEO because of practices introduced at Foxconn.

However, while it seems that Foxconn management did indeed show a strong commitment to motivational programs and initiatives, many continued to argue that Foxconn's management style, based on a scientific and 'militaristic' approach, was inadequate and did not support an enriching work environment. But the question arises: was the introduction of such a management style necessary in order to ensure quality control in the production line, especially for famous customers such as Apple?

■ The solution to 'Made in China'?

Many management practitioners agree that poor quality control (QC) is one of the most widely recognised problems associated with the 'Made in China' label (Barboza 2007). The problem of QC has several facets (e.g. Libcom 2010). For instance, at Foxconn there was a lack of qualified and appropriately trained workers. This was reflected in the fact that a large number of Chinese workers were migrant workers who came from low educational backgrounds. These migrant workers constitute the majority of the workforce in many manufacturing industries in China. Many workers stay at the factory for years, living in factory dormitories or similar accommodation, and rarely visiting their families. This can lead to many workers suffering from feelings of isolation, loneliness and stress, which can impact on their performance on the assembly line. Many companies have reported difficulties in maintaining the quality of their products, especially when managing migrant workers. This was a key factor when it came to working with top-of-the-line clients such as Apple.

An engineer from Hon Hai stated:

> The poor QC of Chinese factories can be a nightmare, perhaps, to all multinationals in China. Foxconn produces major components for iPods and iPhones. It goes without saying that our clients are very demanding in terms of our quality.

An ex-HR manager (also from Hon Hai) identified a possible reason for the poor quality of 'Made in China' products:

> Workers in Chinese factories often go through the motions, possibly because they lack 'motivation'. We have tried many ways to maintain a decent quality level, including an increase in their salaries, but most failed.

While many Chinese factory workers may indeed go through the motion and pay little attention to the quality of their products, the quality issue may also reflect the cultural difference between Taiwan and mainland China, because many of Hon Hai's managers seem to have the impression that 'poor QC is synonymous with Chinese factories'. Nevertheless, for Hon Hai's management, 'motivation' is the key issue. An operational manager (from Hon Hai) said:

> In the Chinese manufacturing context the combination of a militaristic style of management and scientific management largely improves productivity, but it may nevertheless cause more errors and bring down the overall quality of assembly-line products.

Policies to reduce assembly-line errors – and, by extension, improve quality, inceptives and motivational programs – were implemented by Hon Hai as the parent company, and extended to Foxconn at virtually all levels of the subsidiary.

For example, Hon Hai is famous for its prize draw, held during the annual end of year banquet, prior to the Chinese New Year's Eve celebrations. More specifically, in 2009 the company spent NT$1.2 billion (new Taiwan dollars – approximately US$40 million) on its end-of-year banquet and celebrations, with NT$524 million (approximately US$17.46 million) paid in Hon Hai's stocks to prizewinners. These prize draws have been offered to and welcomed by employees as incentives. An Account Manager from Hon Hai recalled: 'Motivational schemes play a critical role. Some might win NT$27 million [about US$900 000] in the New Year party.'

Foxconn also regularly offered the chance for high-performing workers to travel to Taiwan, where they were publicly recognised as 'valuable' workers. Prior to the 14th suicide case, the company organised a 'morale-boosting' rally in August 2010, at which many young workers held up posters that said 'Love me, Love you, Love Terry', referring to Terry Guo, CEO of the company (Chan & Pun 2010). The company also organised an 'I love the company, the company loves me' speech competition to build morale (Foxconn 2010). Apart from these 'motivational' activities the company also offered generous bonuses for its employees. In 2008, for instance, most of the

Hon Hai workers received a year-end bonus equivalent to six months' salary. At the same time, the redundancy rate was about 10–15 per cent.

In Foxconn, the pay system is quite complex, and perhaps more flexible because it runs parallel with a severe punishment system. According to a report released by SACOM (2010a), a production-line leader may punish a worker for making a mistake (e.g. forgetting to fix a screw in a mobile phone) by asking the worker to copy Terry Guo's quotations 300 times, imposing a fine or by demanding self-criticism in front of other colleagues. Guo's quotations include some of his principles of 'Tao' (the word here means 'the Way', which originates from Taoism) (Chang, Chang & Lu 2002). Moreover, Guo's Tao also assumes that employees older than 45 should not be working for money, but instead for 'ideals' (Chang, Chang & Lu 2002). While the former denotes the present-day ideology of flexible working, in reality the latter signals the theory of self-actualisation and self-esteem in Herzberg's motivation theory (Herzberg, Mausner & Snyderman 1959).

To some, Foxconn seemed to solve the problems of poor QC in the Chinese context by closely linking motivation to QC. An ex-HR manager suggested:

> Several famous clients choose Foxconn, because Foxconn has excellent QC and it produces highly reliable goods. This makes Foxconn very distinct from other Chinese factories. Hon Hai has rich experiences in the industry (since the 1970s) and knows how to 'motivate' employees.

In response to criticism about working conditions in the Foxconn factories, Guo insisted that the company was by no means a sweatshop, as it offered decent wages and a welfare system for employees. In a letter to the employees, Guo confidently claimed that the workers committed suicide in order for their families to obtain huge amounts of compensation from the company. He also suggested that the workers had personal and psychological problems, such as 'debts' and 'poor interpersonal skills' (SACOM 2010a). In June 2010, following the spate of suicides, Foxconn announced that it would raise the salaries in its Chinese plants. However, by November it was clear that, despite the series of suicides, there was little evidence that the company intended to honour its promise to raise salaries, even although Guo publicly promised to do so (SACOM 2010b).

An ex-HR manager (from Hon Hai) also holds the view that low salaries were by no means the cause of worker suicides: 'Comparatively, Foxconn offers generous salaries, and numerous people want to work for Foxconn.' Indeed, when Foxconn in Wuhan City opened its recruitment process on 5 August 2010, there were more than 50 thousand applicants applying for a job (Culpan 2010).

After a series of worker suicides, Terry Guo attempted to extend his control over the trade union. Guo purportedly appointed his senior PA as president of the union. This implies that Foxconn serendipitously sought to generate consensus and control in order to maintain a 'harmonious' working environment. The extent to which Foxconn addressed and solved the problem of poor QC in a Chinese context is less clear, because its approach produced further problems at different organisational levels that went beyond the organisational boundary of the company. In 2012, Apple asked the Fair Labour Association to launch an audit of Foxconn's working conditions (Bonnington 2012).

Discussion questions

17.1 Evaluate the effectiveness of Foxconn's motivational strategies. Did Foxconn fail to motivate its employees? Give reasons for your answer.

17.2 Recommend and discuss other approaches to motivating workers in the workplace, and in an international context such as China.

17.3 Did Foxconn successfully solve the problem of poor quality control (QC)? What were Foxconn's main strategies and how could they be improved?

17.4 Historically, there are three important models associated with management and ways to achieve corporate efficiency. Outline the basic assumptions of scientific management, the human relations school and motivation theory regarding how organisational efficiency can be achieved.

References and further reading

Barboza, D 2007, 'China finds poor quality on its store shelves', *The Telegraph*, 5 July.

Bonnington, C 2012, 'Apple's Foxconn auditing group "surrounded with Controversy", critics say', *Wired*, 13 February, viewed 12 November 2012, <http://www.wired.com/dadgetlab/2012/02/apple-foxconn-investigations>.

Chan, J & Pun, N 2010, 'Suicide as protest for the new generation of Chinese migrant workers: Foxconn, Global Capital, and the state, *The Asia-Pacific Journal: Japan Focus*, viewed 10 July 2012, <http://www.japanfocus.org/-Ngai-Pun/3408>.

Chang, W-I, Chang, D-W & Lu, C-F 2002, *300 Billion legend: Hon Hai's empire*, Commonwealth Magazines, Taipei.

Culpan, T 2010, Foxconn to hire 400,000 China workers within a year, *Business Week*, 18 August, viewed 10 October 2011, <http://www.businessweek.com/news/2010-08-18/foxconn-to-hire-400-00-china-workers-within-a-year.html>.

Duhigg, C & Bradsher, K 2012, 'How the U.S. lost out on iPhone work', *New York Times*, 21 January.

Fortune 2012, 'The world's most admired companies', vol. 165, no. 4, 19 March, pp. 139–40.

Foxconn Technology Group 2010, *2010 CSER Annual Report: Corporate, Social and Environmental Responsibility*, viewed 10 December 2012, <http://www.foxconn.com/ser/2010%20Foxconn%20CSER%20Report.pdf>.

Hammer, M & Champy, J 1993, *Reengineering the corporation: a manifesto for business revolution*, Nicholas Brealy, London.

Herzberg, F, Mausner, B & Snyderman, BB 1959, *The motivation to work*, John Wiley & Sons, New York.

Lau, M 2010, 'Struggle for Foxconn girl who wanted to die', *South China Morning Post*, 15 December.

Libcom 2010, 'China's migrant workers', 12 January, viewed 10 July 2012, <http://libcom.org/history/chinas-migrant-workers>.

Maisto, M 2010, 'Foxconn, maker of Apple, Dell products, sees 12th suicide attempt', eWeek. com, 27 May, viewed 5 May 2012, <http://www.eweek.com/c/a/Desktops-and-Notebooks/Foxconn-Maker-of-Apple-Dell-Products-Sees-12th-Suicide-Attempt-843233>.

SACOM 2010a, 'Workers as machines: military management in Foxconn', viewed 14 July 2012, <http://sacom.hk/wp-content/uploads/2010/11/report-on-foxconn-workers-as-machi nes_sacom.pdf>.

—— 2010b, 'Another suicide case at Foxconn reveals predicament of worker remains', 12 November, viewed 14 July 2012, <http://sacom.hk/wp-content/uploads/2010/11/ 20101112-statement-on-pay-rise-at-foxconn.pdf>.

Tam, F 2010, 'Foxconn factories are labour camp', *South China Morning Post*, 11 October.

Quality through culture: Organisational development at New American Ice Cream

Diane Ruwhiu and Graham Elkin

New American Ice Cream began as an ice cream parlour catering to US armed forces personnel visiting Auckland (New Zealand) for rest and recreation during World War II. At the time of this case study, New American had grown under the influence of two young food technologists to have four production sites scattered across both main islands of New Zealand, including a large new state-of-the-art factory in Auckland, and had become jointly owned by a large company (Goodman Fielder) and an industry marketing body (the New Zealand Dairy Board).

New American was very much the minor player in a New Zealand ice cream industry dominated by the US food giant General Foods and its pervasive brand Tip Top. New American made and distributed a full range of ice cream products to corner shops, wholesalers and supermarkets. The company's production capacity, with the new Auckland factory in the mix, was at least double its sales volume. As a result, the business was unprofitable with a net loss of NZ$2 million on turnover of NZ$28 million. There were 300 employees from a variety of ethnicities, including New Zealand Europeans, New Zealand Maori and those from Pacific Island nations.

The chief executive sought help and advice from a friend who worked at a university business school on how to turn the company around. The management team met with the consultant and identified a number of problems. There was the lack of profitability; the quality of the ice cream; variable or poor service and distribution; and a workforce that was believed to be apathetic and unresponsive to suggestions from management – the latter being entirely of European origin. The production workforce comprised mainly first-, second- and third-generation immigrants from Pacific Island nations, with a well-established collaborative way of life. Despite a deep sense of care for individuals, the CEO was perceived as driven and impatient in the loss-making environment.

His immediate aim, as might be expected, was for the company to become more profitable. The CEO was persuaded to try to achieve this through a change in the organisational culture to one that was more inclusive of staff, emphasising multiple dimensions of quality and management styles. An early decision was made to involve all staff in all locations and at every level of the organisation in identifying just how they thought the business should to be managed and improved. This was at a time when quality circles and Japanese approaches to management were being adopted all over New Zealand. There was a growing feeling that employees on the shop floor knew a great deal more about problems and shortcomings in the operational side of the business than some of the executives, and that they had the ability to deal with product quality issues and deal with related organisational problems more effectively.

In this context, all employees were invited to participate in a quality improvement process, based on the 'Delphi' problem-solving approach, in which they would be asked to review and provide feedback on or modify a number of statements relating to the organisation. These would be summarised and the results presented to staff for reflection. They would then be invited to comment again, and modify or add comments to the results. The process would continue until no more substantial modifications were needed. It was envisaged that three of these cycles could be needed.

To start the process, the CEO and consultant worked on producing a list of qualities that would be desirable at New American, to improve the organisational culture and performance. Appendix 1 shows the qualities (listed in no particular order) and two scales. The first three-point scale indicates the current state of affairs at New American and the second indicates the way people would like things to be in the future. Space was also provided to write free-flowing statements. Appendix 2 presents the note to staff that explained the process.

In the first phase of the intervention, all employees were invited to complete the forms and the responses were scored. The second phase of the intervention was to summarise the responses and provide the results to all the staff. Employees were then asked to rank order the importance of the highly scored items (Appendix 3). These results were collated, and a 'Principles of New American' statement was drafted (Appendix 4). The production of this statement, drawn from the responses, initially was problematic. There were, for example, no references to the dimension of 'profit' and financial viability in the responses, which was of great importance to the management team. The notion of 'profitability' was then included in the key words and incorporated into the core statements.

The philosophy statement was widely discussed during the third phase of the intervention, in a series of group meetings, and then agreed upon. In meetings, public support was offered by the CEO and senior management team. Presentations by the consultant were made and training in groups commenced. The statement that captured the changed beliefs and philosophy was put up in every place of business, every workplace and every delivery van, and listed in every manual and office in the company. The implementation phase continued with training in group techniques and the setting up of quality groups to address problems. The groups were cross-functional and involved people of different status working together. The groups were tasked to identify quality problems and suggest how to fix them. The objective was to engage in activity that supported the new statement of culture by 'walking the talk'.

In terms of product improvement and quality, an example was changing the previous common practice of beginning to run new flavours through the ice cream-filling pipes without first cleaning the pipes of the previous flavour. This led to a number of boxes of ice cream that were somewhat mixed! Customers buying banana ice cream may get banana with a brown (chocolate) stain! Another example was the change of practice in packaging the ice cream. Previously the company's marketing staff had changed to the cardboard packaging for 2 litre ice cream products without consulting floor staff, who were fully aware of the problems that could arise – that is, when the cardboard packages had been filled and were stacked on pallets and blast frozen, ice cream oozed out of the lower packages. This had continued for months, with consequent product returns and poor product image. Now employees could have input into the decision-making on best practice in packaging.

In terms of relationship improvements, decisions by senior management could be questioned if they were detrimental to workplace relations. In the new environment, the cultural patterns of consultation and collaboration were encouraged. Employees now felt more empowered and able to deal with hierarchical decision-making. It was made clear by the CEO and the senior team that instructions from supervisors could be challenged if they were going to lead to a drop in quality. Then was more of an 'open door' approach, and individuals could refer matters to the CEO if there was a problem. Conspicuous success in promoting quality spread the quality culture to areas beyond manufacturing. This was done with no quality manuals or forms, but rather individual members of staff feeling that their contributions were valued and that they were empowered to refuse instructions that would have compromised the 'principles' document.

The major changes to workplace practice and improvements in workplace morale brought benefits. New American Ice Cream became the top ice cream supplier to the Auckland market in just 12 months, and broke even the following year. The shared values that were built changed New American from a place where only managers made decisions and workers carried out the instructions to one where everyone cared about outcomes and acted directly within the cultural framework. Many came to a basic understanding of who they were, why they were there and what their purpose was. It highlighted and spread the issues of responsibility for positive outcomes. New American became better at change, more focused on the desired culture and adept at effective problem-solving. The roles of status, task differentiation and decision-making became more fluid. Focus on outputs emerged as crucial.

Subsequently, Goodman Fielder Ltd and General Foods Ltd merged, becoming one company; this gave the new entity control of almost the entire ice cream industry. In the interest of competition, the NZ Commerce Commission insisted that the new company divest itself of one of its ice cream businesses, so New American was sold to a dairy farmers' cooperative. The cooperative was largely concerned with how much milk could be processed into ice cream, so the nature of New American changed radically, concentrating on bulk ice cream for supermarkets rather than the full range of manufacturing consumer products.

▪ Appendix 1: New American – what it is like now and what I would like it to be like

Please tick	New American NOW			New American SHOULD BE		
	Not	A Little	A Lot	Not	A Little	A Lot
Values:						
risk-taking						
consultation						
teamwork						
rigid procedure						
people relationships						

profitability	
growth	
quality of product	
quality of service	
productivity	
creativity	
rules	
Listens	
Communicates	
Gives personal scope	
Is: encouraging	
sociable	
structured	
pressurised	
ordered	
regulated	
free	
enjoyable	
challenging	
cautious	
trusting	
driving	
autocratic	
efficient	
a happy place	
approachable	
(add your own)	

■ Appendix 2: Working with New American: What do you want it to be like?

We are only going to succeed if we are all involved and committed to New American and to being successful. It is much easier to feel committed if we all have had a say in helping decide what sort of a company we are going to be and what it will be like to be a member of the New American team. (By 'what sort of company' we don't mean whether we should be a boat building company or a garage – but we mean the sort of things we care about and what matter to us at New American – like quality and teamwork, service, profit and caring for other members of the team.)

YOUR VIEW REALLY DOES MATTER!

The way we are all going to be involved is:

■ Phase 1

Everybody will be given the chance to complete the form attached. It has some ideas to get you started and spaces for all your own ideas. *YOU NEEDN'T SIGN IT* unless you are happy to talk about it.

■ Phase 2

We will collect all the forms and then take all the ideas and produce a new form which includes the new ideas people put in the first form and leave out the ones no one seemed to care about. We will give everybody a chance to comment again. This time we will ask them to put things in order of priority.

■ Phase 3

If, when we collect the second forms, most people have agreed about their view, we will try and turn the views into a one-page (or less) statement about the way we will be as a company. This will be called the Company Philosophy and will guide everything we do in the company. You will have a chance to comment on it.

■ Phase 4

MAKING NEW AMERICAN HOW WE WANT IT

The last phase will be to change the way we do things – our attitudes, beliefs, priorities and actions to make New American the way we want it to be. It will probably take us six months or even a year to change our way of doing things.

■ Appendix 3: Working with New American: What do you want it to be like? Phase 2

Thank you for taking part in Phase 1. The results have been very helpful. From the replies, we have produced a list of things which most people wish to see in terms of changes from how we are as a company to a new way of operation.

Please number the 12 most important changes you would like to see. Please start by putting (1) against the item which you would change if you can only change one thing; then put (2) against the second thing you would do if you can make two changes – and so on. If you have the patience we would be interested in you numbering every item. Please do at least 12.

More emphasis on:	efficiency
	communication
	creativity
	listening
	encouragement
	teamwork
	consultation
	trust
	people
	quality of service
	quality of product
	profitability
	personal scope
	productivity
Less:	risk-taking
	pressure
	dictatorial behaviour

Please return this form to: _____

▪ Appendix 4: New American corporate culture

As a result of the 'Delphi' questionnaire exercise about how most members of New American would like the company to be, the top six characteristics in rank order are:

1. (1) 2. Communication 3. (4) 4. Quality of product

5. (2) 6. Quality of service 7. (5) 8. Teamwork

9. (3) 10. Consultation 11. (6) 12. People

Two themes are dominant – people and quality. The third area of obvious interest – profit – is missing, but will come naturally with a culture that emphasises the six characteristics. These characteristics could be turned into a simple series of statements against which to measure any action or policy (i.e. does this decision or action reinforce or endanger our commitment to (1) to (6) above).

PRINCIPLES OF NEW AMERICAN

At New American we will
1. BUILD TEAMS and give individuals a valuable role
    we will (1) Communicate openly
    – talk and listen to each other
    – see everybody knows what is going on
    we will (2) Consult
    – welcome and encourage the sharing of opinions
2. SERVE THE CUSTOMER
    all of them
    – distributors
    – owner drivers
    – dairy (corner shops) owners
    – consumers
3. PRODUCE EXCELLENT QUALITY PRODUCTS
    – that we can be proud of
    – that our customers really want to buy

▇ Discussion questions

18.1   Why did New American Ice Cream need an 'external' person to initiate and lead the intervention to improve the company's performance?

18.2   Discuss the intervention strategy and its implementation.
a. To what extent does the intervention reflect the Beckhard (1969) model of an organisational development intervention?
b. Alternatively, select any other theoretical model of organisational development and intervention that you may have studied, and explain the extent of the synergy with the intervention used by New American Ice Cream

18.3   How do you account for the success of the company in making the changes that it did?

▇ References

Beckhard, R 1969, *Organizational development strategies and models*, Addison-Wesley, Reading, MA.

Okoli, C & Pawlowski, SD 2004, 'The Delphi method as a research tool: an example, design considerations and applications', *Information and Management*, no. 42, pp. 15–29.

Part IV

Operating in International Markets

19

Learning from experience: Purchasing industrial machinery from China

Sergio Biggemann and André M Everett

Andrew Protheroe, the general manager of Calder Stewart Roofing (a division of Calder Stewart Industries Limited, a New Zealand construction company), arrives at his office at nine o'clock on the morning of 23 September 2009. A few minutes later, Andrew is at his desk dealing with urgent correspondence when Linda Evans, his personal assistant, enters his office to remind him that Alan Stewart, the company's CEO, will be arriving soon for the meeting they have at ten o'clock. Andrew asks Linda to bring Robert Cash, the financial manager, to his office. Robert and Andrew have been working on a project to produce a new roofing profile (the shape that is given to metal sheets to be used in roofing), which Calder Stewart Roofing plans to launch on the market in the next few months. Demand estimates look promising enough to justify investing in new bending machines. However, both acquisition and operation costs vary depending on the machines' origin. Andrew is confident about the figures (see Table 19.1), but he wants to review them with Robert once again before the meeting commences. The company is considering the acquisition of three additional plate-bending machines. Andrew has to decide whether sourcing from a Chinese supplier instead of from one of its traditional suppliers in Germany, Switzerland, the United States, New Zealand or Australia is best. These machines form metal sheets used for roofs. Buying a new machine would normally not be a difficult decision, but the company experienced several problems in the acquisition of a new machine from the same Chinese supplier two years ago, and the issues regarding this purchase are still fresh in the minds of managers at Calder Stewart. Andrew knows that there are more than just 'cost calculations' that weigh on the final decision.

■ The company

Founders Lance Calder and Bruce Stewart began their company in 1955 with one car, a trailer, £25 (NZ$50) and aspirations for growth. During the next two decades, they focused on building their company, which they called 'Calder Stewart'. It became known as an innovator with quality products, particularly in terms of the use of steel in constructing farm buildings. When Lance Calder unexpectedly passed away in 1974, management control rested with the Stewart family, and continues to do so. The four sons of Bruce Stewart – Peter, Alan, Andrew and Donald – jointly run the company, as well as being active in daily operations. The two eldest sons serve as managing directors.

Unlike many other successful firms originating in small towns, which tend to move their national offices to large cities, Calder Stewart is thoroughly grounded in Milton, a small town 50 kilometres south of Dunedin on New Zealand's South Island, retaining its home base in this 2000-person township throughout the course of nationwide expansion over 50 years. The company has gained a respected position in the industry, with customers generally preferring its products and services to other providers of roofing. The company aims to achieve the highest quality standards and the lowest level of materials wastage by offering to the industry extremely low variation in its product dimensions.

Table 19.1: Data for demand and cost – new profiles	
Demand forecast kg/year	180 000
Demand growth rate	10.00%
Machine purchasing cost	
China	$128 000
Germany	$300 000
Net output kg/hr	150.00
Time calculation values	
Hours/day	8
Days/week	5
Weeks/month	4
Months/year	12
Depreciation time (years)	5
Delivery time (weeks)	
China	6
Germany	8
Efficiency of use of material	
Chinese machine	85%
German machine	90%
Coil cost $/kg	1.80
Operation costs $/kg produced	0.70
Sales price after taxes $/kg	3.10

Most customers of Calder Stewart are large building companies that work under tight schedules. Hence Calder Stewart guarantees its customers that roofing materials will be at the site precisely on the day requested. Laying the roof on a large building requires expensive cranes and specialised people on site; thus plates, beams, fittings and all other elements required for roofing need to be delivered on time. At the same time, as they are bulky items, customers do not want them in advance because they normally have no spare storage place, and tasks scheduled for action before putting on the roof could be disrupted.

Andrew Protheroe, an experienced and well-trained manager, with a Master of Science (Engineering) degree, was appointed general manager five years ago. Since then, he has led the company to an even stronger position by developing manufacturing materials appropriate for residential and commercial construction in Invercargill and Christchurch. Andrew reports to Allan Stewart (the grandson of Bruce Stewart), who looks after the interests of the family in the business. Allan tends to leave Andrew free to manage the business, but when a major capital expenditure proposal arrived a few weeks ago, designating the potential supplier from which a machine was purchased two years earlier, it drew his attention. Allan requested more information from Andrew and decided to have a meeting to make sure the right decision would be made in relation to this new investment.

■ The Milton Penitentiary

The case of the Milton Penitentiary is important because it tells the story of Calder Stewart's previous experience with the Chinese supplier, which currently is still influencing the company's decision-making process to decide on the most suitable and reliable source of machinery for its new project. In 2006, the New Zealand government decided to build a new prison in Milton. The project attracted the interest of many and, following protracted controversy, it was finally ready for tender. Milton residents were concerned about the security issues accompanying a jail, and were largely opposed to the project. However, they were also interested in the positive externalities of having a large government facility in the town. Businesses anticipated that demand for goods and services would increase, not only in the construction phase, but also once the prison commenced operation. To deal with people's concerns, the government agreed to increase the safety requirements of the jail. However, this decision affected the prison's design.

Calder Stewart Roofing was the most likely supplier of roofing materials for this project, as it was one of the few companies in New Zealand with the capability to comply with the new design requirements caused by the security improvements. The new design had implications for the type of steel profiles the roof was going to require and, although this would bring challenges for Calder Stewart, the company was pleased to have the opportunity to secure the project for the company.

The project ultimately was awarded to a group of four different contractors, with the roof going to Calder Stewart Roofing, and requiring close coordination among the contractors to keep the project on schedule. Calder Stewart Roofing knew that complying with the new design requirement meant buying a new plate-bending machine capable of profiling the steel accordingly. It had approached its traditional suppliers of machinery in Germany and found no problems in receiving the machine on time. Thus the company was confident about fulfilling its commitment to the project, and doing so on time. It had no way of knowing how things would change, or of anticipating the problems it was about to face.

The four companies involved in the project were confident that they could meet the deadline set for completion of the project. They knew their decision would place significant stress on their suppliers, but were counting on their experience in managing stringent deadlines and accommodating challenges. Calder Stewart Roofing was about to face its first challenge. To the company's surprise, when it wanted to confirm the purchase order for the new machine with the German manufacturer, the supplier indicated that the original deadline was impossible to meet, partly because it could not deliver on the shorter lead time, and partly because demands from the global market had increased. Everyone appeared to be building something! Since its last communication with Calder Stewart, the supplier had received several new orders to manufacture plate-bending machines, and therefore was completely booked for the next several months. The German manufacturer sales manager commented:

> This is an extraordinary situation. In my 25 years in the industry, I haven't ever seen so many customers buying at the same time. It looks like developers have lost their mind.

Calder Stewart's management could understand the situation as the company also was trying to cope with the demand from several customers who were building at a feverish pace. However, the Milton Penitentiary project was worth $5 million, more than 10 per cent of the company's annual revenue, and Calder Stewart could not afford to lose this project. The company had to act quickly.

■ Finding an alternative supplier

Andrew reacted to the German supplier's blunt news by immediately contacting alternative suppliers in Switzerland, the United States, Australia and New Zealand with whom Calder Stewart had worked in the past; unfortunately, however, their answers were no different. Calder Stewart rapidly realised that sourcing a new machine on time to meet the project's deadline – considering the quality of the equipment it was used to buying – was going to be almost impossible. Desperation started to mount as the options continued to reduce. Aware of the high importance of this project, Andrew began to think outside the square. For the first time in his professional life, he included China in the equation of potential suppliers.

Like almost everybody else in the world, Calder Stewart was eager to take advantage of the China phenomenon. China's economic reforms, initiated in the 1970s, had created the conditions for a level of economic development never experienced before, having converted the rural-based economy into a highly industrialised country. It was no longer a secret that China was capable of manufacturing the most complex electronic devices at prices that it was impossible for most competing countries to match. However, Calder Stewart had sourced steel coil from China in the past and concluded that the low quality of the product – which in principle was 30 per cent cheaper than the price of the traditional supplier in New Zealand – potentially caused large amounts of wasted material, quickly eating away at the savings and ultimately resulting in a more expensive finished product. Besides, Andrew knew that it was one thing to establish a factory for manufacturing iPods in China, but something completely different to buy industrial machinery from an unknown and untested Chinese manufacturer.

Nevertheless, desperate situations require desperate measures. Time was running out, and so the China option became stronger. A quick search on Alibaba.com delivered 62 194 hits for 'roll forming machine for steel', 6680 of them being specifically for 'bending machines'. Andrew knew that identifying the right supplier was an almost impossible task. However, he had heard about a smaller roofer named Max Brough up on North Island who had bought a plate-bending machine from China.

Even though Calder Stewart's quality standards were significantly more stringent, Andrew began to toy with the possibility of approaching Max.

Andrew met with Alan (the CEO) and Robert (the financial manager), and they concluded that the only option available to the company if it were to comply with the Milton contract's tight deadlines would be finding a manufacturer in China capable of delivering the machinery in six weeks (the German manufacturer would normally require 12 weeks, but under the current circumstances was not even prepared to consider a lead time of 16 weeks). Going to China was the last resort, and there were still issues that would need to be resolved. In Andrew's eyes, Calder Stewart had two options: to hire Max to help them with the purchase in China and leverage his experience to find the right supplier; or simply choose one of the potential suppliers from the 6680 he had encountered on the internet. After some discussion, it was decided to approach Max and ask for his help in buying the machine from China.

Max's involvement paved the way to approach the right Chinese supplier. Max had experience and knew a supplier in China from whom he had purchased in the past, and he gave Calder Stewart his assurances about the supplier's reliability. The supplier had produced several machines for the local market; among its customers was the builder of the Shanghai Airport, which Andrew estimated had used ten times the amount of steel that Milton's prison would need. Another positive point about this supplier was that it was supplying Toyota with windscreen washer pumps, which created the expectation of a supplier with quality assurance capabilities. Max was hired as purchasing agent and liaison between Calder Stewart and the Chinese supplier. His job consisted of placing the order and following it up to its successful completion. In addition to knowing the right supplier, Max was deemed to be more knowledgeable about Chinese culture, so he was expected to be better suited to manage the relationship with the Chinese supplier. Max would be paid a fixed amount for his services to Calder Stewart. The order for a new plate-bending machine was confirmed. The NZ$128 000 price was less than 50 per cent of the NZ$300 000 price tag of the traditional German supplier, and promised delivery time was six weeks. What a deal!

■ Five weeks later

Andrew and Alan were feeling rather nervous about the order, and therefore decided to join Max in China to see how the order was progressing. In China, they were warmly received by the company's sales manager (who could speak English) and the owner (who could not). The supplier thought that its customers were just going to visit, have a meal, sign off on the deal and go home. They did not realise that Andrew, Alan and Max were actually going to check the machine closely. When Andrew put on some overalls and said, 'Look, I'm going to check this dimensionally', the suppliers were horrified. They did not want Andrew on the shop floor. Andrew was also horrified when he saw the machine still in pieces on the shop floor. However, the Chinese sales manager kept promising that they would deliver on time. After a few days in China, the following conversation was recorded:

Andrew:	Will the machine be ready by Friday for shipping?
Chinese Sales Manager:	Yes, it will.
Andrew:	It can't be because it's still in a million pieces.
Chinese Sales Manager:	When do you need it by?
Andrew:	Well, look, if you can't make it this Friday ... we really have to get it on the water, because we start production in a month or six weeks. If you can't, can it be the following Friday?
Chinese Sales Manager:	Yes.
Andrew:	Well, which date is it?
Chinese Sales Manager:	Which one do you need?
Andrew:	Well I need it by this Friday, but you're not going to do it ...

The conversation continued like this until Andrew realised that what the Chinese manager wanted was to please his customer, and would say what he wanted to hear. Getting an honest answer was very, very difficult. Max was then faced with the question of what the *real* lead time was going to be for the delivery of the machinery and how he should advise Andrew without inflaming the situation. He quietly commented that 'the delivery dates with products from China are fluid'. Andrew ignored Max's liaison role and, in desperation and almost shouting at the owner of the company while they were still on the factory floor, said: 'Look, we must be on the water, if not this Friday, then the following Friday!' The next day, three times the number of people were working on the machine.

After this meeting, Andrew was so concerned that he decided to stay for as long as necessary. By spending two weeks on the shop floor, Andrew uncovered a number of quality issues that had not been visible on the surface. One issue was the wiring, as the workers used any kind of wiring. Andrew made them rewire it with the appropriate colours. He said: 'Look, you've got a colour-coded wiring diagram. You guys on the shop floor just don't follow it.' Then he checked the rims and noted that one of them was about 10 millimetres higher than the rest. The whole roof would be in jeopardy: 'That's no good. You're going to have to take them all off. Make new profiles, get them chromed, and re-fit them.' His close scrutiny of the machine revealed more problems, such as inappropriate quality of the metals that were supposed to be used in the machine, the bearings, bushes, shafts, hard-faced rollers and guillotine blades. So Andrew stayed for two weeks on the shop floor, fixing problems with the supplier's engineers until the machine was ready for shipment.

Andrew recognised that the supplier's engineers were competent; they knew their jobs and they understood the principles behind the machine's operations. But he felt that they were not used to paying sufficient attention to detail while putting everything together.

Machine arrival

When the machine arrived in New Zealand, new problems emerged. First, all the chroming that was supposed to protect the surfaces had fallen off. As the machine passed through the tropics in a container on its way to New Zealand, it collected condensation, so several parts were rusty. Andrew noted: 'We had to get the whole thing shot blasted and re-chromed and other parts repainted.' When the machine started to operate, the bearings that the Chinese supplied for the shafts started to collapse. At first, Calder Stewart did not realise that the bearings had collapsed, so the company wound up with thousands of dollars of material scrap in the form of unusable bent roofing sheets. The company thought it was a material issue, as everything appeared to be working well – until it marked every shaft to see whether the shaft ends were turning and discovered that one of them was not. The bearing housing had collapsed and jammed. As Calder Stewart could not afford unexpected breakdowns, it decided to change the whole 128 bearings, at a cost of around NZ$50 000.

After all the changes and amendments, including synchronising the machine's motors with the appropriate software (a task that should have been completed in the factory), the initial cost of around NZ$128 000 – which, compared with the NZ$300 000 that traditional suppliers would charge, was initially very attractive – ended up being around NZ$220 000, which was not as cheap as expected. Nevertheless, the machine was able to produce quality steel profiles and Calder Stewart was able to deliver the required roofing materials with no significant delays.

▪ Buying new machines

In retrospect, Andrew reflected on all the things that had gone wrong, only to realise that even though the story had a happy ending, it could have been much worse. Now he has an opportunity to undertake a new project for Calder Stewart, and is faced with the option of dealing with the Chinese supplier or going back to the German one. After his experience of doing business with the Chinese company, he thinks he is better prepared to make the right decision. Besides, he is not facing the same time pressures that he had with the Milton Penitentiary project. Looking at the figures that Robert submitted (see Table 19.1), Andrew can see the cost advantage that buying new machines from China could bring to the company. However, he knows that some of those figures may change. He meets Allan in the corridor; with no prior warning, Allan asks: 'Have you decided where we are going to bring the new equipment from?'

▪ Discussion questions

19.1 Should Calder Stewart buy the machinery from the Chinese supplier again? Why?

19.2 How would your decision change, if you knew in advance that the same kind of problems would occur with this new order?

19.3 If the best source for the machinery was China, should Calder Stewart continue using the services of Max?

19.4   What have both Calder Stewart and the Chinese supplier learnt that could help
       them to avoid making the same type of mistakes in the acquisition or sale of
       such large custom-made goods?

■ Reference

Calder Stewart 2011, website, viewed 20 November 2012, <http://www.calderstewart.co.nz/index.php?history>.

Country of origin labelling and the New Zealand seafood industry

Glenn Simmons, Christina Stringer and Eugene Rees

20

The news that Thomas Fishbone, the CEO of OceanFresh,[1] one of New Zealand's largest seafood companies, had been dreading could not have come at a worse time. The Ministry of Agriculture and Forestry (MAF)[2] had approved the importing of Vietnamese farmed fish (aquaculture)[3] for sale on the domestic market. Even more worrying for Thomas was that MAF might soon approve the importation of Chinese farmed fish as part of New Zealand's obligation under the recently signed Free Trade Agreement with China. Slumping back into his chair, Thomas thought about the impact of even more imported farmed fish on the domestic market. It was difficult to compete when this fish was sold for less than half the price of locally caught seafood. Price-conscious consumers could not tell the difference between locally caught fish and farmed fish. An increase in imports of cheap farmed fish would further stress the company's cash flow.

During the past year, OceanFresh had experienced a 10 per cent drop in sales, which impacted on already declining margins and a stressed balance sheet. The company had little room to move in the face of this new affront to its competitiveness. Furthermore, there was no immediate sign of improvement on the horizon. A second affront facing the company was the increasing move by OceanFresh's competitors to process New Zealand-caught fish offshore. Increasingly, their competitors were shipping fish to be processed in developing countries in Asia, to take advantage of lower production costs. The processed fish was then exported to European and American markets, and even back to New Zealand.

Thomas, a veteran of 20 years in the industry, cast his mind back to the time when Australia first imported cheap Asian farmed fish. The impact on OceanFresh was devastating, as export of the popular New Zealand hoki fish to Australia fell by a massive 90 per cent (FIS 2009a). Despite being fiercely patriotic, Australian consumers could not tell the difference between cheap imported fish and higher quality Australian and New Zealand fish. For many consumers, only price mattered. OceanFresh did eventually claw back much of its market share, but only after savage price cuts and the adoption of country of origin labelling (CoOL)[4] by Australia[5] in 2004.

Thomas looked forward to CoOL's introduction in New Zealand. However, the New Zealand seafood industry, together with other primary industries, convinced the government to refrain from following Australia's move to adopt CoOL. Their key argument was that CoOL was just a costly label for which consumers were unwilling to pay. Thomas could not comprehend why the seafood industry did not understand that CoOL was more than a label. Consumers had a right to know where their food came from, and CoOL would ensure that this information was made available to them. Moreover, for many countries CoOL was viewed as a valuable brand – instantly recognisable and respected around the world. Thomas did not consider New Zealand fish to be just another undifferentiated commodity – or was it?

Thomas was very concerned that once the Chinese fisheries industry – the world's largest, both in terms of aquaculture and reprocessing – gained a foothold in the local market, no company would be able to compete against the inevitable flood of cheap fish. Thomas wondered about the irony of it all – New Zealand-caught fish processed in China for far-away markets, while Asian-farmed fish became the fish of choice domestically. This could be the straw that finally forced not just OceanFresh, but the entire industry, against the wall.

Thomas had a good reason to be worried. In less than an hour, he had to face yet another senior management team meeting. The team would be looking to him for answers about the threat to their domestic market by the importation of Asian-farmed fish. What was he going to say?

Opportunity or threat? Asian aquaculture production

According to the Food and Agriculture Organization (FAO 2011), in 2009 total global seafood trade was estimated at almost US$190 billion (145 million tonnes). Of this, aquaculture accounted for 46 per cent. Since 1970, aquaculture has achieved an average annual growth rate of 6.6 percent and is expected to surpass wild capture[6] fisheries production in the future (2011). Asia supplies 89 per cent of aquaculture in terms of quantity and 79 per cent in terms of value. Increasingly, the most important globally traded whitefish are low-value farmed freshwater species such as carp, tilapia, basa and pangasius catfish, which are mostly farmed in China and Vietnam. China accounts for 62 per cent by quantity and 51 per cent by value of the world's total aquaculture production. Between 1970 and 2008, China's aquaculture production achieved an annual average growth rate of 10.4 per cent (2011).

However, despite China's achievements in the aquaculture sector, the Chinese fishery presents a diverse range of problems, including the use of unapproved drugs and unsafe chemicals during production (USDA 2008). For example, melamine may be used illegally to increase the protein content of fish. Laboratory studies of melamine-fed catfish, trout, tilapia and salmon by the US Food and Drug Administration's (FDA) Animal Drugs Research Centre found that imported fish had melamine concentrations of up to 200 parts per million. This is 80 times the maximum permitted amount (Lee & Hsu 2008). Moreover, in a sampling of imported Chinese seafood from October 2006 to May 2007, the US FDA found residues of unapproved drugs.

In 2010, Vietnam exported 659 000 metric tonnes of farmed pangasius to 140 countries. The exports were valued at US$1.43 billion and reflected an increase of 7.4 per cent in volume terms from 2009 (Vietnam Association of Seafood Exporters and Producers 2011). The FAO (2011) reports that an increase in imports of pangasius in many countries is leading to a displacement of higher priced locally farmed pangasius. According to the Vietnam Association of Seafood Exporters and Producers (2011), the quality of Vietnam's pangasius is comparable to expensive white fish, and can be found not only in fast food outlets, but also on the menus at expensive restaurants. While Asian-farmed fish is seen to be a strong competitor to European whitefish, it is not regarded as being of the same quality, and there are concerns that imported pangasius will 'tarnish' the image of locally farmed fish.

According to Neville (2009), 'the World Wildlife Fund has concerns about the use of antibiotics and chemicals in basa farms. The potential presence of a toxic chemical called malachite green is a particular worry.' Russia has at times banned the import of pangasius from Vietnam. More recently, Alabama in the United States not only banned the sale of pangasius from Vietnam, but also from Indonesia, Thailand, Cambodia and China, because of positive tests for antibiotic fluoroquinolones. Nevertheless, aquaculture production is likely to continue to grow due to increasing demand for low-cost fish that are not dependent on expensive fish-feed from wild fisheries. Aquaculture supply is more predictable and manageable than wild-capture fisheries.

The signing of the Association of Southeast Asian Nations (ASEAN), Australia and New Zealand free trade agreement in 2010 paved the way for Vietnamese companies to export fish and fishery products to New Zealand. As Vietnam enjoys a low-cost business structure, its seafood is expected to be very competitively priced. New Zealand's MAF Biosecurity said that 'a scientific risk analysis found the fish [basa] was safe to import' (Neville 2009). However, a key concern for Thomas is that Vietnamese pangasius, when filleted, can easily be mistaken for wild-caught snapper or terakihi, two key domestic species (FIS 2009b; Neville 2009). In addition, the initial impact on the local industry was such that local fishermen were 'told to temporarily stop fishing domestic species as companies are struggling to sell New Zealand fish' (McCorkindale 2010). This would further compound problems for OceanFresh, but would not affect the company's competitors as much, as they were somewhat shielded by the cost benefits of processing their wild catches in lower-cost Asian countries.

Wild-capture processing in developing countries

In recent years, developed countries such as New Zealand increasingly have outsourced the post-harvest processing of fish to developing countries (Stringer, Simmons & Rees 2011). Despite its competitors doing so, OceanFresh remained committed to processing in New Zealand. According to the FAO (2011), 80 per cent of the world's production of fish and fishery products occurred in developing countries in 2008, with a clear trend towards more value-added processing occurring in these countries. Raw material is caught, frozen and exported to a developing country, where the product is thawed, reprocessed and refrozen for re-export. China has emerged as the key player in the post-harvest processing sector and, as the world's largest exporter of seafood, enjoys an extensive reprocessing trade. This is due to its perceived competitive advantage in terms of low-cost labour and processing skills. The shift in production is attracting attention in many source countries, as increasingly consumers and even industry are expressing disquiet about the value-added reprocessing of fish in China (*Sunday Mirror* 2008; *Campbell Live* 2008).

According to the Möller (2007), the Chinese processing sector works on extremely tight margins, and thus it is difficult to see how it can be profitable, given high raw material prices. Attaining higher yields in processing is a major contributing factor for outsourcing, but this has raised questions about the excessive use of additives, such as sodiumtripolyphosphate (STPP). Seafood may be soaked in chemicals such as STPP in order to maintain taste and freshness. By soaking seafood in STPP overnight, the weight of the final product can be increased to artificially increase recovery rates. Some Chinese processors using this method claim recovery rates as high as 80 to 100 per cent (Möller 2007). In 2006, the European Union (EU) issued warnings and the China Inspection and Quarantine (CIQ) Bureau subsequently implemented corrective actions, including a ban on the use of STPP in products for the EU.

FDA reports of carcinogens, pesticides, bacteria, drugs and heavy metals in imported foods have alerted US consumers about the risks of sourcing food globally, especially from China. Recent incidents have caused concern and raised public awareness about the potential perils of the global food supply. Increasingly, more consumers and food processors are demanding tighter food safety regulations (Roth et al. 2008), which is forcing China to take action. According to China's state-run Xinhua News Agency, boric acid, lye and formaldehyde (used to improve seafood appearance), and carbon monoxide, are now listed as illegal substances in seafood processing. Given the importance of China to the global food chain, chain-of-custody certification of processing facilities and audit processes are crucial for food safety. Traceability problems are compounded by the fact that once seafood is reprocessed in China, the country of origin changes to China unless the product is returned to the original exporting company.

Food safety and hygiene problems are also present in the Vietnamese industry. Almost 1500 cases of seafood poisoning occurred between 2001 and 2007, from which nearly 500 people died. Most incidents were caused by a lack of awareness and knowledge about food hygiene by workers. Investigations carried out at several seafood processing facilities revealed some common factors – almost all female workers wear rings, bracelets and have long nails. Lax regulations, a lack of environmental hygiene, dirty processing equipment and poor storage conditions are also major contributing factors. In addition, misrepresentation of product expiry dates, inappropriate packaging, and unlicensed or excessive use of additives are common features among Vietnamese seafood processors (Ministry of Foreign Affairs of Denmark 2009).

During the last 15 years, there has been a substantial increase in the amount of fish exported from New Zealand to China for further value-added processing (Stringer, Simmons & Rees 2011). Value-added products are then exported to New Zealand, as well as to large fast food companies and distributors in developed countries – particularly in Europe, the United States and Japan. This has far-reaching implications for the New Zealand seafood industry, and in particular for the 'Product of New Zealand' brand. A globalised fisheries value chain means that seafood traceability and food safety issues frequently transcend international borders. This was of major concern to Thomas, who in response implemented traceability systems at OceanFresh. Ultimately, though, Thomas believed that only CoOL would truly isolate OceanFresh from any negative fallout from competitors' global value chains.

Importance of country of origin labelling

Increasing concerns about traceability and food safety issues have resulted in the simultaneous developments of regulatory frameworks at the global, regional and national levels by both the public and private sectors. In the late 1990s, concerns about food security and the potential for economic loss led the Food and Agricultural Organization's (FAO) Codex Alimentarius Commission[7] to focus on certification and labelling initiatives. This included the implementation of regulations pertaining to CoOL. At the same time that the FAO was focusing on CoOL, the EU became concerned about food safety due to the Bovine Spongiform Encephalopathy (BSE) (more commonly known as mad cow disease) outbreak, and subsequently introduced CoOL and ingredient regulations. In the early 2000s, the EU built on the FAO's work, by focusing on traceability-related issues and implementing additional policies aimed at improving transparency along the seafood supply chain as well as combating illegal, unregulated and unreported (IUU) fishing. In 2002, the US Congress introduced the *Bio-Terrorism Act* due to security concerns about their food supply chain. CoOL, required as part of the Act, necessitates retailers to identify the country of origin.

The Codex Alimentarius Commission requires the country of origin of all food products to be identified, except that 'when a food undergoes processing in a second country which changes its nature, the country in which the processing is performed shall be considered to be the country of origin for the purposes of labelling' (FAO, 1985). For example, one-quarter of tins of canned tuna are labelled with Thailand as the country of origin (the processing country), even though the tuna are caught elsewhere (Jacquet & Pauly 2008). Given that FAO requirements change the country of origin for processed fish, some nations adopt their own seafood labelling policies.

Food product labels have an important influence on buying behaviour. Consumers in developed countries increasingly are concerned about food safety, and are demanding more detailed labelling (Knight, Holdsworth & Mather 2007). In Germany and Italy, perceptions about the country of origin play an important role in determining the quality of seafood, particularly with regard to trust in production methods, absence of additives, contamination and hygiene. Jaffry et al. (2004) found labels that contained information about sustainability, quality, origin and production methods had a significant positive influence on consumer choice. Roheim (2008) contends that CoOL legislation would provide consumers with vital information to make more informed choices.

Globalisation has also resulted in CoOL becoming an important competitive differentiator (Dinnie 2004). Consumers increasingly are valuing CoOL, as it embodies important product attribute information – such as perceived health risks and quality (Knight, Holdsworth & Mather 2007). Consumers also use perceptions about a country to evaluate its products. One New Zealand study (Knight, Holdsworth & Mather 2007), looked at the importance of country of origin for European food distributors. They found that a country's image had a clear impact on trust in a food product, which was the essential element necessary for buyers to determine quality and value. Importantly, trust also reinforced a desire to buy. The study also revealed that food safety was the overriding consideration for consumers, and a key aspect of trust is the ability to trace products back to the original producer. Hence the country of origin serves as a proxy for trust, and in this respect New Zealand food products are viewed as being more trustworthy than products from other nations. While price – especially in price-sensitive markets – plays a crucial role, it is moderated by quality, which in turn is moderated by trust, particularly in respect of the original producer and any intermediaries along the value chain.

The CoOL debate in New Zealand

For OceanFresh, the CoOL debate has been frustrating. All developed nations with which New Zealand trades, such as the United States, EU, Australia and Japan, have mandatory CoOL legislation for seafood. Following an extensive review of CoOL in 2005, the New Zealand government decided not to join Australia in making CoOL compulsory. Four years later, however, there was optimism when New Zealand agreed to work with Australia on a comprehensive review of food labelling laws and policy. In a submission to the Food Labelling Review Secretariat in March 2010, the New Zealand Seafood Industry Council said: 'Our preference remains that country of origin labelling should not be mandatory' (New Zealand Review of Food Labelling Law and Policy 2010). At the same time, the New Zealand government's submission also supported continuation of the existing voluntary CoOL regime.

Opposition by the business community in New Zealand has been strongly against mandatory CoOL, due to perceived economic costs. The government estimated that the cost of implementing CoOL would be in the vicinity of NZ$60 million a year, and that this cost would most likely be passed on to consumers. Furthermore, New Zealand prides itself on having an open economy, and CoOL is considered by many to be a non-tariff barrier. Even so, consumers have often complained that food manufacturers do not provide them with enough information on food product labels. A recent New Zealand study by Impact PR found that 53 per cent of consumers believe food manufacturers provide insufficient information on their labels. A majority of consumers particularly want CoOL, and it is seen as very important to those aged over 45 (Kloeten 2011). Thomas could not agree more with Fleur Revell, the study's managing director, who stated that 'there is a considerable gap between consumers needs for information at the point of purchase and what is being provided currently on product'.

At present, international food processing companies selling products in New Zealand can charge a premium for brands that are considered by many New Zealand customers to be 'home grown'. Research undertaken by Research International in 2007 suggests that at least 80 per cent of New Zealanders will buy products made in New Zealand over foreign-produced products. But not all consumers are aware that the 'Made in New Zealand' statement does not mean that the product has been produced entirely in New Zealand. It only means the product was put together in New Zealand. Nevertheless, there is widespread consumer interest for New Zealand to make CoOL mandatory. If CoOL were implemented, it would require a change to the Food Standards Code, which in turn would necessitate a transition period.

The senior management team meeting

As Thomas entered the boardroom, he noted the sombre mood, and wondered whether his Senior Management Team had already got wind of the news. Sure enough, he spotted a MAF Biosecurity press release in front of each manager. Herbert Fritter, the accountant for the past decade, looked up as Thomas took his seat: 'Well, Thomas, history has caught us up after all, but this is not Australia. What do you propose we should do this time?'

As Thomas paused for thought, he was struck by an idea – but first he needed to hear what his managers had to say. He told them that OceanFresh was facing two key dilemmas: first, the impact of imported pangasius on the domestic market; and second, customer perceptions towards New Zealand fish processed in Asia and sold not only back into the domestic market but also internationally. Both had serious implications for the company's competitiveness.

Thomas asked the senior managers to first share their views about the looming increase in Vietnamese and potentially Chinese imports and then about customer perceptions of fish caught in New Zealand, but processed in China. The New Zealand Country Manager responded:

> We're competing with these farmed fish because simply the consumer doesn't differentiate and [is] not prepared to pay the higher prices. Once you put some batter on it and it becomes a Friday night fish and chips, do you know any different? And providing it's white and doesn't smell and is flaky . . . even top restaurants in Sydney now sell this Vietnamese fish.'

The mood remained sombre as they contemplated how to retain market share in an increasingly competitive market largely dominated by price-conscious consumers. Horace Jones, the recently promoted New Zealand Marketing Manager, remarked that customer perceptions about New Zealand-caught fish processed in China were changing:

> Any seafood product from New Zealand processed in China will be marked as a product of China and in the beginning there was some impact, but China production is now better than in New Zealand, so now consumers focus more on where the fish comes from, not where it was processed.

For many international buyers, while quality is a major factor, price is the most important issue. Additionally, OceanFresh's China Manager commented:

> The process could just about be identical, as far as the end-product's concerned, but because it's Chinese processed it has to be cheaper. New Zealand-processed product or Chinese-processed – effectively the same product. Which one do customers want? Some will continue to buy the New Zealand-processed product because they're their clientele, whatever the reason, they're used to it, it works for them and they don't want to change. Others will simply die for the cheaper product.

He further argued that CoOL would have little impact, as many buyers saw fish from New Zealand as merely an intermediate commodity:

> Raw materials have always been sold out of New Zealand. It's not a 'Product of New Zealand' brand that ends up in substantial re-processors in mainland China where it's turned into fish fingers, it's whoever's brand is on the final product. Your brand worth is how your customers value you as a supplier of that fish. If we produce a better, consistent quality of product for customers in Europe, they may value our hoki quality as a better purchasing option for them than a competitor. But they're not necessarily valuing the fish as coming from New Zealand.

However, OceanFresh's International Marketing Manager argued back that customers don't necessarily want products from China. There were those who were willing to pay more if it was 100 per cent produced and processed in New Zealand. Surely CoOL was an advantage?

> Because at the end of the day anything processed in New Zealand is achieving a premium. United States supermarkets will buy all of the hoki processed in New Zealand but won't touch orange roughy as it is processed in China.

This was supported by the Vice President of Corporate Sales, who shared what premium international foodservice buyers were saying:

> Price is always an issue, but quality is number one, price number two. Having a story around the product is very important. Knowing about where a product comes from is very important for the story. They [premium foodservice buyers] like to meet the producer and understand about the area from which it comes from. They want authentic products at a conscientious price.

As Thomas pondered these comments, he reflected on two important, but contrasting views pertaining to importing of farmed fish. Andrew McKenzie, Chief Executive of the New Zealand Food Safety Authority said 'New Zealand's reputation for high quality seafood is at risk' (McKenzie 2009). Conversely, the General Manager of the New Zealand Seafood Industry Council was of the opinion that there were no health and safety issues associated with Asian-farmed basa (*Capital Times* 2009).

■ Discussion questions

20.1   Why is CoOL considered to be of importance in the food industry?

20.2   What actions should Thomas take to influence and bring about change to the industry's opposition to CoOL?

20.3   Outline the steps that Thomas could take to enhance market perceptions of New Zealand-caught and processed seafood. What would be the impact of such steps?

20.4   Given that many Asian seafood companies enjoy significant cost advantages, what else can Thomas do to improve OceanFresh's competitiveness?

▓ Notes

1   While this is a research based case, OceanFresh is a fictional company.
2   In 2011, the Ministry of Agriculture and Forestry was merged with the Ministry of Fisheries and the New Zealand Food Safety Authority, and is now known as the Ministry of Primary Industries.
3   Aquaculture is the aquatic farming of species such as fish, shellfish and plants. The term 'aquaculture' refers to the cultivation of both marine and freshwater species, which can be land- or sea-based production.
4   Broadly defined as a label on the food indicating the country where the food originated or from which it was imported. Where food is processed in a second country, the second country is considered the country of origin.
5   CoOL was introduced by Food Standards Australia New Zealand (FSANZ), an independent Australian government statutory agency that develops and sets food standards for Australia and New Zealand.
6   Wild-capture fish are wild fish caught in the ocean as opposed to fish that are commercially farmed.
7   The Codex Alimentarius Commission was established by the FAO and World Health Organization (WHO) to develop food standards.

▓ References

Campbell Live 2008, 'Mmmm New Zealand fish, processed in China?', viewed 20 October 2009, <http://www.tv3.co.nz>.

Capital Times 2009, 'Something fishy', viewed 21 February 2011, <http://www.capitaltimes. co.nz/article/2511/Somethingfishy.html>.

Dinnie, K 2004, Country-of-origin 1965–2004: a literature review, *Journal of Customer Behaviour*, vol. 3, no. 2, pp. 165–213.

FAO (1985), 'Codex general standard for the labelling of prepackaged foods', in CODEX STAN 1985 (Rev. 1–1991)[1], viewed 20 March 2009, <http://www.fao.org/docrep/005/Y2770E/ y2770e02.htm>.

FIS 2009a, 'EU adds 30 firms to exporters list', viewed 20 February 2013, <http://fis.com/fis/ worldnews/worldnews.asp?l=e&ndb=1&id=32495≥.

——2009b, 'Fishers fear industry collapse due to Vietnamese catfish imports', viewed 18 May 2009, <http://fis.com/fis/worldnews/worldnews.asp?monthyear=&day=15&id=32372&l=e& special=0&ndb=0.

——2011, *The state of world fisheries and aquaculture – 2010*, FAO, Rome.

Jacquet, J & Pauly, D 2008, 'Trade secrets: renaming and mislabelling of seafood', *Marine Policy*, no. 32, pp. 309–18.

Jaffry, S, Pickering, H, Ghulam, Y, Whitmarsh, D & Wattage, P 2004, 'Consumer choices for quality and sustainability labelled seafood products in the UK', *Food Policy*, no. 29, pp. 215–28.

Kloeten, N 2011, 'Labels still confuse Kiwis', *National Business Review*, 6 September, viewed 12 April 2012, <http://www.nbr.co.nz/article/monday-labels-still-confuse-kiwis-ng-p-99977>.

Knight, J, Holdsworth, D & Mather, D 2007, 'Country-of-origin and choice of food imports: an in-depth study of European distribution channel gatekeepers', *Journal of International Business Studies*, vol. 38, no. 1, pp. 107–25.

Lee, D. and Hsu, T 2008, 'Now China's fish are suspect', *Los Angeles Times*, viewed 27 May 2009, <http://articles.latimes.com/2008/dec/24/business/fi-melamine24>.

McCorkindale, W 2010, 'Basa lobs NZ fish out of water', *The Southland Times*, 26 May, viewed 14 April, <http://www.stuff.co.nz/southland-times/news/3737853/Basa-lobs-NZ-fish-out-of-water>.

McKenzie, A 2009, 'International trends in food safety: optimising the opportunities', viewed 3 April 2012, <http://www.seafoodindustry.co.nz/f1501,70816/70816_Seafood_Conference_0509.pdf>.

Ministry of Foreign Affairs of Denmark 2009, 'Food safety and hygiene control in Vietnam's food processing industry', viewed 10 March 2009, <http://www.ambhanoi.um.dk/en/menu/CommercialServices/MarketOpportunities/Sector+Analysis/Food+safety+and+hygiene+control>.

Möller, AB 2007, 'Seafood processing – local sources, global markets (No. TAD/FI/GLOB(2007) 6): workshop on opportunities and challenges of fisheries globalisation', jointly hosted by the OECD Committee for Fisheries and FAO Fisheries and Aquaculture Department, 16–17 April, viewed 20 April 2012, <http:// www.oecd.org/tad/fisheries/38484834.pdf>.

Neville, A 2009, 'Fish and chip shop fright – biosecurity', *New Zealand Herald*, 5 July, viewed 9 July 2009, <http://www.nzherald.co.nz/biosecurity/news/article.cfm?c_id=500816&objectid=10582550>.

New Zealand Review of Food Labelling Law and Policy 2010, Submission documents provided by New Zealand Seafood Industry Council, viewed 15 February 2011, <http://www.foodlabellingreview.gov.au/internet/foodlabelling/publishing.nsf/Content/foodlabelreview_displaypub_parts?OpenDocument&referenceno=1WCME-85F5GT20100514125717ECDQ&partno=3>.

Roheim, C 2008, *Seafood supply chain management: methods to prevent illegally caught product entry into the marketplace* (No. IUCN World Conservation Union-US for the project PROFISH Law Enforcement, Corruption and Fisheries Work), University of Rhode Island, Kingston, USA.

Roth, A, Tsay, A, Pullman, M & Gray, J 2008, 'Unravelling the food supply chain: strategic insights from China and the 2007 recalls', *Journal of Supply Chain Management*, vol. 44, no. 4, pp. 22–39.

Stringer, C, Simmons, G & Rees, E 2011, 'Shifting post production patterns: exploring changes in New Zealand's seafood processing industry, *New Zealand Geographer*, vol. 67, no. 3, pp. 161–73.

Sunday Mirror 2008, 'There's something fishy going on here; we're buying back EUR177m haul caught in our own waters', 12 October 2008, p. 2)

USDA 2008, *US seafood exports to China are re-exported to third countries*, Washington, DC: USDA Foreign Agricultural Service.

Vietnam Association of Seafood Exporters and Producers 2011, Developing the *pangasius* market, viewed 19 February 2011, <http://www.vasep.com.vn/vasep/edailynews.nsf/87abdd0d40924a754725714200323ea3/9734A4BC28B3E0DF47257834000EB877?OpenDocument&Start=19>.

21

Ubisoft: Competing in the global video gaming industry

Eliseo A Aurellado

Yves Guillemot, CEO of Ubisoft Entertainment SA (UBI), mulls over the two documents sitting on his office desk: the latest PriceWaterhouseCoopers (PWC) study of the video gaming industry and a 10-year summary of his company's financial performance. UBI had recently celebrated 25 years of corporate life with a record of 500 million games sold. While the past years had been studded with numerous achievements, the company's financial performance was inconsistent. The industry was promising and dynamic, but it was not very forgiving. Guillemot ponders over the future of his company, and how it can continue to respond effectively to the challenges and prospects of a rapidly changing and highly competitive environment.

■ Historical performance of UBI

UBI is one of the leading developers, publishers and distributors of video games in Europe and North America. UBI derives its name from 'ubiquitous software', which reflects the company's mission to permeate cyberspace with its games. Founded in 1986 by the Guillemot brothers in France, UBI has creative studios in 18 countries, and the second largest workforce in the industry.

UBI holds the franchise of some of the world's best-selling video games, such as *Assassin's Creed* and *Tom Clancy's Rainbow Six*. In 2012, it registered sales of over one billion euros, capturing 7 per cent market share in the United States and 8.3 per cent in Europe. Guillemot fondly recalls the following milestones in his company's history:

- Opened distribution subsidiaries in the United States, Germany and the United Kingdom, and development studios in France and Romania, in 1989.
- Released its first internally developed game, *Zombi*, in 1989.
- Shifted from being a mere distributor to a creator of video games, and opened additional distribution offices in Switzerland and Japan between 1989 and 1994.
- Offered the first game from a well-known franchise, *Rayman*, in 1995, with 20 million units sold worldwide.
- Listed UBI on the Paris Stock Exchange in 1996 and expanded its production by going into China.
- Opened and acquired more studios in Canada, Morocco, Spain and Italy, and opened distribution offices in Spain, Italy, Belgium, Denmark, Austria, Australia and Korea from 1996 to 2006.
- Launched its gaming portal, ubi.com, in 2002.
- Made three strategic acquisitions: (1) Blue Byte Software in Dusseldorf, Germany; (2) Red Storm Entertainment; and (3) the game division of The Learning Company in the United States. These expansion activities catapulted UBI into the top 10 independent publishers worldwide in 2006.
- Pioneered in the casual video gaming market in 2006 with its *Games for Everyone*.
- Expanded with new distribution offices in Mexico and Poland, and development studios in Bulgaria, Ukraine, China, India, Singapore, Canada, the United Kingdom, Sweden and Japan between 2006 and 2010.

- Created the best-selling game, *Assassin's Creed*, in 2007, which led to the company being ranked the third independent publisher worldwide.
- Acquired a French company in 2009, with a popular brand, *Trackmania*, which has 10 million registered players.
- Released its *Just Dance* franchise in 2009, using the new Wii platform, transforming over 28 million living rooms into dance floors.
- Launched its online services platform for gamers in 2011.
- Created Ubisoft Motion Pictures, a business segment that will bring creative worlds to TV and cinema, in 2011.

■ Vision and mission

Guillemot's vision is for UBI to be the shaper of the entertainment industry by making video games the major entertainment of the future. He considers his mission to be the leading international developer, publisher and distributor of interactive entertainment products. His approach has been the creation of strong brands through in-house development, utilising a vast global distribution network.

■ UBI financial performance

Figure 21.1: UBI revenue by source, 2007 (a) vs 2012 (b) as charted by the author
Data source: <http://www.ubisoftgroup.com>, viewed 20 June 2012.

Reviewing UBI's 10-year financial performance, Guillemot observes that the company registered a sales increase from €450 million in 2003 to €1 billion in 2012. Sales revenue comes from three sources, as shown in Figure 21.1.

(a)   (b)

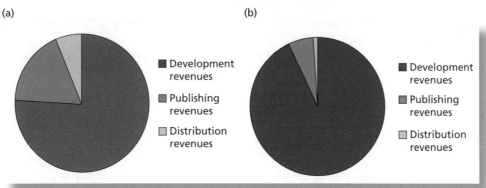

In Figure 21.1, *Publishing* relates to games published by the company but developed by third parties, while *development* involves games developed by the company that it publishes and distributes, and *distribution* concerns games developed and published by other companies but distributed in certain geographic areas by UBI. Publishing and distribution are secondary to developing activity, but they are also important sources of revenue. The company is the second publisher in Europe, the fifth publisher in the United States and the fourth publisher worldwide. The geographic sources of its revenues are shown in Figure 21.2.

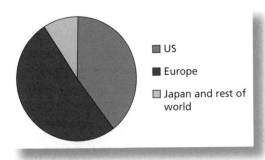

US

Europe

Japan and rest of world

Figure 21.2: UBI 2012 revenues by region, as summarised and charted by author

Source: Ubisoft (2012).

The following should be noted about these figures:

- Sales growth is lower when compared with Nintendo and Activision Blizzard, although it is ahead of Electronic Arts. These competitors are the three leaders in the video games market.
- Operating costs have squeezed profits, resulting in deteriorating profit margins. However, costs of debt have decreased because of a lower debt ratio.
- The company's productivity has improved, with a higher total asset turnover of 97 per cent compared with 73 per cent two years earlier.
- Net income has been inconsistent, peaking in 2008 but showing net losses in two consecutive years. Earnings per share have been erratic.
- Operating cycles have steadily improved through faster receivable and inventory turnover, resulting in more significant cash flows.
- During this period, the company invested substantially in new-generation consoles and in buying brands and licences. However, the company's resources were deemed inadequate to invest in some very profitable game types, such as multiplayer, virtual life and sport games. The company also suffered from inadequate budgets for product development and investments in new technology and people.

The following have also presented challenges:

- UBI develops software but does not manufacture hardware, which forces it to adapt its video games to the new consoles on the market.
- It has not fully tapped the Japanese market, which represents 25 per cent of the global video games market.
- The company still lacks the talent to exploit the emerging trends in the industry.
- A competitor owns 15 per cent of UBI company shares, which is both challenging and disconcerting.

■ The video gaming industry

The video gaming industry has grown exponentially over the past two decades. Sophisticated computer technology and the enabling connectivity of the internet have contributed to the popularity and growth of the industry. PriceWaterhouseCoopers (2009) placed the video games global market at US$67 billion in 2012 (See Figure 21.3). It is estimated that sales revenue will reach over $73 billion by 2013.

Video games are popular in developed countries such as the United States, Japan and European nations (primarily France, the United Kingdom, Germany, Spain and Italy). The United States registered revenues of $12.1 billion in 2007 for a less than stellar annual growth rate of 7.9 per cent. This was despite the success of the Xbox 360 consoles launched by Microsoft in 2005 and Nintendo's Wii and PlayStation 3 introduced in 2006. In 2012, US revenues were predicted to reach $17.7 billion. The

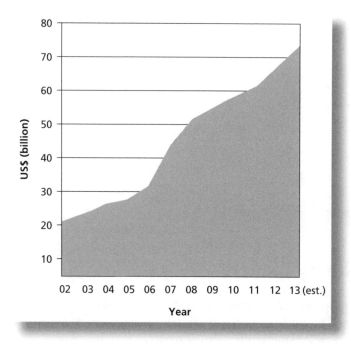

Figure 21.3: Global sales of video games, 2002–13 as charted by the author
Source: PriceWaterhouseCoopers (2009).

Japanese video gaming industry comprised 50 per cent of the global market in 2002, but has declined due to changing game preferences and the country's economic recession. However, the market still showed $20 billion sales in 2009. The Europe–Middle East–Africa (EMEA) bloc represents the biggest video game market, with France, Germany, Italy, Spain and the United Kingdom accounting for $15.2 billion in 2009, nearly 30 per cent of the global market. In France alone, the market represents $4 billion, with a growth rate of 47 per cent.

The PriceWaterhouseCoopers study predicted that the Asia-Pacific video game markets would grow from US$22.2 billion in 2010 to US$38.7 billion in 2015. Figure 21.4 shows the composition of the global market by region.

Products and services

There are two types of product in the industry: hardware and software. Hardware comprises consoles and computers that read video signals and project them on to an electronic screen. Examples of hardware are the Playstation 3, PSP, Xbox 360, Nintendo Wii and Nintendo DS. Software consists of video games in the form of CD, DVD or cartridge, or online downloads, which are loaded into the hardware. Examples include *Doom 3, Oblivion* and *Call of Duty*. Hardware companies usually peg the price of games sold with their hardware, thus limiting the pricing strategy of software developers. Generally, the video game market is replete with hardware featuring all kinds of software that carries the same price.

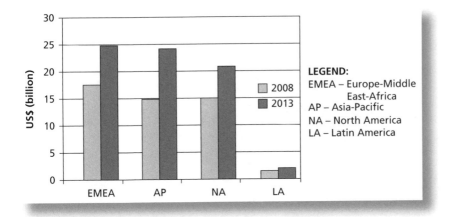

US$ (billion)

30
25
20
15
10
5
0

EMEA   AP   NA   LA

LEGEND:
☐ 2008
■ 2013

EMEA – Europe-Middle East-Africa
AP – Asia-Pacific
NA – North America
LA – Latin America

Figure 21.4: Video games market size as charted by the author *Source:* PriceWaterhouseCoopers (2009).

■ Major industry players

The major industry players include console manufacturers, software publishers, distributors and retailers. The big console manufacturers are Microsoft, Nintendo and Sony. Aside from the console manufacturers that also publish their own games, some of the major software publishers in the industry are Activision Blizzard, Electronic Arts and Konami – the largest publisher in Japan. The distributor segment of the value chain is heavily fragmented, with thousands of distributors globally. They usually obtain their games directly from the publishers. Retailers are generally classified into brick-and-mortar hubs (such as Walmart and Radio Shack), virtual hubs (for example, Amazon) and specialty shops (for example, GameStop or EB Games).

■ Prospects and challenges of the industry

■ *Growth directions*

The PriceWaterhouseCoopers (2009) study indicates that the future of the industry is bright. Console games are expected to continue to lead the way, with US$34.7 billion in sales estimated for 2012 – a growth of 6.9 per cent from 2007. Sales of online games are also likely to grow rapidly, with a predicted increase from US$6.6 billion in 2007 to US$14.4 billion in 2012. The study indicates that the industry growth will be fuelled by social gaming, especially online games, outstripping the sale of console games. The mobile gaming market is expected to grow vigorously at 19 per cent, with the use of handheld devices. Sales from mobile video games were predicted to increase to US$13.5 billion in 2012 with the popularity of 'casual games' such as *Angry Birds*. Casual games are perceived to be simpler and easier to play. Besides casual gaming, another growth area is the 'free-to-play' business model, where consumers can buy low-priced gadgets that can access games online for free. At the same time, the study forecasts a decline in PC gaming, from US$3.8 billion in 2007 to

US$3.6 billion in 2012, resulting from a general downtrend in the number of quality PC game releases.

■ *Emerging markets*

Emerging markets such as China, Russia, Brazil, Mexico, India, Eastern Europe and South-East Asian countries present another huge area of potential for video games. To reach these markets, video game companies have to create subsidiaries and development studios, and establish good distribution networks. As can be expected, the growing demand for video games has encouraged intense competition. The natural consequence is the death of many video game companies that cannot provide the required financial resources to remain competitive. Major players in the industry resort to acquisitions and takeovers, branding, copycat practices, licensing and innovation to expand their market and to survive. Video game companies also rely on manufacturers to provide the appropriate software media (CD, DVD or cartridge) and product packaging. They constantly seek the assistance of major distributors, such as retailers that sell video games through specialised shops, consumer electronics products providers, and hypermarts and department stores.

■ *Video game consumers*

Video game consumers are financially challenged to buy because a console is priced from US$190 to US$800 while the price of a game ranges from US$45 to US$100. Computers that enable video games to be played are sold for between US$1200 and US$4500. A console or computer has a maximum useful life of around five years. A customer can be considered a video gamer if he or she procures at least one game a month for a minimum period of one year (Urban Dictionary 2012).

A media survey (Video Game Industry Statistics 2010) shows the following demographics:

- Fourteen per cent of teenagers consider themselves serious video gamers, while 46 per cent are merely interested.
- Video gaming among female teens has increased from 10 per cent to 40 per cent of gamers since 2009 because of MP3 players, the internet and the need to make use of high-tech gadgets such as computers, mobile phones and iPads.
- Thirty years ago, there were few seniors and adults interested in video games. Today, they represent about 10 per cent of gamers. Adults are encouraged to learn this new trend in entertainment because of their children or grandchildren. Video games are becoming a family activity. A recent report (PRWeb 2013) shows that seniors play Wii games in nursing homes.
- Games used to be played in two dimensions with pixels and squares. Nowadays, games are shown in three dimensions and offer astonishing realism and incredible colors. *Mario*, the first and most famous game in the history of consoles, featured

a two-dimensional character on the Nintendo when it was launched in 1985. Seventeen years later, *Super Mario* was presented in three dimensions on the Nintendo Gamecube.

■ Changing trends

Video games have evolved over time using artificial intelligence that now approximates reality. These games are supported by more content, a wider emotional range of characters, better sounds and musical background, and a realistic atmosphere. This provides the gamer with a powerful virtual life experience. Advanced technology has also shortened game loading time to almost nil, allowing gamers to enjoy their experience without any break. Multiplayer game format is a strong general trend in video games. For example, the multiplayer game *World of Warcraft* is played by 10 million players worldwide via the internet. Another trend has also been observed in casual games that feature animal care, music, fashion, cooking, brain teasers, education, board games (e.g. Chess, Scrabble and Monopoly) and TV show spinoffs (e.g. *Who Wants to Be a Millionaire?*).

The cost drivers in video gaming are technology, people skills, and sales and marketing. Each new generation of games and consoles requires more expensive technology, computer specialists who demand higher pay for increased quality and shortened creation turn-around time, and more marketing campaigns and promotions. The average annual R&D budget for a console game is approximately US$7 million, with some games registering budgets of US$20 million. These figures do not include marketing budgets.

■ Piracy and social concerns

All game publishers face the problem of piracy. Several organisations have been created to combat this nefarious activity, such as the Syndicat des Editeurs de Logiciels de Loisirs (SELL) and the ESA, the North American equivalent of the SELL. These organisations take legal action against hackers and force the withdrawal of games that have been placed illegally online. Companies also protect their brand by registering them with the World Intellectual Property Organization (International), the Patent and Trademark Office in Washington, DC (United States) or the Office for Harmonization in the Internal Market (Europe). Games can be covered by international copyright laws.

The industry has to manage growing concerns about violence in video games and the danger it poses to young viewers and children. Organisations such as the Pan European Game Information in Europe (except Germany), the Entertainment Software Rating Board in the United States, the Computer Entertainment Rating Organisation in Japan, the Office of Film and Literature Classification in Australia and the Unterhaltungssoftware Selbskontrole in Germany have also been established to fight against violence in video games. An established mechanism for classification is that every game in every country has a specific rating, depending on its degree of violence – which is usually indicated clearly on the product packaging. This practice enables game developers to create any game possible – including X-rated ones – and still be protected legally.

UBI's vision for the future

Despite the challenges, Guillemot is optimistic about UBI's growth and prospects. He knows that the video gaming industry is constantly reinventing itself, forcing the company to be even more creative and innovative each day. Resting on one's laurels is therefore not an option in the video gaming industry. He is confident that his company's culture can cope well with industry demands. There is open communication throughout the organisation, with every employee having access to information regardless of their position. There is no strong hierarchy, and no barriers exist between decision-makers and employees. Working spaces are open, and nobody works in an enclosed room. The company encourages creativity, and leaders give value to ideas and individual initiatives.

He believes the company has a strong ethical code, an advocacy for environmental protection through recycling policies, and a strong social responsibility through outreach projects such as sending video games to poor countries each year. Guillemot considers that his team's online expertise, know-how from recent acquisitions and recruitment of specialised talent are powerful tools, which will enable UBI to fully seize the numerous current and future opportunities in the industry.

Discussion questions

21.1 What strategies did UBI adopt to become one of the leading players in the video game industry? What are the key factors that contributed to its growth? Explain.

21.2 How would you assess UBI's financial performance? Was it able to take advantage of the opportunities presented? Discuss.

21.3 What are the opportunities and challenges facing the industry? How should UBI respond to these external factors? Rank these factors in the order of importance in terms of their impact on UBI.

21.4 What do you think are UBI's major strengths? Do you see any vulnerabilities present in the organisation? Discuss.

21.5 Prepare a SWOT analysis to assist the CEO in crafting new directions for the organisation. Using the results of the SWOT analysis, what constitutes the most significant and relevant strategies for the company? Rank them in terms of attractiveness.

References and further reading

Caron, F 2008, 'Gaming expected to be a P68 billion business by 2012', ars technica, 19 June, viewed 3 June 2012, <http://www.arstechnica.com/gaming/2008/06/gaming-expected-to-be-a-68-billion-business-by-2012>.

De Prato, G, Feijóo, C, Nepelski, D, Bogdanowicz, M & Simon, JP 2010, *Born digital, grown digital: the future competitiveness of the European videogames software industry*, viewed 3 June 2012, <http://ftp.jrc.es/EURdoc/JRC60711.pdf>.

Entertainment Software Association 2011, *Essential Facts about the Computer and Video Game Industry*, viewed 9 June 2012, <http://www.theesa.com/facts/pdfs/ESA_EF_2011.pdf>.

Nayagam, J 2011, 'Video games industry set to boom', *The Edge Financial Daily*, 17 November, viewed 28 May 2012, <http://www.theedgemalaysia.com/index.php?option=com_content&task=view&id=196308&Itemid=99>.

PriceWaterhouseCoopers (PWC) 2009, *The evolution of video gaming and content consumption*, viewed 3 June 2-12, <http://www.pwc.com/us/en/industry/entertainment-media/publications/assets/pwc-video-gaming-and-content-consumption.pdf>.

PRWeb 2013, 'Senior citizens extending health and wellness with video games' viewed 20 February 2013, <http://www.prweb.com/releases/2012/1/prweb9131772.htm>.

Ubisoft 2012,<http://www.ubisoftgroup.com>.

Urban Dictionary 2012, Gamer definition, viewed 20 February 2013, <http://www.urbandictionary.com/define.php?term=gamer>.

The Video Game Industry n.d., viewed 10 June 2012, <http://sites.duke.edu/soc142-videogames/global-value-chain/evolutionary-value-chain>.

Video Game Industry Statistics 2009, viewed 9 June 2012, <http://sites.duke.edu/soc142-videogames/global-value-chain/evolutionary-value-chain>.

Video Game Industry Statistics 2010, Website, viewed 20 February 2013, <http://www.esrb.org/about/images/vidGames04.png>.

Wikipedia 2012a, 'Video game industry', viewed 3 June 2012, <http://www.en.wikipedia.org/wiki/Video_game_industry>.

—— 2012b, 'Video gaming in Japan', viewed 9 June 2012, <http://www.en.wikipedia.org/wiki/Video_gamin_in_Japan>.

—— 2012b, 'Xbox', viewed 9 June 2012, <http://www.en.wikipedia.org/wiki/Xbox>.

22

Taobao vs eBay: The fight between a local nobody and a global giant

Zhu Hang, Chai Wenjing, Su Xing and Wu Ziwei

One evening in January 2004, at Alibaba's headquarters in China, Ma Yun, a famous Chinese internet entrepreneur, met with executives from Taobao, a new customer-to-customer (C2C) website founded by Alibaba. The leader of Taobao's management team, Tongyu Sun, reported that the fledgling company was struggling against eBay Eachnet's stranglehold on the industry. In 2002, eBay purchased a 33 per cent shareholding in Eachnet, the largest Chinese e-business company, and in June 2003 purchased the remaining shares, renaming the company eBay Eachnet. Following the acquisition, eBay announced that China would be its second target market following the United States, and began to make aggressive moves to block Taobao's marketing channels in the Chinese market. This resulted in nearly all the main portal websites refusing to promote Taobao because of their exclusive contracts with eBay. Although Ma had foreseen a heavy attack from eBay and prepared a large promotion budget for Taobao, Sun found he had difficulty in spending the money effectively. If it were unable to attract more customers quickly, how could Taobao survive?

■ The birth of Taobao

Alibaba.com, the flagship company of Alibaba Group, was not widely known in 2004, despite the company being established in 1999 by Ma and 18 employees. Ma's vision for Alibaba was to build a 'bazaar online', establish a world-class Chinese brand and become one of the world's top 10 websites. When the company was established, there were several e-commerce business models operating, mostly in the United States: business-to-business (B2B), business-to-customer (B2C) and customer-to-customer (C2C). Amazon, one of the top five US websites, was a model in the field of B2C and eBay was the world's largest C2C marketplace.

Alibaba focused its target market on small and medium-sized enterprises (SMEs), defined as businesses with annual sales less than RMB 10 million (about US$1.2 million). Manufacturing companies with about a hundred employees, small foreign trade companies with only five or six clerks or even small family-run shops were typical examples of SMEs. SMEs can include manufacturing companies with a hundred employees, small foreign trade companies with only five or six clerks, or even a small family-run shop.

For many SMEs, there was an urgent need to expand their business and find more buyers in the global marketplace. Although the scale of these companies was small, according to Ma's calculation there were more than five million enterprises eager to do business with foreign customers annually, as well as RMB 3 trillion (about US$362 billion) merchandise inventory in China. Alibaba built an online platform to showcase the SMEs' products in order to attract domestic and overseas buyers. In this way, Ma set up a unique B2B model in China. Alibaba's B2B platform initially was designed to provide commodity information, so that buyers and sellers could identify each other via their trading information. Alibaba charged members a fixed annual membership fee.

In 2003, Alibaba become the world's largest B2B website, with a daily income of RMB 100 million (about US$16 million). Although focusing on the B2B field, Ma was keeping an eye on eBay, the largest C2C website in the world. Taking a closer look at eBay, Ma found that the platform structures of eBay and Alibaba were almost identical, and transactions on Alibaba were not much different from large transactions on eBay Eachnet. Ma was concerned that 'it is only a matter of time before eBay enters the B2B market'. If he did not take any action now, it could be 'a disaster' for Alibaba a few years down the track, when the global giant eBay entered the B2B market with a strong brand and abundant financial resources (Shen 2007).

Mr Masayoshi Son, a friend of Ma's, and a Japanese investor in the internet industry, helped Ma to make the decision about entering the C2C market. Son urged Ma to compete with the giant eBay in the Chinese market. In February 2003, Ma went to Japan with a few executives to study the Japanese e-commerce industry. Son contacted Ma and requested an urgent meeting with him. Foreseeing the dissolution of boundaries between B2B, B2C and C2C, Son proposed the idea – which coincided with Ma's own thoughts – that Alibaba should enter the C2C market. Ma believed that Alibaba's only choice was to take action before eBay became established in the Chinese market. 'I believe eBay's model is the best opportunity for us,' said Ma (Shen 2007). Due to eBay's acquisition of Eachnet, Alibaba sped up the pace of entering the C2C market (Shen 2007). Japan was the only one of 17 markets where eBay had not gained an overwhelming advantage. Yahoo! Japan, in which Masayoshi Son had heavily invested, accounted for 70 per cent of Japan's C2C market share. Son thought that eBay's operation model was not suitable for Asia, which could prove to be its Achilles' heel. As a result of the meeting, Son provided Ma with US$82 million to found a new C2C company in China, thereby taking the initiative to challenge eBay. This new company was Taobao.

In April 2003, Alibaba arranged development and testing for a C2C platform. When Taobao.com was established, it imitated some features of eBay, such as page design and categories of products. With no fees charged to open an online shop, the number of sellers increased rapidly. However, the buyers were few, resulting in a small volume of transactions taking place on Taobao. Ma and Sun found that, while 93 per cent of Chinese internet users had visited online shops, only 33.8 per cent of them had actually purchased goods online. Given this situation, was it possible for Taobao to find a more suitable way to meet the online shopping habits and needs of the Chinese people? Considering that the main obstacle to online transactions was the lack of interpersonal trust among strangers, Ma suggested encouraging transactions within the same city, beginning with Beijing, Shanghai and Hangzhou. Thus the first three markets for Taobao were established.

▪ Trading problems for C2C

The payment of online transactions had been a choke point in popularising e-commerce in China, as credit cards and electronic payment were not widely accepted at that time.

Successful e-commerce sites such as Dangdang and Joyo were both operating a B2C model. They introduced a home delivery service where customers paid by cash, enabling B2C platforms to gain high levels of consumer acceptance. At the time, the world's leading electronic payment instrument was PayPal (which was acquired by eBay in 2003). From a functional viewpoint, PayPal – as a third-party payment platform – had solved the problem of making online payments. PayPal was able to ensure the quick transfer of money from one account to another through its platform, charging 3 per cent of the total amount as a trading commission. In the United States, PayPal's electronic payments accounted for 90 per cent market share of electronic payments. However, in China there was no third-party payment platform and only a few banks had begun to provide online payment services. Because of security concerns, this service was not widely accepted. In most areas of China – especially in the small and medium-sized cities and in the countryside, people were accustomed to paying with cash, as the market for paying by bank cards was still in the early stage of development.

Compared with the credit problems, the building an online payment system was not such a big deal. Due to a lack of relevant laws and business credit records, most people did not buy anything online. Successful B2C e-businesses were using credit, but in the field of C2C there were no guarantees, and businesses obviously could not operate in this way. In the past, eBay's paid service filtered out sellers with bad credit histories and reputations. However, because of its free-of-charge strategy, Taobao had no threshold for eliminating bad sellers. This was a major concern for buyers when they compared Taobao with eBay. Consequently, while Taobao experienced an increasing number of page views after its launch, this did not translate into increased trading volume. A survey found that buyers had two main concerns, which were expressed in response to the following questions: Is the product exactly the same as the pictures displayed on screen? And are the transactions safe and reliable? Apparently, the buyers' credit concerns represented an obstacle to the transaction.

Ineffective communication between buyers and sellers was also a problem. Because of the wide variety of goods, sellers did not always provide enough product information to meet the needs of potential customers. For example, when purchasing clothing, some consumers were concerned about the texture and colour of fabrics, whereas other consumers were more concerned about the quality of the fibre. On eBay, buyers could seek product information through the message board, but it might take several hours or even days for the buyer to receive a response from the seller. If a buyer needed further information, the whole process of communication between the buyer and the seller could be more time-consuming. In addition, Chinese consumers preferred to bargain, even if the seller set a fixed price. Those wanting to purchase large quantities of goods liked having the option of bargaining with the sellers in order to get a discount or free delivery. Both parties were reluctant to make this personal bargaining process publicly visible on the message board.

There was also the problem of logistics and distribution. The majority of the urban population is concentrated in large cities in China, while the population outside of the large cities is more dispersed. The problem of logistics and distribution seemed to present an insurmountable obstacle. In particular, customers in the third- and fourth-tier cities were eager to buy goods sold on Taobao – for example, perfume, cell phones and Nike shoes. The primary Taobao sellers were also eBay sellers, so their goods were also quite similar, and these products could easily be bought in Shanghai or Hong Kong, but for customers in smaller cities they were difficult to buy locally. Compared with taking lengthy shopping trips, online shopping was more convenient and the cost seemed acceptable. At this time, there were 80 million internet users in China, but even the largest C2C website, eBay Eachnet – which occupied 90 per cent of the online C2C market – had only four million users.

■ EBay Eachnet: The competitor

Founded in 1995, eBay was committed to 'helping people on the planet to buy anything they want'. It was praised as the 'perfect store' because of its unique business model, which was using the internet to solve the difficult problem of finding 'long-tail' products across the globe.[1] By charging clients to post product information online and through successful transactions, eBay reached its break-even point only one month after it was established. It was one of the fastest growing companies in the history of US business. In 2003, eBay became the world's largest C2C website, with an annual income of more than US$3.3 billion, more than 120 million active users and local sites in 28 countries or regions. By way of acquisition and direct operation, at the time eBay dominated the markets in many countries, with the exception of Japan.

With the boom in online auction of second-hand personal items, eBay also attracted big companies selling industrial goods. Having noticed this trend, in January 2003, eBay created a channel to sell industrial products. The business was so popular that even the flourishing Motorola company sold mobile phones through eBay. By 2003, the number of wholesale retailers on eBay was 23 000. In the same year, eBay acquired an American B2B company named fairmarket.com.

Eachnet was founded by two Harvard MBA graduates in Shanghai in 1998. This was the first C2C e-commerce company in China. Regardless of language, Eachnet was simply a clone of eBay. From style, colours, page structures and functional buttons to the business model, the two sites were almost identical. Eachnet charged sellers between US$0.16 and US$1.3 to display their goods online, as well as 0.25–2 per cent trade commission (using the lowest traded price of each product as the baseline). The founders of Eachnet believed that this fee-charging model would ensure not only the quality of the transaction, but also the product quality and the trading turnover ratio. In October 1999, Eachnet received a US$6.5 million venture capital investment, which helped the company in its growth stage. Later, as a result of advertising, Eachnet attracted the white-collar market in first-tier cities in China. This group was an ideal target market for many global internet companies and Chinese business followers. The office buildings in Shanghai, Beijing and other big cities were filled with highly educated internet users, many of whom were IT-savvy and willing to try new and intriguing things.

Eachnet was a rare exception among the Chinese internet companies, at a time when free services were prevalent. Despite charging its users, it was still able to achieve rapid growth. By 2003, Eachnet had 400 million registered users and more than 300 000 products, and had obtained around a 90 per cent market share in China's C2C market. In 2002, eBay paid US$30 million to acquire a 33 per cent share of Eachnet and in 2003, eBay acquired the remaining 67 per cent of the shares for US$150 million. This demonstrated eBay's strong interest in the Chinese market, as well as its recognition of the rapid growth that Eachnet had achieved. At a press conference, eBay's CEO and president, Meg Whitman, said:

> This partnership with Eachnet is an extremely important step in eBay's global strategy. In the next three to four years, Chinese e-commerce will grow 12 times to US$160 billion, and we will help Eachnet exploit the immense potential of the market, and build up an integrated global market in the future together. (Whitman 2005)

After the acquisition of Eachnet, eBay integrated its operations in China with those in the United States. eBay first undertook the centralised management of data, and made the daily routine maintenance work of the website 'internationalized', which in time proved to be problematic. For example, even a small change on the Chinese website took a long time to complete. First, the engineer had to complete an application document in Chinese, which was then translated into English. Second, the job was transferred to US engineers who undertook the development and testing work in the United States. Then the change could finally be made. Even if the Chinese engineer just wanted to change a few words on the website, it could still take two to three months to get the final approval from the United States. Furthermore, the centralised management approach was not only a technical problem, but also became a cross-cultural problem. It was difficult for eBay America's management to truly understand the Chinese culture as well as China's market. The lack of cultural awareness from some US managers can be illustrated in the following joke about the company. A senior manager brought some presents from the United States for his Chinese colleagues. His Chinese colleagues were shocked to see that he had brought everyone a green hat. Unbeknown to him, a green hat in China signals that a man has been betrayed by his wife!

▪ Taobao under siege

In July 2003, Alibaba held a news conference in Beijing announcing its plan to invest US$16 million to build up Taobao.com in order to enter the C2C market. This decision seemed crazy at the time, as eBay had purchased Eachnet just a month earlier. Until then, Alibaba had only focused on B2B e-commerce. If it were to enter the C2C market, a severe conflict with the world's largest opponent might be around the corner. At the press conference, a reporter asked Ma: 'Alibaba has focused on the B2B market, and made good profit – why suddenly enter into the C2C market?' Ma answered: 'The new trend of e-commerce is that the boundaries among B2B, B2C and C2C will no longer exist.' ('Alibaba Market Imagination' 2007).

When Alibaba announced its entry into the C2C e-commerce market at a formal press conference, Taobao had already been quietly online for two months. The main difference between Taobao and eBay was that the former promised that listing of the products and transaction would be free. eBay Eachnet retained its charging policy, deciding to let Chinese internet users adapt to the charging model. It disparaged Taobao's 'free model', and declared that 'free is not a business model' ('Alibaba: Market Imagination' 2007). At the end of 2003, with its free-of-charge policy in place, Taobao had obtained 8 per cent market share in China's C2C market. Although the market share of Taobao was insignificant compared with eBay Eachnet's 72 per cent market penetration, Taobao attracted the attention of eBay. Ma had never expected that competing with eBay would be an easy job, and he defined the war as 'an ant fighting against an elephant'.

Whitman dismissed the newly created Taobao, commenting that it would only be able to survive for 18 months ('Alibaba: Market Imagination' 2007). She also budgeted US$100 million for eBay's competition in the Chinese market. This accounted for one-third of eBay's global marketing budget, indicating the great importance Whitman placed on the Chinese market. As a point of comparison, US$100 million was almost the total amount of China's online transactions in 2003. eBay planned to use most of its budget on advertising – particularly TV commercials, outdoor media and mobile advertisement on buses.

Furthermore, having the strong financial support of its parent company in the United States, eBay Eachnet had signed exclusive advertising contracts or established joint auction channels with several big Chinese portal sites, search engines and even some main vertical sites. It was stipulated in the contracts that if these sites signed an advertising contract with Taobao, Yahoo Auction or another similar auction site, eBay would impose high fines on them. Sun found that almost all main online advertising channels had been blocked by eBay Eachnet, based on those exclusive contracts. This situation made him feel helpless when the newly launched Taobao encountered stiff opposition immediately after its launch. For a newly launched website like Taobao, the primary goal was to promote itself and attract people's attention. However, because of the pressure from eBay, the most conventional ways to realise this goal – such as online advertising – were not available to Taobao. Although Ma had allocated a large amount of money for Taobao's marketing campaigns, Taobao could not find enough channels in which to spend it.

Taobao: Where are the solutions?

Encircled by eBay, Taobao was clearly in a confusing cycle. In order to attract more buyers, Taobao had to encourage sellers to put more goods online. More volume was essential. However, eBay had essentially monopolised the market, and it was extremely hard to attract sellers and buyers without effective promotion. Due to the blocking of promotion channels, it was difficult for Taobao to reach potential customers. What might the solutions be for the newly born Taobao?

■ Discussion questions

22.1 What are the key differences between the e-commerce markets in China and United States?

22.2 Are there conflicts between eBay Eachnet's model and Chinese consumption habits? Discuss.

22.3 Identify the strategies that Taobao used to enter the Chinese market. Evaluate their effectiveness.

22.4 How can Taobao overcome its difficulties in competing against eBay Eachnet in the Chinese market?

■ Note

1   The term 'long tail' is derived from Anderson (2006), and means a large number of unique items with only relatively small quantities sold of each.

■ References

'Alibaba: Market Imagination' 2007, *21st Century Business Review*, September.

Anderson, C 2006, *The long tail: why the future of business is selling less of more*, Hyperion, New York.

Shen Weifeng 2007, *Taobao, hand stander wins: the legend story about how Taobao defeated eBay*, Zhejiang People Publishing House, Hangzhou (in Chinese).

Whitman, M 2005, Presentation to the Shanghai Fortune Forum.

23

The internationalisation of COSCO and its investment in New Zealand

Yan Shi, Christina Stringer and Gloria Lan Ge

The China Ocean Shipping (Group) Company (COSCO)[1] is one of the world's largest shipping companies and the fifth largest container carrier (Alphaliner 2013). In 2012, COSCO ranked 384th on the Fortune Global 500 company listing, with US$28.7 billion in annual revenue (*CNN Money* 2012). COSCO was one of the first major Chinese companies to invest in New Zealand, and is regarded as a successful Chinese investment pioneer in New Zealand. This has major implications for other Chinese companies considering investing in New Zealand. Since the free-trade agreement (FTA) between New Zealand and China came into effect in 2008, there has been significant growth in trade. Exports from New Zealand to China have increased by 152 per cent, and today China is New Zealand's second largest bilateral trading partner. Recognising the economic importance of China to New Zealand, in 2012 the New Zealand government announced priority goals of doubling trade between the two countries by 2015, as well as increasing bilateral investment (NZTE & MFAT 2012).

COSCO's development

COSCO owns or controls over a thousand companies globally, with shipping and logistics being the company's two main business activities. In 2012, COSCO operated over 800 modern merchant vessels with a capacity of 50 million deadweight tonnes (DWT). In addition to shipping and logistics services, COSCO has expanded its global value chain to include ship-repairing and port-management services. From a small shipping company to a key operator in the global shipping market,[2] COSCO's development can be divided into four distinctive stages:

Stage 1: Initial development (1961–78)

COSCO, formerly known as the China Ocean Shipping Company, was established as a state-owned enterprise (SOE) in 1961. It owned four ships with a carrying capacity of 22 600 DWT. During the 1960s and 1970s, COSCO's fleet size developed rapidly by utilising finance from banks. By 1975, the company's fleet capacity surpassed 5 million DWT. During the initial stages of growth, COSCO focused its expansion domestically. It established subsidiaries in five major ports in China: Guangdong (in 1961), Shanghai (in 1964), Tianjin (in 1970), Qingdao (in 1976) and Dalian (in 1978). However, there was no significant differentiation among the five subsidiaries in terms of vessel types and services offered, leading to intensive competition among the five subsidiaries.

Stage 2: Independent development specialisation (1979–92)

Following the Chinese economic reforms of 1978, COSCO developed a separate market strategy for each of its five subsidiaries in order to reduce competition. They also shared shipping routes, depending on the location of subsidiaries and fleet features. For example, the Qingdao and Dalian Ocean Transportation companies mainly specialised in bulk carriers and tankers, in addition to carrying general cargoes such as fertiliser, cereal and steel. The Guangzhou, Shanghai and Tianjin Ocean Transportation companies all had very large fleets comprising a variety of ships, and each operated its own specialised shipping routes. This market strategy increased the efficiency of the company.

In November 1988, COSCO established its first wholly owned subsidiary overseas through the purchase of shares in the Zhonghao Shipping Agency Limited. The subsidiary was renamed COSCO (UK) in 1989, and this marked the beginning of COSCO's internationalisation strategy. In 1992, the Chinese government approved the renaming of the China Ocean Shipping Company to China Ocean Shipping (Group) Company (COSCO Group) and on 16 February 1993, the COSCO Group was officially established in Beijing.

■ Stage 3: Diversification (1993–98)

Following the establishment of the COSCO Group, the company's operation expanded into more than ten industries, including ocean transportation, cargo ships agency, ocean fuel supply, ship repairing, real estate, international trade, travel and finance. Shipping remained the company's core business. During this stage, COSCO further restructured its five shipping subsidiaries, and thereafter established specialised shipping companies. In July 1993, COSCO established Container Headquarters in Beijing in order to operate the containerships of the Guangzhou, Shanghai and Tianjin Ocean Transportation companies. When the Container Headquarters was first established, the management rights for the container ships remained with each subsidiary, which in turn greatly limited the operation of the Container Headquarters. The COSCO Container Lines Company Limited (COSCON) was established in 1998 following the merger of Shanghai Ocean Transportation Company and the Beijing Container Headquarters. COSCON has since operated and managed all the container ships that COSCO Group owns. In turn, in 1998 COSCO Bulk Carrier Co. Ltd was established to operate all the bulk carriers owned by the Tianjin Ocean Transportation Company and Guangzhou Ocean Transportation Company. During Stage 3, the COSCO Group also established its own shipping agency network for air, land and sea transportation, which was essential for providing a comprehensive logistic service for its clients. The transformation of the COSCO Group during Stage 3 laid a solid foundation for the company's future global development.

■ Stage 4: International expansion (1999–present)

From 1999 onwards, the COSCO Group focused on transforming the company into a global logistics service provider. The Group adopted new market strategies – for example, the company gradually reduced its investment in non-core businesses such as travelling, finance and real estate to place more emphasis on shipping-related businesses. In January 2002, the COSCO Logistics Company Limited was founded in Beijing. During the same period, the Group adopted a strategy of moving 'from owning ships to controlling ships' (Wei 2008). Traditionally, the Group had purchased

Table 23.1: COSCO listed companies, 2012

Name of company	Stock exchange	Date of listing
COSCO Corporation	Singapore	1993
COSCO Pacific Company	Hong Kong	1994
China International Marine Containers (Group) Company	Shenzhen	1994
COSCO International Holdings Ltd	Hong Kong	1997
COSCO Shipping Company	Shanghai	2002
China COSCO Holdings Company	Hong Kong Shanghai (A-share)	2005 2007

Source: Table generated based on data obtained from the COSCO website, <http://www.cosco.com>, viewed 20 December 2012.

ships with capital borrowed from banks. However, this financing model could not meet rising market demand, and this limited the expansion of the Group. By February 2007, COSCO's shipping capacity using chartered ships outweighed its shipping capacity of the ships the company itself owned.

The COSCO Group sought to raise capital in global markets in order to expand internationally. COSCO Corporation (Singapore), which focuses on the business of shipping and ship repairing, was listed on the Singapore Stock Exchange in October 1993. This was the first overseas-listed company for COSCO (see Table 23.1), as well as being the first overseas-listed Chinese state-owned enterprise. In 2008, COSCO's assets of its listed companies accounted for 75.5 per cent of the total assets of the Group (Wei 2008). The assets proportion of 5:4:1 that was COSCO's original target was achieved – namely, 50 per cent of the capital to be raised from international capital markets, 40 per cent obtained from bank loans and 10 per cent self-accumulated capital. Being listed on stock markets – particularly the international stock markets – not only provided the necessary capital for COSCO's growth, but also put pressure on the management and governance of the Group.

In 2008, COSCO Group's performance declined as the international shipping industry was hit by the Global Financial Crisis (GFC). The Group's net profit decreased from US$3.67 billion in 2007 to US$1.89 billion in 2008; this was the first profit drop in six years (COSCO 2008). COSCO adopted a series of strategies to manage the impact of the economic downturn. By 2009, the company reduced capital expenditure by 37 per cent from its 2008 levels, and reduced its shipping capacity in the container market 'by delaying some of its new-build fleet and by leasing, exchanging vessels among alliances, chartering-out vessels and terminating leases' (*Business Monitor*, 2009). The company also enhanced cooperation with Chinese central banks and transferred deposits and liabilities from foreign banks to Chinese banks to avoid the risk of bankruptcy by foreign banks. In May 2009, COSCO obtained US$1.752 billion in credit facilities for building and operating container ships, as well as US$1 billion in bank loans from the Bank of China. The Group also obtained RMB 40 billion (approximately US$5.8 billion)[3] in equivalent credit facilities from the Agriculture Bank of China. Despite the initiatives to manage the economic downturn, the company made a net loss of US$651 million in 2011.

In order to boost economic development, in 2008 the Chinese government invested RMB 4000 billion (around US$560 billion) to stimulate domestic demand. A large proportion of the amount was invested in China's infrastructure, including inland waterways. In order to benefit from the government policy of stimulating domestic consumption, COSCO adjusted its strategy by placing more emphasis on the domestic market instead of international development (*Business Monitor* 2009).

COSCO in the international market

In order to effectively manage over a thousand operation units in more than 50 countries and regions globally, COSCO established regional headquarters in Asia, Europe, North America, South Africa and Oceania. In 1982, COSCO Americas Inc. was the first regional headquarters established; it was responsible for the group's business in the Americas. Other regional headquarters followed, with the establishment of COSCO Oceania (Pty) Ltd in 1995. COSCO Oceania is responsible for the management, operation and investment of all COSCO's operation units in Oceania (including Australia and New Zealand).

After more than 30 years of development, the COSCO Group has grown into a multinational enterprise, ranked first in China and second in the world in terms of fleet size. In 2011, the Group operated over 80 international shipping routes and 21 domestic services, connecting 155 principal ports in 53 countries and regions across the world; they provided services to the United States, Europe and the Atlantic, a North–South service, an intra-Asia service and an intra-China service to COSCO's global customers (see http://www.coscon.com for COSCO's trade routes). In the port business, the COSCO Group has invested in and operates 32 ports worldwide, with 156 berths (COSCO 2010). Table 23.2 provides an overview of COSCO's performance in the period between 2005 and 2011.

Table 23.2: COSCO Group's performance, 2005–11							
	2005	2006	2007	2008	2009	2010	2011
Total ships owned and chartered	575	715	841	835	770	799	743
Carrying capacity (DWT million)	33.06	42.19	51.85	53.21	53.07	57.78	55.32
Revenue (US$ billions)	13.7	15.41	20.84	27.43	17.39	24.24	28.79
Profit (US$ billions)	1.61	1.09	3.67	1.89	0.185	1.16	–0.651
Global 500 ranking	Not listed	Not listed	488	405	327	Not listed	399

Source: Table generated based on data derived from COSCO (2011) and *CNN Money* (2012).
Note: The revenue and profit for 2005 and 2009 are based on the authors' calculations using *CNN Money* (2012).

International competitors

COSCO ranks fifth in terms of global market share. Table 23.3 shows the ranking of the top 10 container operators in the world on 3 January 2013.

As cooperation has become increasingly important in the international shipping industry, COSCO has established strategic alliances with competitors in order to improve operational efficiency. In 1997, COSCO cooperated with the K-line of Japan and Yang Ming Line of Taiwan to cut costs while improving overall service to secure new customers. Later in 2001, Hanjin of Korea joined and formed the CKYH alliance, which in April 2010 was renamed the 'CKYH – the Green Alliance' to signify its stance on environmental protection (*Shipping OnLine* n.d.). These alliances have proved to be very successful, as they effectively have improved the operational efficiency and competitive strength of COSCO.

Apart from strategic alliances, the COSCO Group adopted a strategy of innovation to give it core competitiveness in international shipping markets – the successful winning in 2007 of the Airbus A-320 logistic project is a case in point. The agreement is worth over US$201.3 million over a seven-year period (2008–15). COSCO Group provides a comprehensive door-to-door integrated logistic service for Airbus to transport 284 A-320 aircraft and tools from Hamburg, Germany and Toulouse, France to the Airbus Final Assembly Line in Tianjin, China. The transportation process covers not only air transportation, ocean shipping, river feeder transportation and ground transportation of parts, but also includes assembling, disassembling and maintenance of tools and jigs as well as other value-added services. COSCO was awarded 'the most outstanding contribution award in transportation' by Airbus. This project has become

Table 23.3: Top 10 leading service operators of container ships, January 2013

Rank	Operator	Country	TEU	Share of world total, TEU (%)
1.	APM-Mrsk	Denmark	2 583 522	15.4
2.	Mediterranean Shipping Co.	Switzerland	2 233 065	13.3
3.	CMA CGM Group	France	1 388 786	8.3
4.	Evergreen Line	China, Taiwan	723 378	4.3
5.	COSCO Container Lines Company Ltd	China	716 868	4.3
6.	Hapag-Lloyd	Germany	632 049	3.8
7.	APL	Singapore	576 163	3.4
8.	Hanjin Shipping	Republic of Korea	573 977	3.4
9.	CSCL	China	549 192	3.3
10.	MOL	Japan	506 239	3.0

Source: Table based on data obtained from Alphaliner (2013).

a milestone of COSCO's international competitiveness, and has drawn attention from around the world because of its technical standards, investment scale, market influence and development potential (Wei 2010).

◼ COSCO in Oceania

Following economic reforms in China, COSCO began its first international container liner line with the sailing of the *Ping Xiang Cheng* container ship from Shanghai to Australia in 1978. The Group was also the first Chinese shipping company to operate an Australia–China container liner. Today, COSCO Group has four main subsidiaries in the region: COSCO Oceania Pty Ltd (Australia), Five Star Shipping & Agency Company Pty Ltd (Australia), Five Star Bulk Shipping Agency Pty Ltd (Australia) and COSCO (New Zealand) Ltd (hereafter COSCO NZ).

◼ *Developments in New Zealand*

COSCO's development in New Zealand[4] has been very successful. In 1988, the COSCO Group began its container service to New Zealand by establishing a shipping agency in Auckland. However, it was not until 1991 that COSCO NZ, a wholly owned subsidiary of COSCO Group, was established as the agent of COSCO Container Lines Company, for container cargoes to and from New Zealand. The company has undertaken a number of initiatives in New Zealand, including the establishment of COSCO Airfreight (New Zealand) Ltd in 1998 and acquiring a 50 per cent share in United Container Storage Ltd (UCSL) in 1999. United Container Storage Limited (UCSL) was at the time a subsidiary of United Container Ltd (UCL), and six years later in 2005, UCSL was amalgamated into UCL; this resulted in COSCO NZ owning a 27.5 per cent share in UCL. Furthermore, in 2003 COSCO NZ established COSCO Container Line (Fiji) Ltd.

COSCO NZ became the first shipping company to introduce fixed-day weekly services in New Zealand and the first shipping company to offer coastal shipping as an integrated part of the international offerings. Being a specialist in chilled and frozen cargo handling, COSCO was ranked by clients in the top three for performance and service (*New Zealand Herald* 2008). There are approximately 10 main international shipping companies serving New Zealand, including Mærsk New Zealand Limited (Denmark), Hapag-Lloyd Container Liner New Zealand Limited (Germany), and NYK Line (New Zealand) Limited (Japan). These international shipping carriers cover a range of international lines, such as New Zealand–Australia, New Zealand–South-East Asia, New Zealand–North and East Asia, and New Zealand–Middle East–Europe. Mærsk New Zealand Limited is one of COSCO's strongest competitors.

◼ *Shipping lines in New Zealand*

For a long time, COSCO NZ offered a limited shipping line service to and from New Zealand. The ports at which it called were adjusted from time to time according to market demand. Before March 2000, cargo from New Zealand to mainland China and

Hong Kong was transported via Australia, which increased the risks of the goods being damaged and meant untimely delays for customers. With the aim of improving transport efficiency and meeting the market demand, in 2000 COSCO adjusted its shipping lines in Oceania. It extended the China–Australia shipping line to include Japan and Korea (Sydney–Melbourne–Yokohama–Kobe–Shanghai–Huangpu–Hong Kong) and changed the former Japan–Korea–Australia–New Zealand shipping line to Japan–Hong Kong–New Zealand (Auckland–Yokohama–Kobe–Hong Kong–Manila). After this adjustment, COSCO's two separated shipping lines (Australia–East Asia and New Zealand–North Asia) were formed, and COSCO's transport efficiency in Oceania was greatly improved.

At the end of 2001, in order to reduce operational costs and enhance its competitive force, COSCO cooperated with its main competitors, Mærsk, NYK and MOL, to form a Vessel Sharing Agreement (VSA). The VSA provides six integrated container services (ICS) to Japan. As a result of reduced import demand due to the Global Financial Crisis, COSCO and the other ICS members announced a cooperative agreement in 2009 with Hamburg Sud of Russia to reconstruct the New Zealand–Asia shipping line. The service operates weekly, calling at Tokyo, Kobe, Busan, Shanghai, Yantian, Hong Kong, Brisbane, Auckland, Lyttelton, Napier, Tauranga and back to Tokyo. A service to and from Brisbane is offered exclusively by Hamburg Sud. The new service deploys six modern ships, of which COSCO and Hamburg Sud provide two ships respectively while NYK and MOL contribute one ship each. Under the new service, Mærsk and Hapag-Lloyd of Europe are slot charterers, and therefore do not provide ships. Taking into account that the new service would cut capacity, COSCO and its partners also plan to provide a peak-season extra-loader program to ensure that refrigerated trade volumes are accommodated.

The importance of the New Zealand market for COSCO was further highlighted when, in 2009, COSCO added another shipping line: the New Zealand–Europe–Mediterranean shipping line. Ships depart New Zealand for Europe (France, Germany, the Netherlands, Turkey and the United Kingdom) and Asia (the Philippines, Vietnam and Thailand). Due to the rapid growth of the trade between New Zealand and Asia – particularly between New Zealand and China – the volume of freight transported in the New Zealand–Asia shipping line has increased significantly. Notwithstanding the fact that the COSCO Group pays close attention to market risks, director Stuart Ferguson was quoted as saying:

> We didn't over-extend on the NZ trade during those good times. On the one hand, that did have a negative impact on our ability to satisfy the peak demands of our long-term customers but, on the other hand, it allowed COSCO to continue making a solid return on its NZ investment. (Ports of Auckland 2008, p. 8)

In contrast, some of COSCO's competitors in New Zealand have over-stretched themselves during boom periods.

On the outward journey, the company carries mainly commodities such as dairy products, meat, seafood, kiwi fruit and forest products destined for export markets, and on the return journey finished products, such as furniture and shoes. In 2004,

COSCO began to ship dairy products for Fonterra. As Fonterra is New Zealand's largest company in terms of contributions to GDP and the sixth largest dairy company globally, the deal to carry dairy commodities for Fonterra was a significant coup for the company.

New Zealand–China trade and investment

In April 2008, the Chinese and New Zealand governments signed a Free Trade Agreement (FTA), which came into force on 1 October 2008. The FTA has resulted in a rapid increase in trade and investment and, with the reduction in trade barriers between the two countries, opportunities have been created for business. From 2008, when the FTA was just signed, New Zealand's exports to China more than doubled in three years. In 2008 exports were valued at NZ$2.53 billion (US$1.9 billion), and by 2011 this figure had increased to NZ$5.88 billion (US$4.8 billion). At the same time, New Zealand's imports from China increased from NZ$6.44 billion (US$4.8 billion) in 2008 to NZ$7.43 billion (US$6.1 billion) in 2011 – which was even larger than those from Australia (NZ$7.36 billion (US$6.09 billion)). In 2011, China overtook Australia for the first time, becoming New Zealand's largest importing country (Statistics New Zealand 2012). After signing the FTA, China's foreign direct investment in New Zealand significantly increased from US$9.02 million in 2009 to US$63.75 million in 2010. At the end of 2011, Chinese FDI stock in New Zealand totalled US$185.46 million (*China Statistical Yearbook* 2012); however, inward Chinese FDI declined that year to US$23.89 million (net overseas investment).

With a free trade agreement in place, links are strengthening. In 2011, the Hon. Tim Groser, New Zealand's Trade Minister, commented:

> We now trade with China in six hours the same value [that] we traded in a whole year in 1972, when diplomatic relations were established with China. China's booming economy now plays a central role in New Zealand's economic future . . . The FTA has opened the door for more of our companies to reach into China, and put China firmly in their focus. (Groser 2011)

COSCO is a successful Chinese investment pioneer in New Zealand. The company has grown from a small base in China to become a key operator in the shipping industry. In so doing, it has expanded its shipping line capability to and from New Zealand. The investment by COSCO in New Zealand has implications for other Chinese investment in New Zealand. For many years, Chinese investment in New Zealand was limited, both in value terms as well as with regard to industry sector, and until the mid-1990s investment was mostly constrained to the resources sector. Since this time, Chinese investment in New Zealand has diversified – for example, into property, health care, manufacturing and tourism. In particular, New Zealand's agribusiness sector is an attractive one for Chinese investment. Recent Chinese investment in New Zealand has included Agria Corporation's purchase of a 13 per cent stake in 2009 in PGG Wrightson Limited, New Zealand's largest agricultural provider. Within three years, Agria had become the majority shareholder, owning 50.22 per cent of the company. A very controversial investment was finalised in 2012, after months of conflict, with the purchase of Crafer Farms by the Shanghai-based Pengxin international company. Another significant investment was the acquisition in 2009 by the Haier Group of China of a 20 per cent stake in Fisher & Paykel, New Zealand's largest household appliance company. In late 2012, the New Zealand Overseas Investment Office removed the last regulatory barrier, thereby allowing a complete takeover, subject to shareholders selling shares in Fisher & Paykel.

In 2012, the New Zealand government announced its strategy to develop further linkages with China, and in particular the goal of increasing two-way trade and bilateral investment. The challenge for COSCO is how to tap into potential growth, in terms of both trade and investment.

◼ Discussion questions

23.1 In less than five decades, COSCO has grown from a small state-owned shipping company to one of the largest multinational shipping companies in the world. What are the drivers of the internationalisation of COSCO?

23.2 Competition in the world shipping industry has been very intense. What are some of the factors contributing to the success of COSCO in China and in the world?

23.3 With the signing of the China–New Zealand Free Trade Agreement in 2008, the trade volume between New Zealand and China increased significantly. It is expected that the two-way trade volume between the two countries will double by 2015. What are the implications of the growth of China–New Zealand trade and investment for COSCO?

23.4 Does COSCO have a role to play in facilitating increased investment in New Zealand? What can companies that are planning to globalise their operations in New Zealand learn from COSCO?

◼ Notes

1 Unless otherwise shown, the principal source for this case study is information obtained from COSCO's website (in Chinese).
2 See COSCO Internet TV, Global COSCO at <http://www.coscotv.com> (in English) for further insight into COSCO.
3 All currency converted using Oanda's mid-point historical conversion rates.
4 The major source of information in this section, unless otherwise stated, is a semi-structured interview with a senior manager at COSCO.

◼ References

Alphaliner 2013, 'Top 100 Operated Fleets', viewed 3 January 2013, <http://www.alphaliner. com/top100/index.php>.

Business Monitor 2009, 'Company profile – China Ocean Shipping (Group) Company (COSCO), viewed 12 January 2010, <http://www.businessmonitor.com>.

China Statistical Yearbook 2012, viewed 3 January 2013, <http://www.stats.gov.cn/tjsj/ndsj/2012/html/R0619e.htm> (In Chinese).

CNN Money 2012, 'Global 500 companies', viewed 10 December 2012, <http://money.cnn.com/magazines/fortune/global500/2012/full_list/301_400.html>.

COSCO Group 2008, *Sustainable Development Report 2008*, viewed 10 September 2009, <http://www.cosco.com/GC_report/GC_report2009/gcreport2009.pdf>.

—— 2010, *Sustainable Development Report 2010*, viewed 25 April 2012, <http://www.cosco.com/GC_report/GC_report2011/index-en.html>.

—— 2011, 'Part II: General information of COSCO Group', viewed 20 February 2013, <http://www.cosco.com(GC_report/GC_report2010/web-en/a/2-1.html>.

Groser, T 2011, 'China FTA delivers economic benefits', viewed 23 February 2013, <http://www.beehive.govt.nz/release/china-fta-delivers-economic-benefits>.

Ports of Auckland 2008, *Interconnect*, December, viewed 23 February 2011, <http://www.poal.co.nz/news_media/publications/interconnect/interconnect_081200.pdf>.

New Zealand Herald 2008, 'COSCO looks forward to good year',19 February, viewed 23 February 2011, <http://www.highbeam.com/doc/1G1-175374397.html>.

New Zealand Trade and Enterprise (NZTE) & Ministry of Foreign Affairs and Trade (MFAT) 2012, *Opening doors to China: New Zealand's 2015 vision*, viewed 27 December 2012, <http://www.tpk.govt.nz/_documents/nz-inc-china-strategy.pdf>.

Shipping Online n.d., 'CKYH join environmentalists as the Green Alliance', viewed 4 January 2013, <http://www.shippingonline.cn/news/newsContent.asp?id=15318>.

Statistics New Zealand 2012, website, viewed 20 February 2013, <http://www.stats.govt.nz>.

Wei, J 2008, 'Globalization plays a vital function in COSCO development', Viewed 22 February 2012, <http://mnc.people.com.cn/GB/6912928.html> (translated from Chinese).

—— 2010, 'Promoting development by innovation to win the future of COSCO', viewed 28 February 2012, <http://www.cosco.com/cn/news/forum.jsp?leftnav=/5/7> (translated from Chinese).

24

Developing education exchanges between China and the West: The case of Bricknowledge and Mericia

William X Wei, Kimberley Howard and Evan Goodwin

Institutions are now, more than ever, seeking opportunities to provide global exposure and learning for their students through international exchange. In 2009, three business students from Grant MacEwan University in Edmonton, Alberta, Canada travelled to Beijing to fulfil the practicum requirement of their Asia-Pacific Management program and attain this learning. Their placement was with a non-governmental organisation (NGO) called Bricknowledge Education Group (hereafter Bricknowledge) in China. Bricknowledge was formed in 2003 with the goal of establishing an international platform to address issues facing the development of education in emerging markets and to promote innovation, policy-making and cooperation (and therefore cross-cultural understanding) in the education sector among the BRIC (Brazil, Russia, India and China) nations and developed nations, and in particular between China and the West.[1]

The director and staff of Bricknowledge welcomed the MacEwan students and helped them to settle in and adjust to life in Beijing. The students were given the opportunity to learn about the structure of education in China. Importantly, the Chinese government is focused on ensuring quality education, and has sought to raise education levels. As part of their learning, the Grant MacEwan University students analysed the significant similarities and differences, and sought to identify possibilities for collaboration, between North American and Chinese educators, in order to propose ways in which Bricknowledge might develop and capitalise on education exchange opportunities.

■ Bricknowledge

The students spent considerable time conducting research on Bricknowledge and interviewing its director and employees. They learned that 19 countries were represented at the inaugural meeting where Bricknowledge was given the mission

> to promote a more relevant, more dynamic, and a higher quality education in BRIC countries; improved access to basic education for poorer children and communities across the region; and identification and development of lifelong learning opportunities that assist populations to adjust to the rapidly changing work environment (Bricknowledge pamphlet).

Bricknowledge's goals are outlined in Appendix 1.

To ensure that these targeted goals are achieved systematically, Bricknowledge's focus from the start has been to organise forums that provide networking and information exchange opportunities for educational organisations. These forums allow attendees to navigate China's bureaucracy by giving like-minded people the opportunity to meet and build relationships. As can be expected when engaging with multiple groups and cultures, a particularly challenging aspect of Bricknowledge's work is the communication and coordination across these multiple parties. In addition to forums, Bricknowledge holds an annual meeting of the primary initiators of Bricknowledge, including each member nation's Education Minister, United Nations Educational, Scientific and Cultural Organization (UNESCO) representatives, former prime ministers and any other key figures in education. In this respect, Bricknowledge is providing the means for BRIC nations to work together and cooperate in improving education in their regions. This annual meeting serves as a means of recognising achievements and celebrating the successes of the previous year; however, the networking opportunities are usually considered to be the most valuable aspect of the annual meeting.

Bricknowledge's internal portfolio is already expansive and complex, but the organisation is well aware of the priority the Chinese government has placed on international exchange, and the value of promoting educational exchange between China and the West for both students and faculty members. To that end, Bricknowledge is considering becoming an agent to facilitate Western foreign teacher placements in English teaching schools in China. Having an organisation like Bricknowledge in this role can help alleviate foreign teachers' concerns, provide assistance in navigating the Chinese bureaucracy and bring needed accountability to the current system. This is an important role, but more targeted strategies are required.

◼ The Bricknowledge and Mericia collaboration

The students learnt that Bricknowledge was currently engaged in such targeted strategies – for example in a cooperative project with Mericia Group, a privately held education group based in Beijing, China. The aim of the Group is to develop relationships between Western educational institutions and Mericia Group's schools in China. Mericia Group has strong ties with Chinese officials, which helps it navigate through the often daunting Chinese government bureaucracy. As demand for international exchanges grows, Mericia Group is experiencing increasing pressure to create a system that benefits and works for all parties, locally and internationally. Visiting scholars from several prominent educational institutions, from both the United States and the United Kingdom, have toured Mericia's facilities and campuses to explore opportunities for global education and exchange for their students as well as sources of international students.

The students discovered that one sample program that appeals to both sides is the Advanced Placement (AP) program at Mericia. It has been designed to offer Chinese students who demonstrate academic excellence the opportunity to spend a period of their high school education in the United States, and to help them with a smooth transition into a Western post-secondary educational institution. Their strategy of adopting the 'Advanced Placement' program in an attempt to create a standardised curriculum will be effective in helping students with the transition process. However, the indication is that the majority of Chinese students, in the current context, do not meet the eligibility requirements for the AP program, and there are many issues relating to just how the common curriculum (that is, some form of standardisation) can be attained or studied.

Challenges to international education exchanges

Equipped with a growing understanding of Bricknowledge, the three Grant MacEwan University students continued to explore the challenges of education exchange between China and the West. They gleaned further understanding and learned that education exchange had become a major priority for Chinese institutions since they had undergone a massive transformation over the last decade. Educational facilities are striving to catch up to the pace of economic growth and meet the capacity requirements of the world's most populous nation. Although the desire for exchanges is great, several barriers remain on both sides.

From the Chinese perspective, there is no standardised global or Western curriculum, and Chinese students planning to study abroad can sometimes be significantly ahead of or behind the curriculum. Credits for post-secondary education are often non-transferable across countries. These disparities in curricula and grading standards can lead to studies in a foreign country not counting toward credits at a Chinese student's home country institution. Although the increasing wealth of China's middle class bodes well for an increase in international education, the cost of international education currently is extremely high, and it is available only to those who have above-average means.

From the Western institutions' perspectives, they value reputation, and are therefore reluctant to form relationships with institutions with which they are unfamiliar, or that are lower in ranking. For Chinese institutions, this is complicated by the fact that Western institutions are far better known in China than Chinese institutions are in the West. Reciprocity in instructor exchange is also difficult to achieve, as many Western teachers are unwilling to move to China to teach. Most Western students studying in China must be instructed in English, due to the perceived difficulty of Mandarin. Chinese students, on the other hand, learn English throughout their education. The desire of Chinese students to study in the West is also far greater (due in part to population size and the good reputation of Western education) than the desire of Western students to come to China for their education. Currently, Western schools do not have the facilities to accommodate the numbers of Chinese students interested in studying in the West. See Figure 24.1 for the imbalance between Chinese and American exchange students, and Figure 24.2 for the top 10 international destinations of Chinese students.) The imbalance in potential student numbers is problematic for both sides. Figure 24.3 provides an indication of the overall global destinations of international students.

Although post-secondary education is fairly common in China, international tertiary education exchange is not, largely

Figure 24.1: Education exchange imbalance: China and United States, 2000–12

Source: Derived from Institute of International Education (2012).

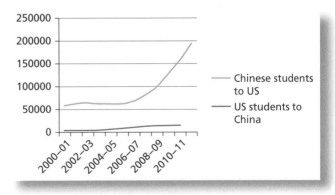

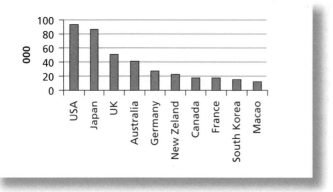

Figure 24.2: International destinations of Chinese students
Source: Derived from <http://www.atlas.iienetwork.org>.

due to parents wanting to maintain proximity with and influence over their children. Computers and the decreasing cost of international communication may help diminish this concern. Chinese students have a strong desire to experience Western culture, and in some of the bigger cities in the West, large Chinese immigrant populations exist that can provide support to Chinese students. Conversely, many Western students are open to experiencing Eastern culture, as people worldwide develop a more international perspective. Differences in educational priorities in Eastern and Western contexts can create friction in the negotiation process – for example, the importance of university entrance exams.

■ Potential strategies

In their research, the Grant MacEwan University students found that, despite these obstacles and challenges, Bricknowledge and Mericia Group are both focused on helping Chinese students to become global citizens. Some of their goals and strategies include offering dual degrees and diplomas, where students graduate from both a Chinese and a Western institution; recruiting highly skilled bilingual teachers who can instruct in both English and Mandarin; developing agreements that allow English proficiency to be demonstrated by other methods than the International English Language Testing System (IELTS) or Tests of English as a Foreign Language (TOEFL) examinations; and collaborating on developing a curriculum suitable for both Eastern and Western institutions.

Although these strategies are a start, there are many factors that are beyond both Bricknowledge and Mericia's control. Perceptions of foreign nations can often be negative, and there has been much negative propaganda directed toward both the United States and China over the last 50 years. While interest in studying in China is increasing, a marketing strategy to build greater demand in the West could help the process significantly. (For global destinations of international students at the post-secondary level, see Figure 24.2.) Political differences also have a strong impact, particularly with regard to the choice of country parents make for their children's education.

Bricknowledge strongly believes in the inevitability and importance of global education cooperation, and views it as one of its primary goals over the next several years.

However, as an NGO, it is constantly facing financial restrictions. Building relationships and a network of people who are able to accomplish these educational tasks is of great importance. So too is its ability to create awareness in the general population about the opportunities that are available in terms of educating students.

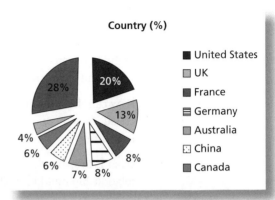

Bricknowledge has some important decisions to make over the next year in order to capitalise on new international opportunities and keep up with the changing education industry. In order to remain a sustainable and relevant, it must develop new international relationships and gain a more universal understanding of modern education. It is accountable to the Chinese government rather than shareholders and, as a non-profit organisation, it will be judged on positive results in education rather than on positive income statement returns. Both Mericia and Bricknowledge are trying to adapt to the new education environment, but they are working with quite different mandates. Bricknowledge is an NGO with a strong relationship network. Mericia is a privately held company, somewhat lacking in international know-how and the connections necessary to make any truly effective international projects possible. Both of these organisations need to utilise each other's strengths, and they need to constantly be monitoring the expectations of international institutions and organisations with which they wish to partner.

Figure 24.3: Global destinations of international students *Source:* Derived from www.atlas.iienetwork.org

▪ Appendix 1: Goals of Bricknowledge

- Meeting the demand for an educated and skilled workforce
- Investing further in the educated population and providing educational opportunities to those in underprivileged communities
- Improving communication and cooperation across BRIC regions and the West through educational mechanisms
- Developing plans to:
  - increase professional development opportunities of education professionals and policy-makers in both the private and public sectors
  - host annual conferences
  - provide an informal consultation mechanism for education policy-makers
  - foster communication and exchange among students, teachers, and scholars
  - explore the feasibility of offering financial and intellectual support and services
  - organise events to foster cultural and educational exchange

Discussion questions

24.1   Analyse the differences that the three Grant MacEwan University students found between the education expectations and approaches to learning in China and its Western counterparts.

24.2   How can these differences be managed or overcome in order to successfully collaborate in education exchanges between Chinese and Western institutions?

24.3   What is Bricknowledge's role in this situation and how can it assist in relationship-building and networking capacities?

24.4   Why is global education becoming increasingly important? How can it be facilitated even further?

Note

1   The authors may have disguised certain names and other identifying information to protect confidentiality.

References

Gallagher, M, Hasan, A, Canning, M, Newby, H, Saner-Yiu, L & Whitman, I 2009, *OECD reviews of tertiary education: China*, Paris: OECD, viewed 20 February 2013, <http://oecd.org/edu/skills-beyond-school/42286617.pdf>.

Institute of International Education 2008a, 'China 2008', in *Atlas of International Student Mobility*, viewed 10 June 2009, <http://www.atlas.iienetwork.org/?p=53467>.

——2008b, 'Country Profiles', in *Atlas of International Student Mobility*, viewed 10 June 2009, <http://www.atlas.iienetwork.org/?p=48027>.

——2012, 'Open Doors' database, viewed 20 February 2013, <http://www.atlas.iienetwork.org>.

People's Daily n.d., 'China becomes "hot option" for Americans', viewed 15 June 2009, <http://english.peopledaily.com.cn/90001/90776/90883/6544524.html>.